D.103

THE STOLEN DESERT

Freedom Deferred. *A girl from Kenya's Somali district (part of former N.F.D.).*

THE STOLEN DESERT

A Study of Uhuru in North East Africa

THE EARL OF LYTTON

MACDONALD: LONDON

First published in 1966 by
MACDONALD & CO. (PUBLISHERS) LTD.
Gulf House, 2 Portman Street, London W.1.
Made and printed in Great Britain by
THE ALDEN PRESS (OXFORD) LTD.

CONTENTS

Author's Note   ix

1 Kenya Echoes   1

2 The Halting of Kush   16

3 Kenyattaland   39

4 The White Highlands of Kenya   56

5 Pastoral Nomads   80

6 Dismembered Nation   98

7 Noah's Curse   118

8 Unworthy Causes   132

9 Emperor Amba   144

10 The Ten Plagues of Uhuru   168

11 Maharaja's Well   195

Appendix

1 Centenary Diary   220

2 'Identikit' Revolution   231

3 Translation of Emperor Menelek's Letter   236

4 Bibliography   238

5 Acknowledgements   241

Index   243

LIST OF PLATES

Freedom Deferred. A girl from Kenya's Somali district
                                                        frontispiece
1 Dr. Adan Abdullah Osman   *facing page*   22
2 Mr. Jomo Kenyatta   23
3 The Emperor Haile Selassie with H.M. the Queen   38
4 Amharic text of the Emperor Menelek's letter of
       April 1891   39
5 Somali religious leader: Sheykh Mohammed   86
6 Somali elder: the late Gerad Mohamoud Ali Shirreh,
       M.B.E.   86
7 In the floor of the Kerio valley, Kenya   87
8 Lower slopes of the Kamasia hills, Kenya   87
9 Head of young Somali woman showing non-negroid
       features   102
10 Head of middle-aged Somali woman showing
       non-negroid features   103
11 West African nursing sister showing negroid features 150
12 Successful Bantu 'settler' in Kenya's 'white' highlands 151
13 Young Turkana (Kenya) housewives (1925)   166
14 Young Turkana with her first baby and her first
       home (1925)   166
15 Young Turkana housewife cutting up fish (1965)   167
16 Happy warrior (Turkana)   206
17 Snapshot of the author and his wife with the Governor
       of Lower Juba   207

LIST OF MAPS

                                                        page
Language map   217
Abyssinian Colonial Empire, 1883–1962   218
Political map of North-east Africa   219

ILLUSTRATION ACKNOWLEDGEMENTS

Frontispiece, 7, 9, 10, 15 and 16, Bob Campbell and Des Bartlett, Armand Denis Productions, Nairobi; 1, Dr. Ahmed Shire Lawaha and Luxardo, Rome; 4, original in Amharic and accompanying French translation preserved in the Public Record Office under reference F.O. 95/751; 5 and 6, by kind permission of C. J. Martin, Esq.; 8, by kind permission of John Knight, Esq.; 11, Lynx, Agence Photographique de la Presse, Paris; 12, by kind permission of Sir Gerald Reece, K.C.M.G., C.B.E. The language map and map of the modern Ethiopian Empire are based on those reproduced in *Islam in Ethiopia*, by J. Spencer Trimingham (Oxford University Press), by kind permission of the author and publishers.

AUTHOR'S NOTE

It is a good custom in writing this kind of book to give the name and qualification of all persons upon whose authority the author relies. In most cases I have followed the established custom in this matter but in a few cases, each one of some importance, I have either been asked, or I have thought fit, to conceal the identity of my contributors. In the matter of land management in Kenya, for instance, passions run high and I have suppressed the identity of each one of my private correspondents irrespective of whether their criticisms fall upon the new African government or the former colonial regime. In the matter of self-determination for the Somali N.F.D. (the portion of the N.F.D. occupied almost to a man by Somalis) I do not name those whose Somali patriotism is now treason in Kenya. There is a field of discussion moreover which is a mixture of anthropology, biblical exegesis and theology; most of my correspondents in this mixed field are, like myself, Roman Catholics who not only are, but who much prefer to remain, subject to ecclesiastical authority in matters theological; probable hypotheses and novel inferences in this field are open for discussion but while they are *sub judice* the names of some who from their positions might be thought to bestow finality upon questions still open are usually held back. Since their opinions in particular cases stand up well on their own I have acted upon the old military maxim 'No names, no pack drill'. In this field also I have tried to show a process of transition from 'Victorian' views to positions that seem even to me more probable.

Apart from suppressions I give in Appendix 5 a more than usually long list of persons who have helped me; together with a list of formal copyright permissions to quote from the works of others. All permissions have been granted cordially and without fee, and in thanking authors and publishers for their prompt co-operation

I go further and thank those whose works (like dictionaries, encyclopaedias, Parliamentary reports and the BBC Monitor Service) may be cited without the granting of formal permission. In this category too are 'short' quotations which by some convention are exempt from formality but are often too valuable to use without a general word of appreciation; my gratitude is not less in those cases where a short quotation illustrates a position which I have felt obliged to criticize adversely. I hope that with three exceptions (two white and one black) all whose actions are criticized adversely will find something substantial recorded to their credit. Undoubtedly those three would be better counterbalanced if my book did not have to assess them only on their transgressions over the frontiers of its particular scope.

I

KENYA ECHOES

'We don't want to be governed by a murderer!'

An Arab is speaking; the place is Mombasa, the hot city where racial tolerance is a fact and where heads are usually cool in spite of the heat. Nairobi calls it sloth.

It is the late autumn of 1961 and the red flag of the Arab Sultan of Zanzibar, legal suzerain of the coastal strip, still flies from a mast-head on the turret of old Fort Jesus. The power of the Catholic Portuguese who built the fort has long been dead. The power of the Muslim Arabs who succeeded them is dead too. Now we Protestant British are about to renounce our power and transfer our authority to pagans who have neither wealth nor power: we are on the threshold of a new experiment—the poor in pence are to be installed in the judgment seat of the mighty.

Kenya's wealth still comes mostly from the farming surpluses of the white settlers whose political influence, supreme when I first came to this country forty years ago, is today extinct. Even a year ago the White Highlands were still endowed with a privilege deemed during half a century to be advantageous not only to settlers but to everyone else. Yet at this moment white settlers are living under a threat of dispossession notwithstanding the excellence of their husbandry. Other husbandmen with neither capital nor skill are 'squatting' in the forest verges waiting to re-settle and deconsolidate the white men's holdings.

At first sight it looks like evolution in reverse. Have not Africans always resisted or ignored change? Is this all going to be just another example of their propensity to retrogress?

I avoid discussing the 'murderer' with the Arab.

'Things were very different,' I go on, 'when I stayed with Ali bin Salim in 1926'—Ali had long been the Liwali, or Sultan's representative, of the Kenya coastal strip when I stayed with him the other side of Kilindini harbour.

I

'Oh, you stayed with Ali! He was so fond of the Royal Navy that he bequeathed to them the house in which you must have stayed with him. I know them all quite well. I'll telephone and they will ask you over for drinks.'

There seems to be little resentment about this Arab; I feel that the maxim of 'kismet' or 'shauri ya Mungu' (God's affair) still serves on the coast to put a sugar coating over a bitter pill.

I am staying in Mtwapa Creek with a cousin, a white hunter who reads Swahili newspapers beside the mangroves that grow in his creek. He and his wife would like to move away from Mombasa where the climate is too humid for him, but the bottom has dropped out of the property market and nobody will buy. One morning I hear my cousin muttering over his newspaper, 'This Mzee is letting loose forces that nobody will be able to control. When he addresses white farmers he says, "Uhuru does not mean that we shall take a shop or a shamba (farm) away from its owner just because the owner happens to be an Indian or a European." But then within a few hours of this reassuring speech we find him addressing a crowd of some twenty thousand wildly enthusiastic Africans, telling them in Swahili that they are poor because the white men stole their rich lands, and that when Uhuru (independence) arrives the stolen lands will be restored to the Africans who are their rightful owners. After an interval this is followed by a denial that he said what he said—a denial printed in a corner of an English language newspaper where none of his listeners will even hear of it.'

At the end of a sultry day an up-country rancher of sixty or so arrives by Land-Rover in a cloud of dust from his remote ranch to spend a few days big game fishing on the coast. He counts himself amongst the stayers and can never for long suppress his vitality nor conceal the satisfaction he gets from putting his efforts into pioneer cattle-breeding; his ranching achievements are held to be outstanding throughout the country.

'My bill to protect my stock against robbers,' he says with a laugh, 'is a hundred and ten pounds a month. My Turkana guards will protect me against any raider—they were the only people I had to look after me during the Mau Mau emergency.'

During the evening we talk for some hours. His ranch is away up in a different world from this mangrove creek where little pink one-clawed crabs dart away into holes in the mud as you approach the water's edge. The rancher is deaf, but he can hear so long as people are willing to speak into his obsolete trumpet with tube. He plants one end of this curious instrument into his ear and pushes the other towards me across the table top.

We talk of ranching disasters and ranching successes. He tells of a dozen boreholes that petered out notwithstanding expert advice and of twice as many dams and pumping plants successfully installed without any expert advice. We discuss the choice of indigenous beasts and of imported bulls, the control of cattle diseases by dipping, inoculation and segregation. I hear of the tribe which provides all his guards and of another tribe from which come all his robbers—I happen to know both of these tribes very well. We exchange views on tribal characteristics, how some are lean of frame eating little on safari and drinking less while others are large and muscular and might have been planned by nature to become stevedores.

We examine the causes of African low standards of husbandry and the insuperable problem of creating a market for the pastoral nomads. We compare the grievances of some tribes who have gained most from white colonialism with the tolerance of others who have only been stopped from raiding their neighbours. We ask each other why this tribe is prone to treachery while that other is the mainstay of the army and the police. We try to guess why the members of some tribes seem courageous to a man while others have to generate courage through oaths and invocations to calamity. We agree that Indians all seem to be born shopkeepers while Somalis are the only up-country Africans with any aptitude for trading. We are both doubtful whether European democracy which makes clerks and school teachers masters of martial tribes is going to survive the departure of the Europeans.

'I'm staying,' concludes the rancher.

We are far into the night, and in the middle of further interesting discussions, when he says suddenly, 'I can't hear, what's happened?' We have a look and find that, although one end of the instrument is still in his ear and I am still speaking into the other and the snake-like connecting link appears to be intact, something in the middle has given way and there is now a hiatus which prevents him hearing anything more! So this small mechanical breakdown brings to an end a conversation which seems hardly to have begun.

During the cool of an early morning I am introduced to elder citizens of Mombasa from whom I learn that Mombasa is proud of three hundred years of civilized history—part of it, I reflect, has not really been quite civilized, but let that pass—the Mayor is a Pakistani, his deputy a Giriama. The Sultan, of course, is an Arab of Zanzibar. We British are de facto rulers, the atmosphere is cosmopolitan, the communities see as much of one another or as little as they please and it is just as well like that.

Two hours spent with the assistant superintendent of the docks, a Briton, is an interesting occasion. The stevedores are Africans of mixed tribes, so I learn, the clerks are mainly Indians; the secretary of the Dock Workers' Union is a competent Luo (from Lake Victoria) whom I meet presently to enjoy his sense of humour and cavernous laugh. There is, I am assured by both sides, no trouble in the docks in spite of admittedly low wages and considerable unemployment. There has been no strike during the five years of Secretary Dennis Akumu's term of office to which he was elected by a majority of Africans not of his own tribe—a fact which clearly has given him great satisfaction.

Next day is Sunday. At Sunday Mass in the Roman Catholic cathedral the front part of the congregation is mainly Goan, the back mainly African. A few whites are dotted about here and there amongst the Goans. There is no rule or tradition to stop a 'shirt and shorts' African from moving into the same pew as myself or the beautifully dressed Goan girl kneeling in front of me, but he wouldn't. At the end of Mass the girl picks up her white gloves and goes out to the car-park where she unlocks a Ford Anglia and drives herself off. The boy goes off barefoot with a crowd of other Africans. This is the kind of self-segregation which is based not on race or colour but on economics—the Africans are clearly the 'have nots' of this society and as such they cling together.

The priests are still mostly Irish, but one of them who seems overcome by the heat tells me, 'We're finished,' and then explains that Africans are being trained to replace the Irish as soon as possible.

The British Club still excludes anyone it pleases, and that includes Jews and coloured people of every sort, but nobody seems to mind here—what is a club for anyway? As I think over my answer to this question while sitting a little later during elevenses in the club itself, I come to the conclusion that this all-white enclave might be all the brighter if that smart Goan girl were a member. The hotels here, unlike those of Dar-es-Salaam, exclude nobody except those who cannot afford to cross their thresholds.

Mombasa says in effect, 'We are tolerant down here—we are not bitter in spite of having to put up with many provocations from less civilized quarters—we know how to get on with one another—by contrast look at Nairobi—up at that unsettling altitude they are always at one another's throats—their scandals are all in public—their hatreds are broadcast to the world—they become angry about nothing and are all a little mad. In the Highlands white women unaccustomed to authority in their own homes in England swear like sergeant-majors at black boys in their execrable Swahili—many of them drink too much and have no idea what to do with their surfeit of leisure. Some people up country are much too rich while with others bankruptcy is becoming a way of life. African politicians swagger about on Indian credit—white settlers denounce Westminster politicians with a degree of hatred worthy of the enemy in time of war. Nairobi is a mushroom city without roots or manners—it is as uncouth as the Masai manyatta settlement which preceded it. Her Majesty the Queen would have been better advised to grant Her Royal Charter to Mombasa!'

Moving up from Mombasa to the neighbourhood of Nairobi, I find some of the white men in the Highlands more intense in their resentments than those I have yet met. In fact the further you go from the coast the greater the passion and bitterness except possibly for some business men in Nairobi itself.

In the coffee land near Nairobi a farming settler whom I have known for some years introduces me to the much deeper resentments of some of these white farmers including himself. I am in his company outside a local government building looking up at a plaque on the wall in memory of the Kikuyu Chief Waruhiu. 'He was the best of men—a thoroughly capable man—he was also my friend—I attended his funeral—standing next to me on that day was his murderer—very soon this murderer is going to be the ruler of our country—can you expect me to have any confidence in the future? And quite apart from all that take a look at things and size them up for yourself. You know the Africans, you were here forty years ago, look at them now and draw your own conclusions. Are you prepared to go home and tell your friends in England that the African has been trained and is really qualified to take over the management of this country?'

I promise that when I do get home I will say or write what I do think about all this.

After dark one evening I am sitting in the Norfolk Hotel in Nairobi. A young African porter of about thirty arrives at the door and calls 'hodi' (may I come in) to which I reply 'karibu' (come in). He opens the door and comes in and we start talking. Presently finding that my Swahili is less good than his English he breaks into English in a way that would not have happened forty years ago where it was the ritual for the Bwana to speak in Swahili, however immature, to every African.

'I have brought your fifty pounds in cash from the office where you left your travellers' cheques. Here, sir, is your money. It should be a thousand shillings, please count it. I am a new boy in this hotel. I have only been here a week and I do not want to make mistakes.'

I count.

'It looks like twenty short, but I have counted in a hurry and I'm sure I must have made a mistake. I'll take it as correct.'

'Count again, please, I want to be sure that it is correct.'

I count aloud in front of the Kikuyu porter so that he can join me in numbering the notes as I turn them over.

'My mistake. You see it is a thousand after all.'

'Very good. Are you here for the first time, sir?'

'No, I am not here for the first time, in fact I was here first about forty years ago.'

'Forty years? You don't look as old as all that, sir.'

'I am not old, I am only sixty-one. But tell me, are you looking forward to Uhuru?'

'Yes, sir.'

'You are a Kikuyu?'

'Yes, sir. I am a member of K.A.N.U.'

'Would Tom Mboya make a good leader?'

'Tom is too young to be the head, but the Mzee will keep him in order.'

'You like an old man to be your leader?'

'It is natural to want wise men to lead.'

'The Masai are led by their warrior age group. Is that too young in your opinion?'

'What good is a warrior without war, and who wants war?'

'We Europeans are inclined to believe in youth these days?'

'The Communists all say that too.'

'Tom Mboya is a Luo, is he not?'

'Yes, he is a Ja-Luo, but we are all friends these days, Luo, Kikuyu all the same, but Tom is young and the Mzee is wise. . . . During your stay here if you wish to talk about our country you have only to send for me.'

'See you later, thank you.'

The porter leaves and I reflect that there are clearly more views than one on the 'murderer', but of course a Kikuyu might be expected to have a special regard for the leader of his own tribe.

On the following day I am guest at a luncheon given by the United Kenya Club for the World Bank. The chairman of the club, which has no premises of its own but hopes to acquire some soon, is a well-dressed European business man wearing an old Etonian tie. He comes up briskly, introducing himself, and adds as a description of himself, 'I am a Kenya African.' I am taken aback at this, bearing in mind that my B.B.C. producer used always to insist on my substituting the word 'African' for 'native', 'Negro' or 'black.' Some Europeans who were born in Africa and are citizens of an independent African state now claim an equal right to be called African and really there is no reason why they should not do so even if they force us once more to use those simpler but unpopular noun-adjectives 'Black' and 'White.'

I have heard that this old Etonian is a friend of the 'murderer' and that he holds some official post in K.A.N.U. He is reputed to be one of Nairobi's rich men. I listen with interest while he has a discussion with the leader of the World Bank delegation. I gather from what I hear that he regards the so-called 'murderer' as something akin to Robin Hood.

That same evening I am given hospitality by another Englishman who runs a successful transportation business. He has an attractive house a few miles from the centre of Nairobi. We get into the usual run of conversation.

'The sooner the Africans get their independence the better,' he says.

'What about the "murderer"?' I ask.

'Not sure you can convict like that. After all he was taken out of circulation too soon. Maybe the removal of the only leader with authority had the effect of letting in more extreme men. For myself I give him the benefit of the doubt. Anyway, we have had in our Imperial dismantling to put up with many like him before!'

B

'Are you a newcomer?' I asked.

'Yes, post-war, the last fifteen years.'

'Do you employ any particular one tribe rather than others in your business?'

'I started not knowing one tribe from another and we engaged anyone who turned up and appeared to be suitable. It so happened that the first lot were all Kikuyu.'

'Did you have to get rid of these Kikuyu during the emergency?'

'I got rid of them long before the emergency. After one year we had no further use for Kikuyu in our firm.'

'Are the tribes who replaced them satisfactory?'

'Yes, quite all right. In point of fact, unless somebody gives trouble I am never quite sure that I know one tribe from another even now.'

During the course of a multi-racial party held on another day for our benefit, I meet an Indian called Patel. There are some four hundred and fifty entries under the name of Patel in the Kenya telephone directory so I am not giving away very much by mentioning his name.

'How do you like the prospect of Uhuru?' I ask.

'I am very apprehensive,' he replies.

There is a variety of opinions about the position and value of the Indian community in Kenya, so I try to find out more of what various settlers think about them. I meet a white rancher and put the question, 'What will be the effect upon the Indians of Uhuru?'

'The Indians have been cheating the Africans for so long that the Africans are bound to give them a bad time and take over many of their jobs.'

From this disparaging settler I move on to a white bank director and ask the question in a different form: 'Are the Indians the swindlers that some people make out?'

I give the gist of his reply as far as I remember it in his own words:

'The Indians are the shop-keepers of Kenya. An Indian "duka" is like all the shops of a small English town put together, with post office, bank, petrol station and insurance thrown in. The Indians' prices are competitive, their seasonal borrowings from the banks are quite colossal, but it all returns and their credit stands high. You have to take into account that each Indian community, there are a good many separate ones, is a religious foundation which takes care of all its members, the poor, the sick, the elderly, the orphans, the unemployed, and looks after them all without letting any of them come on the State for their welfare. Most Englishmen and all Africans have a curiously false instinct that anyone can run a shop, but that is not true. The Indians have a keen commercial instinct and the Africans will be the losers if they drive them out of the country. Of course we have to admit that a shop run by Messrs. Patel employs a family of sixteen, or maybe fifty or more other Patels, and very few Africans. It is all a bit of a headache, too, for accountants and tax collectors that every member of the family is in some sense an owner of the business, but there is nothing wrong in that, in fact it is an element of stability.'

Then I have a word with an Indian merchant, who says, in a manner indicating that he would prefer not to be overheard, 'If things don't get more than fifty per cent worse we shall still be better off here than we would be in India!'

I next get in touch with other members of the white farming community. Two ranchers big enough not to mind whether they have to leave the country or not have similar views. One of them says, 'Mixed farming for us is finished. The mixed farms are on the kind of land which Africans want, moreover mixed farming is the type of farming which Africans, not always correctly, think they are capable of managing themselves. For the time being at least the big ranches and coffee and sisal estates, and so on, will continue.'

The other says. 'In the course of time, in my judgment, all white farming will come to an end and will be taken over by Africans. The larger ranches will be run by co-operatives, but that will take a little time.'

I still find quite a number of other people saying, 'I am one of the stayers, at least until I am driven out.'

Over the White Highlands, however, there spreads a sense of betrayal, especially amongst the mixed farmers, who are the middle men with not a great deal to spare of this world's goods. They have been induced to settle in this country with pledge after pledge of living in a privileged region, with a British way of life pendant on those pledges. A deep, almost unspeakable bitterness fills their hearts. The bitterness is sharpened, no doubt, as is everything else here, by the quasi-hysteria which is a special feature of these cool highlands. I find that there are approximately three tiers of bitterness:

The first tier has regard to the pledges, and no doubt there *is* a long record of pledges.

The second tier has regard to the total lack of preparation for self-government, which has preceded this extraordinary experiment of launching untried, untrained people into the complicated management of a mixed industrial and agricultural economy. All stock exchanges in the far north are still taking place by the bartering of beasts while a modern Stock Exchange operates in the capital, Nairobi, for shares and securities.

The third tier of bitterness is perhaps the bitterest of all. Not only has the guaranteed white man's way of life been destroyed without adequate warning and without apology or compensation, but it has been destroyed on the foundation of an abominable lie. The land was vacant and uncultivated when white men took it over, and it is they who have brought golden harvests in place of scrub, prairie grass and weeds. Take any report you like and see what is said of the general level of African husbandry in comparison with the achievements of the settlers. Moreover—so the lamentation continues—white settlers have their own staffs of squatters and other employees who have a certain measure of skill, and who, if any African is to take over should be given the first opportunity of doing so. Instead, 'an uncouth gang' of people lately engaged in one of the most debased and unworthy rebellions of all time is claiming land in all directions without having the least qualification to manage it. For these the white man's employees are the stooges and Quislings of an era that is about to pass, and they will be pushed off into unemployment while their unskilled successors come in to prove their inability to manage a viable agricultural unit.

These resentments are directed exclusively against Her Majesty's Government. In some cases nothing is bad enough to say of the Tory rulers who have in practice outstripped the theories of Socialists in the process of equalizing the unequal at a gadarene gallop.

From this depressing atmosphere of betrayed settlers, I move to the officers' mess of my old regiment, the King's African Rifles. Here I find a totally different atmosphere. The system obtaining in the King's African Rifles has always been that white regular officers are lent by their British regular regiments for a period of about five years to become officers in charge of African askaris and N.C.O.'s. During the period they are on loan to the Colonial

Government. The rank and file soldiers are all Kenya Africans. This is the way things have always been managed.

Now that there is a political wind of change devoid of executive planning in most of the fields of administration, the white officers at Nanyuki are among the first to realize not only that two years is probably the limit of time left before the date of Uhuru, but that a crash programme of Africanization of the officer's mess is a possibility within certain limits, if it is started immediately.

Brigadier Miles Fitzalan-Howard expounds the new scheme. He and his staff are convinced that it is capable of working. The plan for Africanization of the officers is to give commissions to the more promising of the African 'Effendis' who have had experience in peace and war in command of infantry platoons. It is thought that after a short course of training these experienced but rather 'elderly' Africans will be suitable for advancing to commissioned rank, and that in this way it will be possible to have an army officered by men of some experience until there has been time to train young men at Sandhurst, or some other cadet academy, to grow up into Regular Army ways of life.

I learn that most of the suitable candidates are men of the Kamba tribe who have always been excellent supporters of both the K.A.R. and the police.

'Will this programme produce an efficient officer corps by our own standards?' I ask.

'Of course it won't be up to our own standards; how can it be? But within a given context it will produce a reasonable answer in the time available. The alternative may result in a very dangerous situation, and in much confusion: For instance, there is going to be a black African government wholly independent of Great Britain. This government, unless we do something about it in time, will be directing the operations of white senior officers who are subjects of Her Majesty the Queen, commanding black junior officers and black askaris who are subjects of the independent Kenyan Government. The latter, wishing to keep up with the Joneses, might wish to send a contingent to say the Congo, or some other trouble spot, where we would rather British people were not embroiled. This scheme will, in two years, make it possible for British officers to withdraw altogether in case of emergency, and in any case within three or four years it should be possible to have a reasonable first African Commanding Officer.'

'Are you able to persuade the settlers' clubs to accept your African officers as members?'

'For the present they have refused to do so and so I have withdrawn the membership of all the white officers. It happens that we joined as a mess and I am able to withdraw as a mess. That decision will stand until the clubs accept our African officers on precisely the same terms as our European officers.'

Soon afterwards at the K.A.R. annual regimental dinner at Muthaiga Country Club I find myself sitting next to the Minister for Defence, and to make conversation I say somewhat carelessly, 'I suppose there is little risk of serious trouble in Kenya now that the emergency is far behind us?'

'No risk? Far from it! Might be serious trouble at any minute.'

From him and from various other sources I compile a list of the seeds of trouble that seem to be at hand: there are unemployed Africans who demand, as a solution of their unemployment, not merely fresh employment but a piece of land. There are the Mau Mau 'freedom fighters' demanding the restoration of the lands alleged to have been stolen by the settlers; they want particular lands, the 'stolen lands,' restored to them. Every African deems himself by divine right entitled to a piece of land to farm.

In addition to a land-hunger problem there is a racial problem. The Kalenjin and other martial minorities, who are in part non-Negro and who formerly dominated the region, are now placed under the Negro ballot-box majority. There is no certainty that they will be content to remain where we have put them.

There is tension between the tolerant coast and the over-charged highlands.

The Somalis of the N.F.D. are resolved to unite with their mother country with which they have a common boundary of three hundred miles or more.

I come to the conclusion that we are in a thicket of difficulties, and I begin to doubt whether even the habitual resilience of Kenya will enable her to emerge unscathed or at least sufficiently undamaged to stand as a model for Africanization of other countries like the Portuguese territories, Southern Rhodesia and South Africa.

Continuing my tour I attend an all-white cocktail party and there meet the headmaster of a large European secondary school in Nairobi.

'I suppose your school, like many others, has been segregated for whites ever since it was established in this country, in fact until now. Is that the case?'

'Yes, that is so. As you well know there are many good reasons for it, or at least there were until comparatively recently. The school that I run is part of the white man's way of life and without it he would never have come. It is not and never was part of the African way of life, and for many years Africans had no desire to take any part in it; even if they had, it would have been quite impossible to pay for it; even now it is impossible that such schools should be available to all Africans. The change came probably when Africans began to want our sort of education for the first time, and very likely we have been too slow in meeting their aspirations. Now I have been asked to take Africans, as many as I can, and although I am only too willing to do so I have had a very unprofitable search for Africans with sufficiently good qualifications to be capable of taking part.'

At this point an English schoolgirl chips in to say, 'Three Indian girls have just come to our school.'

'What do you think of these three?' I ask.

'Oh, all right,' she replies, as any other schoolgirl at home might say of something that she found rather satisfactory, such as oranges for supper.

The headmaster continues:

'I have combed the whole region for Africans and I can find only three who are remotely suitable. Most of the tiny amount of African educational cream is, at the age of sixteen, no more than just up to the average of white twelve-year-olds.'

Here somebody intervenes with, 'But these African lads surely might in many cases catch up in the end if they were given the chance?'

'That has yet to be proved, but even if it is true, as it may well be, you cannot put twelve and sixteen together in our sort of school. The physical maturity and mental immaturity of the African sixteen-year-olds simply debars the possibility of assimilating them in games and social relationships even if they are able to sit in classrooms together.'

Before returning to England by air from Nairobi I am the guest of the Liwali of the coast during a debate in Leg.Co. The acoustics of the chamber are very bad and I am getting deaf, but my wife, whose hearing is perfect, tells me that apart from Tom Mboya most of the African members seem handicapped in debate owing to their defective command of English. It is not that this defect compares with the immature Swahili in which most Englishmen convey their instructions to their African staff but it is quite inadequate for conducting public business in Parliament.

In one of my last conferences in Nairobi an official charged with African affairs gives his views, views endorsed at every administrative level where I am able to take soundings in Kenya and Tanganyika.

'It is absolutely certain,' says the official, 'that Uhuru will bring not a small but a tremendous falling off in standards of efficiency and integrity. We can only hope that our crash programmes may prevent the fall from becoming catastrophic.'

Last of all I meet the Roman Catholic Archbishop. He has known Britons, Africans and Indians in Kenya for about thirty years. He is Irish, but to Africans he is just a Mzungu (European). In reply to my questions he gives an opinion in approximately the following words: 'I do not think that either Africans or Indians like us very much. It so happens that I have exceptionally keen hearing and I am also completely fluent in Swahili so I hear very easily what is said around me. I have often heard Africans in earlier years commenting in an amusing way, one to another, how a certain district commissioner arrives and wants everything just so. He is only there a very short time and presently he is succeeded by another district commissioner who wants everything quite different. Europeans are a constant topic of conversation with Africans, and they give illustrations like these to indicate that they think we must be a little mad.'

Asked about the alleged 'murderer,' the Archbishop agrees with the business man that he must have the benefit of the doubt. His Grace claims that he gets on very well with African leaders and it will be unwise, in his opinion, to suppose that Africans will not, in quite a short time, be able to manage their own affairs efficiently.

By the time I have finished my visit I have promised so many people in Kenya to 'let people in England know what I think about all this' that this book is the outcome. Looking back with memories of forty years ago it is impossible not to feel that we might well have trained Africans long ago in friendly co-operation with us to share in all our way of life. Had we said whenever an African reached a level of development, 'Come friend, take a seat at my table,' matters might well have been very different. We have, however, dawdled for forty years and have now made things very much worse than they need have been by cramming the preparation into a collection of crash programmes over less than three years. Uhuru is not going to represent the maturity of a developing society like the multi-racial society of Brazil; it will be a sudden and total replacement of the mature by the immature depending for its success on the willingness of the mature to remain subordinate and the immature to show sufficient good will to retain them.

2

THE HALTING OF KUSH

The Region

Unfold a Bartholomew's physical map of Africa, 1:10,000,000, and lay it on the table in front of you with Cairo in the north farthest away, and Cape Town nearest to your belt. Then take a flexible footrule of the plastic sort and put one end of it just short of midway between Cairo and Cape Town, namely on to the clove island of Zanzibar. Next put the upper end against the Red Sea harbour of Port Sudan, and finally bend the footrule in a bow towards the west until it moves beyond the western boundaries of Kenya and Ethiopia. The land space between the footrule and the ocean is the region of Africa which is the subject of this book; it contains the political states of Ethiopia, Kenya and the Somali Republic.

The bowed base of this region on its western flank is about eighteen hundred miles between north and south. On the east from Mombasa along the seaboard of the Indian Ocean to the tip of the Horn at Cape Guardafui is some fourteen hundred miles, and here perhaps I should add that the territory occupied by the Somali peoples is generally known as the Horn of Africa—taking its name possibly from the slight resemblance of this portion of the region to the horn of a rhinoceros protruding from the eastern flank of Africa into the Indian Ocean. From the tip of this horn, running along its upper side and south of the gulf of Aden to the kink near Berbera, is another four hundred and fifty miles. The line then turns north-westwards through the Straights of Bab el Mandeb to the northern extremity of Eritrea. The land surface of the region enclosed is a little less than nine-tenths of a million square miles—eighteen times the size of England, or a quarter the size of U.S.A. Within present boundaries two hundred and twenty-five thousand square miles are in Kenya, two hundred and ninety-eight thousand in Somalia and three hundred and fifty thousand in Ethiopia. Nearly a half of the whole area approximates to desert conditions, but at least a third of the whole is taken up by the largest and most fertile area of temperate highlands in all Africa. The present estimate of population is about twenty-eight million—nearly the whole of it is black, but less than a quarter of it is negroid and little of it is pure Negro. There are small but important settlements of white and brown.

The region lies between the Equator in the south and the Tropic of Cancer in the north, but apart from this single uniformity of being situated wholly in the tropics, almost every other geographical factor makes for diversity.

In the north are the great highlands of the Habash and the Galla, in the south the lesser highlands of Bantu Kenya, extending southwards into Tanganyika. Both are regions of high rainfall, over thirty inches a year in the Kenya highlands and from thirty to sixty inches in the Habash and Galla highlands. Between the Habash highlands and the Red Sea to the east are deserts inhabited by Danakil (Afar) peoples. Between the Galla highlands and the Indian Ocean are the Somali deserts, and these continue south-westerly and then north-westerly to form a desert wedge between the Ethiopian group of highlands in the north and the Bantu highlands south of them. This wedge includes the desert half of Kenya. West of all the region lies the basin of the White Nile. Annual rainfall in the desert regions is nearly everywhere under twenty inches. In many parts it is under ten inches and in some parts under five inches. In few places, however, is it so little as to render the area devoid of vegetation at all seasons.

In temperate climates like that of northern Europe the mountains are the regions of austere pastoral farming, while the fatlings and the golden harvests are to be found in the valleys. For instance, here on Exmoor where I am a farmer, we have a higher rainfall indeed, but the topsoil is thin and the subsoil porous so that the lime and potash which we spread in order to maintain alkaline fertility is leached away by too much water and we revert quickly to acid conditions. We are exposed to fierce winds, our trees are stunted, high-return crops give way to permanent grass and our beasts are all of the hardier and less profitable breeds. Ten miles away in the vale I have a second farm which is fertile, mild, productive and yields whatever profits there may be.

In Africa it is all the other way round. Up on the tropical but temperate plateaux between five and ten thousand feet, rain is more abundant; springs, streams and wells last throughout the year; the soil is deep and rich; good animal management can yield stock of a higher grade; agriculture can produce high return crops and good harvests are expected as the reward of good husbandry. In Kenya that is the position today after half a century of successful warfare by Europeans against the cohorts of diseases that formerly plagued man, beast and plant.

The Presence of Kush

The region is a meeting point between black Africans who are mainly of Negro origin and black Africans who have European features.

Negroid physical features are firmly established in most people's minds, and they include such things as short hair called wool which is tightly kinky; a slight beard or none at all; high cheek bones; protruding lower jaw; shallow eye-sockets; a nose with low bridge flattened and splayed and distended nostrils; large mouth with thick everted lips; large hands and feet and thick fingers.

By contrast European features include long, straight or wavy or curly hair; full beard; deep eye-sockets; thin and straight or aquiline nose with small nostrils and raised bridge; small mouth with thin lips; small hands and slender fingers.

The point can be illustrated if we acknowledge that the celebrated Negro singer, Mr. Paul Robeson, would not look like a European even if he were white, while President de Gaulle would not look like a Negro even if he were black. In East Africa whole tribes of Africans look more like Europeans than Negroes in spite of being black.

Those African groups in the region who have mainly Negro features are called negroid by most people. The term is a purely racial one with two linguistic divisions, the Bantu and the Nilotic; there are non-Negro racial elements in both groups. Groups with European features possibly inherited for thousands of years, are called Eastern Hamites or Kushites; these terms have been used both racially and linguistically with ever-increasing confusion until anthropologists are now suggesting that in a racial sense they have become nonsense. Some of the experts go so far as to suggest that the more spectacular physical features which we notice are offset by less obvious physical features which we do not notice at a glance but which contradict the visual impact or at any rate dilute the viability of traditional inferences.

On the face of it this looks like a re-statement of the old debate between heredity and environment, but a second look suggests a clash between two inheritances, the physical and the cultural. It is as though a team of investigators from Mars were to discover first that half the Latin races were speaking Teutonic languages and then that under microscopic examination of blood groups and hair the difference between Italians and Germans was seen to disappear.

So we are invited either to ignore the visual evidence or to present it in a new vocabulary which is far from having replaced the old.

From criticisms which I produce in a later chapter it may seem that anthropologists are nearing the point where the racial differences between Mr. Robeson and General de Gaulle are of no particular cultural significance, but not everyone is yet with them in this matter, and we are unable to escape from the language still in use to describe such things as the 'coming' of Hamites (Kushites) or the 'Hamitization' of East Africa. We must be attentive of course when we are told that some Hamites (linguistically understood) are almost wholly Negro (racially understood), while others like the White Berbers are strongly Caucasian (racially understood). We must also take careful note that the Habash are Semitic in speech and the Somalis Kushitic in speech, but it is harder to accept that the Caucasian features of both may no longer be termed Hamitic or Kushitic.

Seeing that Kush—racial Kush—has been observed on the move in the region I am to review, and that I am not qualified to correct the language in which for so long the phenomenon has been described by many accepted authorities, I am forced, like the Gerenuk, to stick out my neck and give an account of Kush: Christian Kush, Muslim Kush and Pagan Kush; and I mean to imply by the term Kush the presence of a European racial ingredient which may be like a little whisky in the soda or, for those who may be offended by this analogy, a little soda in the whisky.

Christian Kush—The Habash

The first task in writing of the Abyssinian peoples is to decide what to call them, for here we stumble at once against another confusion. The Habash call themselves Ethiopia, and Ethiopia is a very old name with more than one very old meaning. Habash historians have given to one of these old meanings a twist of their own which is not accepted by other historians, and they confuse the matter still further by applying the old name to their modern East African empire which they acquired not earlier than we acquired our own in this area, that is some eighty years ago, part of it less than five years ago.

The word 'Ethiopia' itself is made up of two Greek words meaning *burnt faces*, and is the same etymologically as the word 'Negro' which is derived from the Latin for black—niger. Budge explains how the classical scholars Homer, Herodotus, Diodorus, Strabo, and Pliny used Ethiopia to indicate the whole region from the Nile to the Indus which they knew to be inhabited by dark-skinned and black-faced peoples. These they divided into Eastern Ethiopians living in Arabia, Syria, Mesopotamia and India, and Western Ethiopians living west of the Red Sea. These classical writers did not include the Abyssinians even amongst the Western Ethiopians, for they knew nothing about Abyssinians or Abyssinia nor the position of their country.

It appears also that those Biblical scribes who translated the Hebrew *Kush* into the Greek *Ethiopia* intended to signify the region of Nubia in the southern Sudan, not Abyssinia further south.

Why then do the Abyssinians claim a name which historically has been used either for all dark-skinned people or more narrowly for people who live to the north of them (e.g., Candace or Meroe) and who have never been Abyssinians?

It seems that those scribes who translated the Bible into Ethiopic (more properly called Geez) applied Ethiopia to Abyssinia perhaps in a spirit of antiquarian imperialism so that the Habash might appropriate for themselves alone the venerable standing in ancient history and holy writ.

But there is another Habash tradition, an oral one, which is accepted everywhere in Abyssinia (Budge); this is that Noah begat Ham and Ham begat Kush who begat Aithiopis who gave his name to Ethiopia, and whose grave is to be found in the city of Aksum in a State of the same name founded by his son Aksumawi.

Abyssinia is a European form of Habash or Habish or Habsha which is the name of the Arab tribe from Yaman who invaded the country some centuries before the Christian era.

Whilst not pretending to decide whether this was a first invasion or a re-occupation by Semitic peoples, it does seem to

suggest that the de-Europeanized word Habash is the most
ancient and most honourable as well as the most accurate term
which is available to name the Abyssinians. The chronicle Kebra
Negast attributes to God a decision to discontinue the line of Ham
owing to Noah's curse, so even if Aithiopis is a person of history he
is tainted with his great-grandfather's curse, while the Habash
from Saba or Sheba in Yemen are more glamorous in their
ancestral Queen and her romance with King Solomon of Israel.

Anyway, Habash is what all the Africans of Kenya used to
call them in my day, and I expect they still do so except for a few
who now use the term 'Amharas' to indicate more accurately the
tribal oligarchy at the head of the empire. My Swahili dictionary
for instance has nothing for Ethiopian but it gives Habeshi for
Abyssinians. So I shall be using Habash for Abyssinians in this
book to cover them in all stages of their history, whether in Arabia
or in Africa, and to distinguish them from the Ethiopia of antiquity, which is something different, and from their own late
Victorian empire.

Budge, in his comprehensive history of Ethiopia, writes that one
of the difficulties of compiling Habash history is the unsatisfactory
nature of native sources and the absence of any others. Although
the Royal Chronicles

> 'are regarded everywhere in Abyssinia as the supreme and final
> authorities for the history of the country it is impossible to accept
> them as historical documents in the true sense of the word . . . the
> truth is that the Abyssinians know nothing about the true history of
> their country in pre-Christian times. They have always had a pas-
> sionate desire to be considered a very ancient nation and the vivid
> imagination of their scribes has borrowed the traditions of historical
> facts preserved by Semites . . . and modified them to suit the aspira-
> tions of their countrymen. . . . The history of Abyssinia during the
> Christian era, as presented by chroniclers and scribes until we come
> to the second half of the 13th century is, to say the least of it, in-
> complete and, in some respects is wholly untrustworthy'.

This trait, as I shall have occasion to point out, has persisted
right up to our own day.

According to Budge again, Abyssinian 'history' records
separately and without reconciliation first that Adam heads the
Abyssinian King list, and here the pedigree is entirely incredible,
then that the first King was Aithiopis the great-grandson of Noah
(in the Kebra Negast however it seems, as we have seen, that God

terminated the line of Ham because they were condemned to be
the slaves of Sem); finally that the first King was Menelek I son
of Solomon King of Israel and Makeda (Belkis to the Arabs)
Queen of Sheba and moreover that Menelek was the founding
father of Aksum in northern Abyssinia (Tigre).

No matter how questionable or unproven these three accounts
may be, the mention of Aksum does indeed bring us to the
meeting point of legend and history. History records that Semites
(Arabs) from Yemen, including the Habashat, did most probably
invade the region of Tigre during the last thousand years B.C. It
is not impossible that a Habashat Queen may have been the
'Queen of the South' who visited Solomon; however, if historical
evidence does not allow the Habashat into Africa as early as 970
B.C. she could have travelled with less difficulty and danger by
camel caravan from Southern Arabia to Palestine.

It appears certain that Aksum was not founded until the first
century A.D., that is about a thousand years after the Habash
claim. Habash historians also claim that St. Thomas the Apostle
converted the Habash to Christianity in the first century A.D., but
Budge considers it beyond any doubt that Ezana who reigned in
Aksum in the second quarter of the fourth century was the first
King who adopted Christianity as the national religion—the
Constantine of Abyssinia.

On this a critic* writes as follows:

> One other point concerns the religious fortunes of Abyssinia. It
> received the faith (papal Christianity) at the hands of St. Frumentius
> in A.D. c. 350. You state that in the following century it was con-
> verted to Monophysism of Coptic heresy. This, indeed, is the legend
> current today, of the nine saints from Syria who fled to Ethiopia and
> preached the doctrine there for the first time. Fr. Coulbeaux, the
> historian of Abyssinia, seriously doubts this story. He thinks the
> actual facts are considerably more complicated. Ethiopia depended
> on Alexandria for its Abuna, or bishop, and it would have been
> unaffected by the theological fluctuations of the Church of Egypt
> until a determined Modophysite patriarch reigned at Alexandria.
> The Syrian story is unlikely. The first undoubted Monophysite
> patriarch of Alex. was Benjamin in 641, who sent the Monophysite
> Abuna Abba Kierlos Cyrille to Abyssinia. The schism dates from
> then (Muslim times) since an Abuna, only, could have effected it—
> not a handful of vagrant monks unconnected with Alexandria.

* See Author's Note. P. ix

1. *Dr. Adan Abdullah Osman, President of the Somali Republic.*

2. *Mr. Jomo Kenyatta, President of the Kenya Republic.*

There were Kushites (a branch of Hamites) in the area prior to the arrival of the Habashat (Semites), and there had earlier been in all probability Negroes who were perhaps in part displaced. The Habashat imported civilization, including their written language, a superior building technique in stone (albeit without lime mortar), better agricultural equipment, better husbandry and a currency system. Unlike the later wave of Muslim invaders the Habashat were settled farmers from the Yemen highlands, not pastoral nomads from the Arabian desert. They preceded Our Lord by half a thousand years at least and they preceded the prophet Mohammed by a whole thousand or more. They may have been pagans worshipping a serpent or they may have already accepted Jahweh from the Hebrews or they may have been pagans in part and Judaised in part.

Having thus acknowledged the Habash historically at Aksum in the century of Our Lord I jump to Budge's description of them today after they have long exchanged most of their Arabian blood for African Kushite blood (if the linguists can be kept at bay) and have sipped at many different cultures during their tenure of the Habash highlands through twenty or thirty centuries:

> In all periods of their history the Abyssinians have *mixed* more or less freely with Semites and people of Negro or negroid origin, but their country produces a type of man or woman, e.g., in Shoa, whose form and physical characteristics approach perfection, and the type is not altered provided that the mixture of Semitic or Negro blood is not too great. The body is tall and well-formed, the features are handsome, straight and regular, the eyes are bold and fearless, the mouth sensitive, the hair dark brown and curly or long and straight and almost blue-black in colour. . . . The young Abyssinian women have in all periods of history been famed for their beauty . . . their great velvety eyes are said to be one of their principal beauties.

Clearly this is not the physical description of Negroes! What is it? *Kush* until lately was the answer, and Budge is in line with many others in ascribing superior intelligence to the descendants of Kush: 'The Abyssinians of Tigre and Amhara are very intelligent and their shrewdness is often mingled with cunning.'

The same author writes thus of Pagan Kush, that is the Galla:

> They are large and powerfully built but their features are savage-looking [a savage-looking photo is produced in Budge's history], and when they shake their long hair which they wear hanging over their shoulders like a mane, their appearance is animal-like and terrifying.

C

And again Kush is associated with superior intelligence, for Budge writes, 'In intelligence they are superior to all the other peoples in East Africa.'

The Foreign Office report of 1920 on Ethiopia confirms the intelligence of the Galla: 'Most intelligent . . . since they invaded the country (the Ethiopian plateau) have become more than once the dominant race.'

The *Encyclopaedia Britannica* of 1929 is fairer to the good looks of the Galla:

> The Galla are members of the Eastern Hamitic family with their neighbours, the Somalis, the Afars (Danakil) and the Abyssinians. There is a strain of Negro blood in the Galla who are a wonderfully handsome race with high foreheads, brown skins and soft wavy hair quite different from the wool of the Bantus. As a rule their features are quite European.

This is not a description of Negroes. Indeed it specifically restricts Negro blood to 'a strain,' differentiates them from the Bantu who are negroid and associates them in appearance with Europeans who are not negroid. What then is the rest of the blood? *Kush* was until lately the answer.

Turn now to the Somalis who, like the Habash and the Galla, are almost wholly African without being wholly Negro. Sir Charles Eliot writes (*The East Africa Protectorate*, 1905):

> At the same time the wildest and most civilised of Africans . . . sharply distinguished from all Negro tribes by their clear-cut and often beautiful features . . . very Apollos cast in dark bronze. . . . knowledge of European law and power of using it to their own advantage without parallel amongst the natives of East Africa . . . only rivalled amongst the Indians. . . . Undoubtedly talented race. . .

I hope that by now I have established by reference to acceptable authorities the presence of Kush in the region: Christian Kush, that is mainly the Habash; Muslim Kush, mainly the Somalis; and Pagan Kush, mainly the Galla—all three branches of Kush occupying a habitat mainly north of the Bantus.

The Halting of the Habash

Racial and tribal movements in Africa sometimes implied the eviction of those who were there before, but often they involved co-existence with exchanges of blood and culture. In this process some of the cultures have predominated notwithstanding an almost total transfusion of blood during the course of centuries by inter-marriage. In the course of reviewing how the Habash have preserved their culture for so long, we have to examine the influence of topography upon history.

The two highland groups already described in outline are sharply dissimilar. Those of Kenya although distant from the coast are easy of access and, with few exceptions, intercommunication within them is not very seriously obstructed except in seasons of unusually heavy rain like the autumn of 1961; even then my wife and I were only occasionally held up during our journeys in a small Ford Anglia. By contrast the Habash highlands are among the least accessible and the most fissured by sheer chasms of any region in the world. Here in a pear-shaped territory so formed as to constitute one of nature's defensive regions the Yemeni Habash slowly grafted themselves upon the Kushite occupiers. They took perhaps a thousand years to occupy the whole of the pear-shaped region now called Abyssinia. Then in this specifically Habash region they have held on tenaciously against many an invasion from outside and many a revolt from within since the sixteenth century.

Here follows my description of some of the topographical features which have helped them to hold out for so many centuries often against superior forces:

All along the eastern flank of the pear-shaped region runs the west wall of the Danakil deserts rising steeply from desert level to a terraced plateau in general eight thousand feet above the desert with mountains yet another six or seven thousand feet above the plateau. For the most part this cliff-like escarpment is broken only by steep, narrow clefts hundreds of feet deep.

The high terraces of the Ethiopian plateau lose height generally towards the west, contributing the great bulk of their high rainfall to the waters of the Nile by means of the Takaze (Atbara) and Abbai (the Blue Nile) and their numerous tributaries. These rivers flow in part through jungle-choked gorges which are often entirely impassable; the rivers, too, are often difficult and dangerous to cross even at the recognized crossing places.

The pear-shaped region is bounded on the south for most of its length roughly along the tenth parallel North latitude by a chasm reputedly greater than the Grand Cañon of the Colorado; the latter world wonder I have descended but so far I have not seen the Blue Nile Gorge. This is the gorge where the Blue Nile

after turning westwards runs for hundreds of miles as far down as
a mile below the lips of the gorge itself, taking a course so difficult
to follow that few if any have been able to do so from end to end.
Only at the upper or south-eastern corner is there a gap where
Addis Ababa now stands affording a vulnerable line of approach
from the south or the south-east.

The region within these external defences of cliff and gorge,
chasm and torrent, is the historic land of the Habash people who
founded the city and state of Aksum in Tigre north of the Takaze
from the first century A.D. onwards, and who after many fluctua-
tions of fortune occupied the region between the Takaze and the
Blue Nile. During the sixteenth century the southern advance of
Christian Kush was finally halted.

David Mathew makes a good summary of this final halting
(*Ethiopia*, 1947):

> During the Middle Ages it was the work of the Abyssinian kings
> to push southwards, to Christianise and settle the provinces of
> Gojjam, Lasta, Amhara, Beghemeder and Shoa. There on the
> southern frontiers of Shoa expansion and conversion ceased alto-
> gether. Enarya, a conquest of the late sixteenth century, was the last
> province gained. Until within living memory there was neither tem-
> poral rule nor spiritual ascendancy over the inhabitants of the
> plateau country which stretches southwards from the present capital
> towards Lake Rudolf and Lake Stefanie. During the whole period
> that we shall consider, these wide territories were the home of pas-
> toral tribes originally pagan, but sometimes, as around Jimma,
> Mohammedan; they did not form a part of Abyssinia.

During the sixteenth century too the Habash finally lost all
control over their former seaport Massawa, they ceased to operate
a single seagoing vessel, they no longer harried the Muslim
Somali, Bedja or Danakil communities for tribute, their Negro
looting grounds south of the Blue Nile were overrun by the
martial Galla, their frail national unity slowly declined and even
their capacity for defence seems to have degenerated. Only their
fissured fastnesses saved them from complete obliteration; even
their historian of the period attributes Galla victories to the fact
that nine out of the ten Habash classes had ceased to provide
combatants in time of war.

The segmented character of the Habash territory is a freakish
and exaggerated association of downland tops and *Cheddar*
Gorges. The Habash plateaux in many places take the form of

dome-topped mountains, some with pyramid or chimney-like features surmounting them. These are self-contained agricultural locations with lush pastures holding a superior grade of African cattle and fertile tillage land yielding two or three crops a year. Here, too, are permanent springs and forested slopes for firewood; each fertile mountain area is severed from its neighbours by narrow chasms or sheer naked cliffs falling to rivers hundreds or even thousands of feet below. So just as the pear-shaped whole is a region naturally formed to make defence from outside aggression the stronger form of war, so by means of cliff, gorge, chasm and torrent is each separate hilltop or *amba* a naturally self-contained subsistence area accessible only by steep and easy-to-defend mule tracks.

Some of these ambas have been strongholds of independent kings or recalcitrant rases, last defences of the Habash when ravaged by invaders, prisons for potential emperors and even in later centuries guarded enclaves for nonentities deemed suitable to sit on the throne of Solomon's son at the discretion of the powerful nobles.

Who then are the enemies of the Habash?

On one flank the rise of Mohammedan Arabs at the end of the sixth century produced a threat from the East which waxed strongly and later waned a little during the course of eight hundred years from about the eighth century to the sixteenth. At the end of this period Islamic power shifted from the Arabs to the Turks and reached a new climax, bringing defeat and apostasy to the Habash during fifteen years followed by victory which yielded but few of the fruits of victory.

From the sixteenth century, too, the martial Galla brought their tribes and herds from the Savannahs of the south-east on to the high plateaux to which David Mathew has referred. Here they made use of the indigenous horses and acquired great renown as horsemen. The Habash had by then lost much of their renown and all of their imperial authority.

Negroes were never a match for Hamites (Kushites); they had endured the Habash who raided them for slaves and went away again like the Arabs, but the Galla needed land, not loot, so the Negroes moved on leaving the Galla face to face with the Habash no longer as a people acting passively as reservoirs for slaves but as warriors who were to prove more than a match for raider Habash during the next three hundred years.

The Halting of Muslim Kush—Somalis

When Muslims first reached Africa from Arabia they were of course Arabs—that is Semites, not African Kushites. And, in spite of the anthropologists, I mean by Semites persons with Semitic noses as well as Semitic tongues, just as we know them today—just as they were known and depicted in the monuments of Rameses II which I saw at Karnak (or thereabouts) in 1932.

The prophet Mohammed stands astride the year A.D. 600, thirty years on either side of the century year. We are accustomed to hearing in connection with the rise to power of his movement the story of military eruptions and great victories won against three established empires, all simultaneously and successfully assaulted in defiance of such authorities as Hannibal, Scipio Africanus, Julius Caesar and other exponents of the principles of war. The jihad spread along the North African coast destroying, it is said, more than two hundred bishoprics and eliminating Christianity everywhere along the southern seaboard of the Mediterranean.

But not all the early Muslims were militant or victorious, and some were even persecuted to the point of becoming refugees. Amongst such refugees were the advance party, in a sense, of numerous later Muslim settlements in the Horn of Africa. They took ship somewhere near Medina with a message of amity from the Prophet himself, and they were so well received by the Habash king that the Habash, notwithstanding their Christianity, were dispensed from the jihad by a fiat of the Prophet; they continued to be thus dispensed for nearly a thousand years even when relations between Arabs and Habash had become very bad indeed.

Some of the Arabs remained Arabs as they have done to this day, but others, following the same processes of blood transfusion and cultural exchange as the Habash, became in the course of time Kushites with an Islamic culture. The assimilating process probably started a thousand years after the Habash, but it continues today four hundred years after the Habash have almost ceased to assimilate.

Before reviewing the history of Islamic Arabian settlers in the Horn of Africa, it is important to compare them with those pre-Islamic Arabian settlers, the Habash.

The Arabian Habashat from Yemen came from cool, well-watered agricultural highlands in Arabia to cool, well-watered highlands in Africa. It is not credible that they could ever have wished to settle and live in the Danakil or Somali deserts, and I can find no indication that they have ever tried to do so. On the other hand post-Islamic Arabian settlers in the lowlands of the Horn came from one desert to another, from one arid region of pastoral nomadism to a similar habitat, from one over-heated Red Sea trading village to another where conditions were very much the same.

These settlers came not as imperial overlords but as occupiers of land and localities which they liked and understood, and moved probably into a land under-occupied owing to the adverse consequences of diseases, droughts and disorders.

After they had ceased to assimilate, the Habash retained their latent imperial ambitions, and whenever they felt strong enough sought to impose their imperial authority over territories where none of them wished to live and which their small population was incapable of occupying. This is the power-hunger of empire-building, not the land-hunger of people faced with a desperate struggle for survival, nor even the economic imperialism of a nation of shopkeepers.

Arabs in addition to their nomadic settlements have always conducted a substantial seaborne trade between the Red Sea ports of Africa and those of Arabia and further afield, using the monsoons for voyages to India and China. So did in turn the Egyptians, the Greeks, the Roman Empire, the Venetian Republic, the Ottoman Turks and the Portuguese. Both Habash and Arabs have been raiders and traders in slaves right up to the present age, but not for centuries have the Habash conducted their own seaborne trade, and most of their external trade by land has always been in the hands of non-Christian minorities mainly Muslims.

Conflicts between the Habash and the Muslim Arab settlements began to occur then in territories where the aggressors with rare exceptions, had no intention of settling and no desire to live.

The first Islamic period which had a serious impact upon the control (as opposed to occupation) of what the Habash called their maritime province (Danakil) containing the ports of Adoulis and Massawa, began in the second quarter of the seventh century; this is how it started.

In the sixth century A.D. the Habash king ruled not only in African Aksum, but in Arabian Yemen as well, and there he

planned to make Sana a place of pilgrimage at the expense of
pre-Islamic Mecca, which was already a holy place attracting
pilgrims. In A.D. 571, when the Prophet was one year old, the
Habash king's army was almost at the gates of Mecca when he
was thwarted by an outbreak of smallpox amongst his troops.

After the Habash withdrawal the Muslim Arabs reacted
strongly against such acts of piracy and pillage and in A.D. 634
even Massawa was in Arab hands; in 640 the Arabs destroyed the
Port of Adoulis and it never rose again. Then between A.D. 636
and 642 the Arabs conquered Syria, Palestine and Egypt. But
Habash pirates were not easily put off, and in the year 702 an
African sea expedition sacked Jedda. Soon afterwards the Arabs,
intending to forestall another assault upon Mecca itself, again
occupied the Habash ports.

In spite of these warlike activities there appears never to have
been a complete interruption of trade, for hostilities were intermittent and port controllers were often tolerant or inefficient or
adequately corruptible for 'business as usual' in spite of hostile
appearances.

Then an empror of the 'restored' Solomonid line brought a
better unity to the Habash state, but made use of his new power,
as so often before and so often since, to persecute his neighbours
and extract tribute from a number of thriving Muslim kingdoms.
Of these kingdoms Adel on the Gulf of Aden was the most
prosperous and the least disposed to co-operate in paying tribute
to anybody. Of these conflicts lasting some two centuries Jones
and Munroe write (*History of Ethiopia*):

> With monotonous regularity the king (of Abyssinia) ravages the
> Moslem kingdoms, burns their capitals and receives the submission
> of their kings. With equally monotonous regularity the Moslem kings
> ravage the Abyssinian kingdom and annexe its border provinces (at
> one time a Moslem state was thus established in eastern Shoa). The
> Abyssinian armies murmur at their continual hardships in the torrid
> clime of Somaliland and return home . . . so the wars go on with
> little permanent result. While the Abyssinian armies are in the field
> some of the Moslem kingdoms temporarily acknowledge the suzer-
> ainty of the Abyssinian king and pay him tribute. When they are
> disbanded they rebel again.

Of these Moslem kingdoms the most famous, and one certainly
never subjugated by the Habash, was Adel. As the star of Christian Aksum began to set so did the star of Adel rise.

Thus did the Arab phase come to an end. It was followed by the Turkish phase which was to last a further three hundred years.

In the middle of the fifteenth century under the sultan Muhammad II the Ottoman Turks launched the last great effort of militant Islam against the Christian west. Constantinople, eastern capital of the Christian world, fell in 1453. Mohammedan Egypt rejoiced rather prematurely, for in 1516 another Ottoman sultan, Selim I, overthrew Egypt's sultan and annexed both Egypt and the Hedjaz to the Ottoman Empire. From 1520 there reigned in Constantinople Suleiman the Magnificent, who formed a great Turkish Navy, and in whose reign Habash piracy in the Red Sea was brought to an end by the occupation of key ports such as Massawa, which was to remain in Turkish hands until 1885. Moreover, armed with firearms (matchlocks) for the first time, Muslim forces began in 1528 to ravage the whole of Abyssinia, bringing perhaps three-quarters of the Habash territory under their control and forcing the Christian Habash to choose between apostasy and massacre. The leader of these inroads, which lasted until 1543, was Ahamed Gran, reputedly a Somali, but the impulse of invasion was undoubtedly an Ottoman impulse, especially as to initiative and the provision of Turkish infantry armed with matchlocks, which the Somalis themselves did not manufacture.

Just prior to these events, and in anticipation of them, the Habash King Lebna Dengel had been negotiating with the Portuguese to secure a Portuguese base in a Habash port. On being shown the position of Portugal on a map, he was unfavourably impressed by the small size of a state claiming to be so powerful, and was with difficulty dissuaded from inviting the Spaniards to establish a second base and the French a third. The Portuguese, however, convinced him in the end of their complete command of the seas without help from anyone else, but they procrastinated in their preparations and Ahamed Gran, Emir of Harar, struck first with overwhelming success.

Lebna Dengel, in the hour of his desperate need, appealed for troops to the Portuguese, and after some further delay a small Portuguese military contingent arrived in time to be wiped out by the Emir—one Portuguese soldier however managed to shoot and kill the Emir himself, and forthwith the tide turned. The Portuguese then proved themselves as good as their word and decisively interrupted Turkish communications across the Red

Sea. The Ottoman thrust was to receive its final and permanent repulse as a sea-power twenty-eight years later when a fleet, assembled in response to an appeal of Pope Pius V, defeated the Turkish fleet at Lepanto.

Even before Lepanto the Habash had begun to suffer more from their blockading allies than they had ever suffered during their seasonal conflicts with the Arabs. The Arabs were raiders indeed, but they were traders too, and sometimes their excursions were a mixture of both raiding and trading. War in any case was not the total thing it has become in modern times, and there might be war along one line of communications and unmolested trade along another line at the same time. But the Portuguese started by sinking a large number of Arab ships, and then they diverted the Far Eastern trade round the Cape to Europe and left the Red Sea a declining cul de sac with only a modicum of local trade.

En passant, it is to be noted that in the sixteenth century Portugal restored freedom to the oppressed Habash, while Britain in the twentieth restored a neglected empire to its Habash oppressors.

The restored Habash freedom in the sixteenth century did not for long leave the Habash with any taste for further imperial adventures. After initial successes against the retreating Muslims, their right to expand and raid their neighbours on the authority of Leviticus was challenged by Kushitic pagans whom they had never feared before— the Galla. But before giving an account of the Galla, the story of Muslim Kush must be concluded.

Amongst the nations formed by the grafting of Muslim Arabs on the Kushites of the Horn were the Somalis, who in the course of a thousand years or so have become what they are today—that is one nation speaking one language, professing one variety of one religion (Islam), having a common nomadic pastoral heritage in the frugal desert. By the end of the twelfth century they were establishing their distinct identity as a desert-dwelling nomadic pastoral people.

Undoubtedly Somali troops took part in the invasion of the Habash under Gran, who also was probably a Somali, but the impulse was more Arab than Somali and more Turkish than Arab. In all normal circumstances Habash and Somali preferred their own habitat and disliked that of the other. In the case of the Somali it is very unlikely that many settlers would have moved up into the highlands, even if Gran had been able to consolidate the power of Islam in Abyssinia. The Somali camel scours and languishes in lush highland pastures while Somalis themselves are prone to suffer from bronchial afflictions at high altitudes.

After the defeat of the Turkish invasion the Habash were barely able to hold off the Galla, but the Somalis took no advantage of their weakness, presumably because they did not covet the Habash plateau. Somali expansion took place south-westwards in the deserts, so that when Bruce visited Abyssinia, he remarked that the Somalis had long ceased to be a threat to the Habash. There was not then, and there is not now, any desire on the part of Somalis or Habash to live in the country of the other. There is something unlikely in the currently accepted story of the Somali advance south-westwards; the desire of the Habash to represent all Muslims as disturbers of the peace may perhaps have dovetailed with the Somali propensity for vainglorious recitations of their prowess in war. The traditional account has it that the fierce Somalis, thwarted in their desire to occupy the Habash highlands midway in the sixteenth century, turned south-westwards, driving the defenceless Negroids along the coast and pushing their less warlike opponents the Galla up into the Ethiopian plateau south of the Blue Nile, where they proved troublesome to the peaceful Habash.

We are given the picture of one continuous advance, with the Somalis crossing in turn three rivers, the Shebeli, the Juba (crossed in 1865), and finally the Tana in Kenya. This story may be true, but I half suspect it of being no more than half the truth, and I hope the Somali historian Dr. Lewis may enlighten us further.

A factor to which I feel obliged to give weight is that any people who could dominate the Habash as the Galla did for some three centuries, would be likely to have done so and to have moved into the coveted plateau without waiting to be pushed from behind by Somalis or anyone else. In the first instance Galla raiders would have discovered for themselves the new weakness of the Habash, and having arrived on the edge of the plateau, and by making use of the indigenous horses, found themselves masters of their new habitat, they would have moved up with their cattle from the less fruitful lowlands to a land flowing with milk and honey which neither Negroes nor Habash could prevent their taking.

The Somalis, with their unique survival animal the Somali camel, are certainly masters of the desert habitat, but it is difficult not to infer that their sudden comparatively rapid southward drive was made fortuitously easy by the voluntary evacuation of lowland territory by the upward moving Galla. While the Habash were going through a long period of decline, the Somalis seem to have shared an era of virile multiplication with their Galla cousins, both nations suddenly finding the endless annual struggle for survival turning strongly in their favour. Such Galla as remained to thwart the Somalis, chiefly the Wardeh Galla, were too few to occupy very easily the territory abandoned by the main body of their race; thus they must at many seasons have left water holes and grazings unoccupied and available for others. I have not heard in the course of studying African occupation of particular localities that any tribe ever recognized what we should call a title deed to ownership on the part of peoples who were unable to become beneficial occupiers of the property. It seems probable, too, that insufficient is known of the impact of small-pox on the movement of African peoples and their capacity to hold what they have at any particular time. The failure of the Habash viceroy Abraha at the gates of Mecca owing to a small-pox epidemic has already been mentioned, and Sir Richard Turnbull in a memorandum entitled *The Darod Invasion* describes how the last stand of the Wardeh Galla in Kenya was rendered abortive by another such epidemic of which the Somalis took advantage.

The foregoing notes are tentatively put forward, bearing in mind that the Somali historian, Dr. I. Lewis, has a book in the press as I write, and I expect it will reveal a more complex ebb and flow, with Somalis re-occupying the N.F.D. at the turn of the century—a region of which they were already in occupation in the seventeenth or eighteenth century. However that may be, the Somalis were on the move at the time when we arrived in Kenya, and it looks as though they were moving out of the habitat, where they have for a thousand years proved their mastery as beneficial occupiers, into the Highlands similar to those from which they were barred in the sixteenth century. Sir Gerald Reece for example thinks it reasonable to believe that Somalis would have conquered the Kikuyu and over-run the Kenya highlands if the British had not arrived in time to halt them. We shall see in the next chapter that the Kikuyu at this time were also victims of smallpox and unable to occupy their traditional lands, so the verdict of Sir Gerald Reece may well be a correct one, but on the whole I feel the Somalis would have been corrupted by the highlands and their vocation for better or worse on this planet is in the desert.

The Halting of Pagan Kush—The Galla

Who and what are the Galla?

They are Kushitic (Hamitic) in race and language, or they were until experts declared Noah's curse to be a myth. (Damn Ham!) When they emerged from total obscurity after the defeat of the Muslim invasion of Abyssinia, they were pagan. They were also pastoral nomads, and it is thought that they occupied a region around the present south-east border of the Ethiopian plateau—some say as far north as the Ogaden province, others nearer the Kenya-Ethiopia border. They are not a single nation, but several —Budge, for instance, gives them twenty-six 'tribes'—nevertheless they were aware of some strong underlying common factor. I am not sure how far their different languages differ in dialect alone or more substantially, but they have a common name for themselves, Orma or Oroma, and they do not like the name Galla any more than the Abyssinians like the name Habash, and they have better reasons than the Habash for their dislike. To the Habash, Galla means 'emigrant,' but to the Arabs it means two words—Gal = he said, and La = no; and that is alleged to have been the reply given by the founder when he received the Prophet's delegates and their summons to accept Islam—he flatly refused and they went back with the message 'Gal la' or 'He said no!' Whereupon the Prophet decreed that they should be known by the answer which they had given. Since those days some have become Muslim and others Christian, and while statistics in Ethiopia are apt to be what Disraeli thought of them, it seems probable that at the present time a third of the Galla may be Muslim, a third Christian, and only a third still pagan.

As a tribute to Galla military ability, it must be repeated that at a given moment in history two powerful slave-raiding communities, the Habash heirs of Aksum and the Arab settlers of Adel, were both successfully attacked by Galla warriors who were far less well armed; while Adel and Habash had access to matchlocks, the Galla had only pikes or spears. The Galla nevertheless put an end to the prosperous Islamic kingdoms based on Adel, and they might even have conquered the whole of Abyssinia (so thought Bruce), in spite of the gorges and cliff-protected ambas, but for a disastrous epidemic of smallpox, which so greatly reduced some of the Galla communities that they forthwith became tributaries of those whom they had conquered. This third epidemic of smallpox completes a trilogy of such epidemics, each one perhaps having had a decisive influence upon history which perhaps may not as yet have received sufficient notice from historians.

Aside from these contacts with the Habash, the Galla seem to have been accorded no *raison d'être* in history. Their valour has been depicted as animal savagery, their success against the Habash during three centuries has been represented as Habash weakness rather than Galla strength, their religion has been sneered at as something more than ordinarily infantile and superstitious, their political qualities have been decried as unstable and inept, and their future assigned to them uncritically as a docile colony of the world's dingiest empire.

Quite frankly my suspicion is that the Habash practice of heaping the most contemptuous abuse upon anyone whom they happen to dislike has in the case of the Galla been indulged in a direction where adequate retort has not yet been possible. Moreover, European historians to some extent seem to have followed the same line; for example, Budge writes: 'About the middle of the sixteenth century the Galla began to disturb the peace of Abyssinia . . .'. Are we not meant in this passage to accept that murderous Habash raiders, with their historic enslavement of their neighbours, their torturings and their mutilations, are just the 'blameless Ethiopians' of Homer? Has anyone ever heard of a Pax Habassina?

Budge follows his remark with a 'translation and summary' of a 'little Ethiopic manuscript'.

I begin to write the history of the Galla to make known the number of their tribes, their eagerness to kill men and their bestial manners and customs.

It is, of course, a Habash who is writing, and, according to Budge, the Ethiopian Empire at the time when he wrote had one hundred and fifty-nine tribes, of which only twenty-six were Galla.

The Habash author of this 'little Ethiopic manuscript' has this to say of Galla superiority:

Learned men often debate amongst themselves and say 'How is it that the Galla conquer us, seeing that we are very many in number and that we have an abundance of weapons?' . . . now as regards the fact that we are many in numbers. Those who are capable of fighting in wars are few in numbers while those who take no part in wars are very many.

So it is all a Habash weakness after all!

The manuscript says of their religion:

The Galla, like most of the people of East Africa, adore the sycamore tree, certain kinds of serpents and vultures. Their chief God, *Wak*, lives in the clouds, but they also worship Oglie (male) and Atatie (female). They believe that eighty-eight devils exist, each of which is able to inflict disease and sickness on man.

In this triangle of pagan, Christian and Muslim Kush, all have received the support and sympathy of some of us Western Europeans, except the Galla. The disparagments of which I read are however so far from corresponding with the little I have seen and heard about them in the field that I offer a few observations in an attempt to start a reassessment of their position in the world.

Those of the Galla on whose fringe I have worked are the small Kenya portion of a large Galla tribe occupying part of Southern Ethiopia—the Boran Galla. It is these who provided the early white settlers with their best indigenous cattle as a foundation for their cross-breeding with European bulls. I do not of course urge that good farming is next to Godliness, but at least good cattle cannot arrive by spontaneous generation from bad farmers, and that is greatly to their credit.

A friend of mine who knows the Boran language and who goes to stay with Boran families tells me that they are a God-fearing people worshipping the one sky God and going out in the early morning to pray to him. They have also a successful inter-clan system of regulating disputes so that they do not degenerate into war. My friend calls this the pax Borana. They are generally monogamous, and not only are very fond of children, but have so high a standard of care for the coming race that a husband may not have intercourse with his wife from the time of conception to the publicly celebrated weaning of the child two years after its birth. Intercourse, so they hold, would risk diminishing the vigour of the mother, whose sole physical duty at this time is to impart her own health and strength to her baby. Before the arrival of Europeans, infringement of this tribal law was regarded as a capital offence, punishable in certain circumstances by death.

By way of illustrating the Boran love of children my friend has told me a story of an occasion when he was staying with a Boran family where the mother of many children was having difficulty with her last—an ailing daughter whose condition did not respond to any remedy or any treatment. One day my friend overheard through a partition wall the woman praying aloud, 'O God, this child has her life in front of her, while I have mine behind me—take me instead of her and let her have life!'

These were the people living as they do far from the boundaries of Abyssinia who were 'shot down like rabbits' by Menelek's soldiers, armed with French rifles, in about the year 1899. Thus did the Habash avenge themselves for the long centuries when, so long as armaments were equal, they could neither raid nor invade the Galla with impunity.

The Halting of Hybrid Kush

I will only add a short reference to one small martial tribe, so mobile, so restless, so violent, so beautiful, so predatory, so wasteful of land use—the Masai. These hybrids carried the blood of Kush (unless the anthropologists have by now drained it all away) all the way from the Boran in Northern Kenya to the Wahehe in Southern Tanganyika. There at their southernmost point in 1850 they were defeated, but it was not this one battle which halted the southward advance of Kush, but the arrival of Europeans, mainly British. Between the Boran in the north and the Wahehe in the south there is a distance as the flamingo flies of about five hundred miles. And the Masai people have probably never much exceeded one hundred thousand.

3. The Emperor Haile Selassie waits to receive from H.M. the Queen the gift of a fine thoroughbred stallion, on the occasion of Her Majesty's State Visit to Ethiopia in 1965.

4. Letter in Amharic addressed by the Emperor Menelek to the Powers in April 1891 (author's translation of part of the French version is given in Appendix 9)

3

KENYATTALAND

Mr. Kenyatta is the first black Prime Minister* of the Kenya
Republic and he is also, inter alia, author of a book on the
Kikuyu tribe from which he himself has sprung. Dr. Leakey, a
Kenya Briton, has also written books about the Kikuyu; he has
only a little less inside experience than Mr. Kenyatta, for he was
brought up with the tribe and belongs to a Kikuyu age-group, and
speaks Kikuyu, it is said, as well as he speaks English. So, with Mr.
Kenyatta as my chief source, Dr. Leakey as a second source, and
with scores of minor contact points of my own, I set out to give a
summary account of a pagan agricultural community of Negroes
in the highlands of Kenya.

Mr. Kenyatta writes lucidly, coherently and persuasively about
the tribe to which he belongs, and of which he has been one of the
leaders during the past forty years. He writes of pre-colonial
Africa as of a golden age, and of European colonialism with
intense animosity. On colonialism he is perverse and extremely
inaccurate, delivering his major attack upon the white settlers for
their virtues rather than their faults—and where he probes their
faults he is not content to do so without imputing malice. In this
respect his book, *Facing Mount Kenya*, is a diatribe, resembling in
its oddly unbalanced sarcasm the passion-raising overtones of the
Communist manifesto, rather than a work of sober history.

On the Kikuyu tribe Mr. Kenyatta follows the maxim prescribed for one selling a horse:

> Be to his points a little kind
> And to his faults a little blind.

The picture is of some tribal Eden before the fall, with advance-
ments in grace and wisdom and responsibility moving sweetly
forward from the cradle to the grave. In spite of this strain on

* Now President.

credibility the picture is an absorbing one, with a great deal that
is most probably true, with other parts of it that one might wish
to be true even if they are not, and with only a few aspects which
we would like not to be true even if they are. When Mr. Kenyatta
gets away from matters directly connected with his own tribe
there is abundant evidence of his great ignorance of African and
even of Kenyan affairs once he is no longer in sight of Mount
Kenya. He seems to depict all Africa in a state more flawless than
anyone has ever reported it to be—but let that pass. I aim here to
do justice to the better parts of the picture painted by Mr.
Kenyatta, and to segregate the lucidity of his tribal picture
equally from the aura of *Paradise Lost* and from the author's unbalanced sneers.

Mr. Kenyatta starts by presenting his credentials: he is a
Kikuyu with a Masai grandmother. He was brought up by his
family in the tribal area and became the leader of his age-group.
The history of the Kikuyu was imparted to him from his earliest
years according to the oral traditions of the tribe. Mr. Kenyatta is
intimate with every custom, and claims, in particular, to be
especially familiar with the procedures relating to land purchase,
land tenure and disputes about land. He has also studied the
Kikuyu methods of waging war, and those too of the Masai,
presumably in the Narok area. Of the Masai and other pastoral
nomads who occupy at least three quarters of Kenya he has
almost nothing to say. He has been abroad for a number of years,
but his story is almost wholly circumscribed by the limits of a
small region of Kenya within the sight of Kenya mountain. It
focuses exclusively upon the way of life of only one of Kenya's
sixty or so tribes. The picture, when we have made reservations
for certain serious omissions, has an authentic ring as an account
of the tribal laws, customs and usages. Its weakness lies in its
failure to carry conviction on the matter of the tribe's main
grievance, and there is absurdity when the substance of that
grievance is extended to the whole of Africa. Only when Mr.
Kenyatta is deeply absorbed in giving an account of the Kikuyu
way of life does his animated narrative fascinate and command
respect.

The Kikuyu live in the temperate highlands, occupying their
small family holdings and living in huts in the same place all the
year round. (Here I am obliged to mention that other reports
indicate that in pre-colonial days the Kikuyu managed their land

wastefully in a semi-nomadic manner.) The Kikuyu till the soil
and grow a variety of consumer crops producing, at any rate until
recently, a very small margin above subsistence needs (until
recently, too, it is a fact that every report describes their methods
of husbandry as of a very poor standard). The more prosperous
members of the tribe keep a small number of humped cattle,
again of a poor quality, and Mr. Kenyatta admits that these
could be better. Every Kikuyu family keeps flocks of goats and
fat-tailed sheep. The sheep and goats were formerly the 'currency'
of the tribe, and were also needed for 'marriage insurance',
sacrifices, meat feasts, magical rites, purification ceremonies and
for the leather garments worn by all. The sequence given here is
that more or less followed by Mr. Kenyatta in his book. Some of
the tribe have donkeys, as I have noticed, but most of the heavy
carrying (firewood for instance) is done by women who bear the
load on their backs with a forehead strap to prevent the load from
sliding off.

Dr. Leakey indicates that in a normal Kikuyu lifetime there
may be over two hundred occasions between the cradle and the
grave when a sheep or goat is sacrificed. Some of the sacrifices are
to Ngai (God), most of them to ancestral spirits. Thus, with a life
expectation of forty years and a population of one million, it seems
that five million victims are needed each year as a tribal consump-
tion for sacrificial purposes alone—here the arithmetic is mine.

Here a critic writes:

> As to the five million Kikuyu sacrifices: these are not wasted from
> a dietary point of view, since, presumably there is a sacrificial com-
> munion in which the animals are eaten. There are a number of
> tribes (cf. the Dinka and Nuer of the Sudan) who never kill a cow
> merely for food, but when they feel hungry find a pretext for a
> sacrifice!

In addition to individual or family holdings of cultivated land
there are (or were) rough grazings of unimproved bush and grass
over which certain family groups have (or had) grazing or
browsing rights in common—a system with which we Exmoor
farmers are familiar.

Mr. Kenyatta stresses the problem of land, and land tenure,
above all others. On the last page of his preface, for example:

> . . . . Nothing is more important . . . it is the key to people's life;
> it secures for them that peaceful tillage of the soil which supplies

their material needs and enables them to perform their magic and traditional ceremonies facing Mount Kenya.

On the last page of his book he reverts to this with a sweeping emphasis and a wholesale indictment of expropriation by Europeans in Africa. Throughout the book the theme of tribal tradition, tribal history, tribal marriage, tribal worship of God, tribal propitiatory sacrifices, tribal veneration of ancestors, tribal reverence for sacred trees—all this is interwoven with land—not any land, but particular land, the land given by Ngai (God) to the tribe in the first instance, and increased by highly respectable transactions some time later.

Mr. Kenyatta's Genesis resembles the Genesis of the Old Testament in several respects, not least in vagueness about the time factor: 'from the beginning' God (Ngai) gave a part of the land to Gikuyu and Moombi (Adam and Eve by analogy) so it is still today their garden of Eden from which, being a blameless people, they have never been expelled by God for misdeeds of their own, but only by the wicked Europeans who expropriated them [sic] in base ingratitude for early Kikuyu hospitality.

According to Dr. Leakey, and many others of great authority the alienation of land to which reference is here made was inadvertent, for the land had been some time abandoned and there was no sign of cultivation when it was taken over: moreover the extent of the alienation was very small indeed, and again it was ultimately made good by the restoration of other good land to compensate. And above all the tribe were protected from the factors which had caused their de-population and lived longer and multiplied more than ever before during the colonial period.

To go on with Mr. Kenyatta's narrative, the freehold of the original Eden is shown to have been acquired by its first occupiers, and moreover it was 'God given'. Mr. Kenyatta writes of a temporary period of nomadism and despotism, after which he resumes a story of continuous expansion. As the multiplying tribe needed more land they increased their holdings by pegging out claims in a forest area from which 'pigmy' inhabitants mysteriously disappeared at their approach.

The Kikuyu are a peace-loving people and the author, notwithstanding his account of their warlike attributes, assures his readers that before the bellicose Europeans arrived only a few smash-and-grab raids ever occurred, and in these there might be one or two casualties, and that was the limit of violence to be found. It is implied that this happy state of the Kikuyu tribe was common amongst all others in Africa. Accordingly, there is no question of the Kikuyu having evicted or exterminated the pigmies. If they did not disappear into the bowels of the earth, as the tradition of the tribe would have it, they must have agreed to assimilation—alas, there are no pigmies left to tell the tale.

Both Mr. Kenyatta and Dr. Leakey intimate that the Kikuyu continued to multiply so that they needed more land, having absorbed what was available from the pigmies. Mr. Kenyatta assures us that there was 'no war of annexation of territory' in Africa before the Europeans came along—so the Kikuyu, finding other forests inhabited by hunters called 'Wandorobo,' negotiated with these forest dwellers for the purchase of more land. As to the time when these things occurred, Mr. Kenyatta suggests no date for the founding of the Kikuyu nation, while Dr. Leakey hazards the suggestion of eight hundred years ago. For land purchases from the Wandorobo Mr. Kenyatta puts some at least of these as occurring in the time of his own grandfather—Dr. Leakey suggests the mid-sixteenth century as the beginning of such transactions. There are still Wandorobo here and there, and I am not sure whether they concur in these oral traditions of the Kikuyu.

The picture drawn by both Mr. Kenyatta and Dr. Leakey is one of uninterrupted increase of the Kikuyu, who expanded first into recently vacated forest land, then into further forest areas so sparsely inhabited that there was plenty of room for their inhabitants to 'move on'.

Just before the Europeans arrived to 'alienate' farming land in 1902 four great scourges had affected the Kikuyu. For the first time in their history, so it is made to appear, they were so diminished in numbers as to be unable to occupy and manage all their lands. Smallpox had reduced the population by twenty to fifty per cent. Rinderpest had greatly reduced the cattle of the rich. Severe drought had dried up their fields, and a locust invasion had devastated what was left of their crops.

Later on, when their numbers had been restored, they found Europeans in occupation, and it was necessary for many of them to become 'squatters' on European farms where they worked part-time for themselves and part-time for the European occupiers. Mr. Kenyatta refers to the Kikuyu as being a source of all labour in agricultural areas occupied by the white settlers, and he omits adequate reference to Masai and other tribesmen who became the herdsmen of the white ranchers in different areas.

With the coming of Europeans many factors combined to cause a rapid increase in the Kikuyu population, increases due mainly to improvements in health and the reduction of mortality at an early age. Of all these factors Mr. Kenyatta mentions only the one which might perhaps be considered unsatisfactory: with the relaxation of tribal controls and taboos, the traditional safeguarding of healthy maternity, by imposing abstinence from full intercourse between man and wife from the conception of an infant to the time of its weaning at the age of two, began to be ignored. A babe a year in place of a babe every three or four years became common for the first time after the Europeans had arrived. To balance the account, Mr. Kenyatta should have mentioned also that Europeans put an end, not without considerable difficulty, to the superstitious practice of exposing ailing infants to the risk of hyenas or pneumonia by leaving them outside the hut at night. Dr. Leakey thinks that perhaps sixty per cent of all children over one year old may have died from this cause alone.

Before taking a plunge into the European era it is essential to go back with Mr. Kenyatta to the heart of pagan Kikuyu society and to examine the character which he gives it—one which seems to have escaped the notice of all leading administrators for quite a quarter of a century. Mr. Kenyatta describes in simple terms the structure of the kinship system as it has grown from a single family to a group of closely related persons consisting of perhaps two hundred people in a few years. Everyone in this group knows everyone else, and there is traditional ritual prescribing manners and conduct in relationships, together with the rights and obligations of individuals and groups.

In time other family groups break off to form a clan: nine clans were established with female names arising from some legendary conflict between men and women of the tribe. From the time the nine clans came to be firmly established, new accretions have been termed sub-clans. The clan and the family group constitute the inner structure of the Kikuyu kinship system, which is then strongly held together horizontally by the age-group system. The age-group bond runs through every family group, every sub-clan and every clan throughout the whole tribal territory. While the organic unities of family group, clan and sub-

clan may tend towards fragmentation between one group and
another, the age-group system forges a tribal unity at every age
level—always supposing that the whole tribe does not expand so
greatly as to attenuate the practical exercise of the rights and
duties involved. In this connection other reports have indicated
that at the turn of the century, while there might be intimate
fusion within kinship groups occupying a particular ridge, it often
happened that there was ill-feeling between neighbouring ridges.

Having followed the structure of the living tribe to this point
we are required to note that it is then linked in a close bond
backwards to the ancestral dead and forwards to generations yet
unborn: this is achieved through the ceremonial and sacrificial
medium of association with the sacred soil which is 'mother' of the
tribe.

From tribal structure we turn to personal and group relations.
Every member of the tribe is destined for marriage. Girls between
ten and fourteen, boys between sixteen and eighteen, all are married. There are no bachelors or old maids and no word designating
such persons. Every woman is required to be in the 'custody' of
a man. The aim of every male Kikuyu is to have a large number
of children: at least four, two boys and two girls, so that there is
someone on earth with whom each of the four departed grandparents may communicate. Family continuity is secured only
through the male line, and for a man to die without a son is a
great calamity, for then there is no one at all left on earth with
whom the family ancestral spirits can commune. Polygamy is
defended by both Mr. Kenyatta and Dr. Leakey. The former
defends it partly on economic grounds, partly on grounds of the
need to multiply more rapidly, partly also on Biblical grounds,
citing scriptural authority for Christian polygamy. Dr. Leakey
uses a further argument in defence of polygamy; he alleges that
the much greater number of women makes it necessary for men
to have more than one wife. As to this last argument, the one
based on surplus women, we have no reliable data until we come
to our own censuses, and on referring to the Kenya statistical
survey of 1960 I see that it offers no support for Dr. Leakey's
argument, as the sexes are shown to be almost exactly equal in
numbers.

On the matter of Mr. Kenyatta's appeal to Scripture, it is
clear that in his view the austere matrimonial precepts of St.
Matthew should be modified by reference to Solomon and other

heroes of the bedchamber. The ordinary Christian regards Christ as having fulfilled, modified, deritualized and restored the pristine excellences of the Divine Mandate, including that of mono-gamous marriage. Mr. Kenyatta will have none of this: taking his stand on the polygamy and even adultery of certain V.I.P.s in the Old Testament, he declares it to be quite proper for a Chris-tian gentleman to have as many wives as he can afford.

In dealing with Africans it is clearer than ever how unsatis-factory it can be to regard the Bible as arbiter between different sets of views.

Here a critic writes:

'There are two theories held about polygamy in the Bible:

(1) At the beginning men were monogamous, but God permitted polygamy to the patriarchs and an easy divorce under Mosaic law because of the hardness of their hearts.

Later, Christ re-introduced monogamy:

(2) There was a progressive evolution of revelation concerning the ideal of marriage through the Bible to the New Testament. When Christ said, "It was not so at the beginning," He was pointing to human nature as God created it—the two in one flesh—as an argument for monogamy which harmonizes and fulfils the pur-poses of God in creation. The revelation was slow and progres-sive because of the hardness of men's hearts.

The second explanation seems more sensible and more in tune with modern theology.'

To revert to the inner relationships of the Kikuyu tribe once more, we start with a young married couple. They have two huts, his and hers, with a garden and some cultivated land. This is the foundation of the family and without it traditional Kikuyu family life cannot be. There are ceremonies and collective rituals in the construction of this round hut with its mud walls and grass thatch. The hut is built with the help of friends in a day, and it is taboo to take longer than a day lest some evil spirit occupy the unfinished premises. It is taboo for the wife's hut to be left un-tenanted on any single night. It is taboo not to light a fire in this hut every day. Marital intercourse must take place in this hut, and only in this hut, and only at night, and only when the children are there, and only when they are already in bed, for intercourse is not only a sacred act, but a collective act implicating the whole family. It is taboo for a stranger to enter a woman's hut, although members of the husband's age group may enter and have intercourse if the husband is informed. Outside the tribal regulations promiscuity is almost unthinkable, but within these regulations both partners have considerable freedom—or licence!

There are many outward signs and obligations of good manners between man and wife, between a man and his father and his paternal uncles whom he calls 'father,' between both partners and their in-laws, so that marriage at once extends the pre-existing collective relationships instead of attenuating them, as happens in a more individualistic way of life.

When a child is on the way a wife may suggest a second wife, for the partnership is an economic one, where every task in the house, in the fields, in the woods and in the rough grazings is allocated by tribal custom to men or women—no man may do a woman's work, no woman a man's. A woman with a child at breast may feel that she needs more help in weeding the fields or in the collection of firewood, both of which tasks are allocated to women and women only. There is no way of getting this help except by adding a wife, for there are no serfs or servants, no stray bachelors or spinsters, and almost every able-bodied person is married. The second wife will have her own hut and her own piece of land. Both wives have a right to be visited by their husband at the time of maximum fertility in the ovulation period.

When the child is born the husband's status in the tribe goes up, especially if it is a boy, but he does not become even a junior elder until he has a circumcised son. Moreover, he is not fully mature until he is a grandfather, perhaps at the age of forty. Birth is one of the four great collective ceremonial occasions in a man's life, when prayer is offered collectively to God (Ngai). If the boy is beautiful he must not be praised or looked at with admiration lest this bring on the curse of the evil eye. The child is in its mother's charge for early education. The mother will sing to it, and its education starts by establishing its knowledge of its relationships with others. Respect due to relatives of differing degrees is inculcated from the earliest years, as also the correct manner of addressing them and referring to them. The relationship between youth and age, between individuals within the family group, between one family group and another, between groups and clans, between members of the same age group, between the circumcised and the uncircumcised. As a child grows so does it learn more

names of persons and groups. It is told the tribal history and
legend, the family history and legends. It learns practices conducive to health and hygiene; also how to carry out planting,
weeding, tillage, harvesting and the management of sheep and
goats. It acquires knowledge of herbs and trees and animals and
their tracks, how to keep the toll of a hundred goats without coun-
ting them, for it is taboo to count them.

All education for manhood and womanhood is focused upon
the initiation ceremony of circumcision, which marks a transition
from youth to adulthood. The surgical operation is said to have
certain practical merits in matters of intercourse, but its chief
importance is that it is an outward sign of inward change
that imparts a new and indelible character—a sacrament by
analogy, maybe a sort of confirmation ceremony. The things
of a child, including masturbation, are then left behind; the
things of a man, including the ngweko, are now licit. The
circumcised youth may have 'fondling' associations with uncircumcised girls, the uncircumcised may not. The circumcised
may marry ('have a hut'), the uncircumcised may not. The
circumcised may go to war as warriors while the uncircumcised
must stay at home. The circumcised youth may grow his hair in
long ringlets, become a dandy and join in the dances and he may
also boast; the uncircumcised may do none of these things. The
circumcised may become an owner, the uncircumcised may not
possess anything. The circumcised is a responsible citizen who can
be called upon to account for his actions, bearing the blame for
misconduct and praise for virtuous acts. For the uncircumcised
blame and praise alike belong to his parents. The circumcised is
a member of a tribal age group and is blood brother to everyone
of that group. The group is known from the great day onwards by
a new name. Members of the group have incurred reciprocal
obligations, and acquired reciprocal rights. They are known and
they know themselves as the destined elders of the future, with
judgment and justice and wisdom and ceremonial in God's name
one day to be entrusted to them. For the uncircumcised there is
nothing of this inspiring forward thrust of youth looking ahead to
its glorious destiny.

The boy to be circumcised arrives at the day of his initiation, to
which he has long and eagerly looked forward. When he has
recovered from the pain of the wound he knows himself, and is
known to others, as a man. He joins in the dances and so do the

circumcised girls, who are now women. A fine youth may h[...]
many open girl admirers. A beautiful girl may have many [...]
admirers. All that they may do, and not do, is meticulously
prescribed by tribal tradition. And there is only one place where
the practice of ngweko may take place—in a hut set aside for this
purpose and no other purpose. A circumcised girl may go there at
any time of day or night. Should she arrange to meet a boy friend
there she will take along with her a meal for them both. Other
couples may be there too, and so may less favoured girls who have
no boy friends, and boys without girl friends. The meal must be
shared with all of these others, and in due course, when one of the
boys present mentions the dramatic word ngweko, it is not the
girl friend whom he will first invite (so Mr. Kenyatta assures us—
I do not know) but another less comely maiden, who will thus
take her share of male beauty. All that the two may do together is
prescribed in meticulous detail. The boy removes all his clothing
(tanned goat skins) while the girl removes hers above the waist—
she then puts her apron (leather) between her legs and tucks it
into the top of the skirt at the back. Thus protected from misadventure the girl lies with the boy face to face, legs entwined
to prevent movement of the hips, and they rub the breasts
together:

> Thy breasts are better than wine,
> There will I give thee my breasts
> —*Song of Solomon*

The couple are expected to talk lovingly to one another:

> Thou art all fair O my love, and
> There is not a spot in thee
> I am black but beautiful
> —*Song of Solomon*.

And thus embracing they fall asleep. What then of the truly
beloved? Has she lost not only a meal but a lover? We learn that
in the end she gets her boy friend, for the couples change round.

In the first case, a boy who dares to interfere with a girl's
clothing runs the risk of being reported by her, with dire consequences to himself at the hands of his age group. In this intimate
association, which Mr. Kenyatta calls 'platonic fondling' ('O
Plato, Plato . . .' *Byron*) he also concedes that the partners
(both?) may experience sexual relief, but this is a second effect
not intended and not essential.

When a girl has a friend of long standing she may allow his sex organ to touch hers, or even to go so far as 'coitus interruptus.' Pregnancy must in any event be avoided, and a girl when she marries should be 'physically' a virgin.

Mr. Kenyatta defends the practice of ngweko against the wrong point. He declares that since Europeans are themselves incapable of self-control in like circumstances their missionaries prohibit the practice, believing that intimate fondling is impossible without copulation. In fact the missionaries—those for example of my own faith which is that of Mr. Kenyatta's first wife—teach that these intimacies are wrong in themselves even if and when they occur precisely as Mr. Kenyatta describes them. But maybe the custom of a popular boy having a duty to take the trouble to give pleasure to a plain-looking girl before he embarks on enjoying the society of his first choice, is one to be commended in replacement of our own growing selfishness where one boy may dance all night with one girl, the one he prefers, except for certain protracted periods when he abandons even her and props up the bar. The point with the Kikuyu is that all are by analogy 'brothers and sisters in Christ' and the charm of the few is God's gift, not to one isolated person to be exploited for his own satisfaction alone, but to be shared with the many, even with the less favoured members of the community. Judged by their own standards, are not the Kikuyu more enlightened in charity than we are? Or is this only giving glamour to promiscuity?

By means of ngweko boys and girls come to decide their marriage partners after a period of friendship and intimate association that falls short of coitus but in all other respects affords premarital sex experience. Mr. Kenyatta insists that the choice of husband and wife is usually that of the partners themselves in the first instance, and that once they have decided between themselves they inform the parents, whose consent is a *sine qua non*. Various other steps are then taken, including an exchange of gifts and the handing of a 'marriage insurance' by the boy's parents to those of the girl.

Here a critic writes:

> Marriage Insurance. The technical word coined by Professor Evans-Pritchard and now used by all English speaking anthropologists is 'Bridewealth'. This word avoids the ambiguities of other terms and is wide anough to include all the social functions of the institution of which 'insurance' is one of the most questionable.

The insurance value of Bridewealth is often attenuated by elaborate rules for divorce and return of Bridewealth in certain well-defined cases. Bridewealth is a 'prestation' between communities, a legal document, an earnest, a religious offering. Bridewealth is also an indemnity and an economic transaction.

By Kikuyu law this marriage insurance is fixed at thirty goats or sheep—one cow being the equivalent of ten of the minor animals, and one bull or bullock the equivalent of five. The receivers of this insurance may not consume or dispose of the animals until it is clear that the marriage is going to be a success. The birth of a child is the usual mark of such success. In the event of the failure of the marriage the insurance flock must be returned.

Wives and land give rise to the main subjects of litigation where questions of stock are involved, and here we may conveniently move from marriage to the law and its administration in the control of crime and the settlement of civil disputes.

First as to crime: disputes between individuals are frequent and are regularly settled by duelling, which seldom has fatal consequences. There are no police and no prisons. Murder gives rise to action under a kind of *lex talionis*, and is settled by payment of a hundred sheep or goats for a man's life, thirty for a woman's life. Thefts can be punished by fines or ostracism—ostracism is greatly feared. Habitual thieves may be burned or flogged to death. Trespass, assault and witchcraft are among other crimes.

Maturity is the main qualification for becoming part of the government or part of the judiciary. The circumcised man joins the Council of Junior Warriors. 'Eighty moons' later he joins the Council of Senior Warriors. At marriage he joins the first grade of Elders. When he has a child of circumcision age he joins the Council of Peace and has a staff of office. When all his children have been circumcised, and all his wives are past child-bearing he joins the Religious and Sacrificial Council, and wears brass earings. Men of this grade are accorded the greatest respect— they communicate with and receive advice from ancestral spirits. Thus it is that age is a *sine qua non* of governorship and judgment.

The detection of crime in a community where everyone knows everyone else is always easier than in our anonymous urban communities, the more so where the handling of cases of crime is a collective family and community matter like everything else in the tribe. It is not alone the criminal who is being tried but his family, while the Council of Elders have in the family of the victim something in the nature of prosecuting counsel. Moreover, it is possible in most primitive communities to examine witnesses in private so as to expose collusion in the case of fabricated evidence, as Daniel did in his defence of Suzannah. But, above all, Kikuyu justice without police is reinforced by reference to the occult.

The Council (Kiama) may accept the prescribed court fees from both sides, but beyond this they take a solemn oath not to accept bribes but to judge justly. The witnesses take other solemn oaths not to lie, not to deceive, not to claim what is not theirs, and the perjurer is burdened in advance with the curses of the court. In the most serious cases the most solemn oath is administered. This oath is so much feared that it is taken only on some barren waste lest the 'evil of the oath symbol contaminate the crop'. The terror of destruction (may this oath destroy me) by occult forces far surpasses anything else as a deterrent to false witness and wrong doing.

Finally we come to the tribal religion. God is Ngai, according to Mr. Kenyatta, although in the early twenties the Kikuyu in Nairobi used to call him Murungu, perhaps a variant of the Swahili Mungu.

Here a critic writes:

> Murungu, Mulungu, Mungu are all common Bantu variants for the name of God. Ngai is Masai, isn't it? The Kikuyu have imitated the Masai in one or two things, perhaps in this?

His attributes are not far from those of God, Allah or Jahweh, but he is more remote than Christ. He dwells everlastingly in the sky, but has a lodging on the earth in Kerenyaga (Kenya Mountain). Men do not pray individually to God but collectively on occasions of importance: 'Ngai must not be pestered'—'regular daily prayers are not advisable'—'there is no one man's religion or sacrifice'.

Here my critic writes:

> Africans did not pray *formally* as individuals, but there is no doubt that they turned spontaneously to God in mental aspirations, on occasion. This is certain for many tribes. Early anthropologists were looking for people saying the pagan equivalent of the Lord's prayer!

Birth, circumcision, marriage and death are the four great occasions for collective religious ceremony in a man's life. Minor occasions are the building of a new hut (which happens more frequently than one would imagine owing to the rapidity with which the borer beetles and white ants destroy existing huts), planting, purification of crops, harvesting and against illness and for the veneration of ancestors. A man communes with his ancestors, while it is the clan alone that offers sacrificial prayer to God. There are sacred trees and sacred groves where sacrifices are made, and the living soil holds the spirits of the ancestral dead.

Over and above this, or maybe altogether on one side, is the feature of magic—one man's magic against another's, good magic against bad magic. There are no tribal priests or missionaries, but there are seers and wise men amongst the Elders, wizards of the medicine-man type who are versed in herbal therapy and human psychology and exorcism.

Then on a lower level are witch doctors of the malevolent sort who traffic in evil, and whose occult powers strike a terror so great that illness and even death may occur through fear engendered by warning received from one of them. Mr. Kenyatta enumerates eleven kinds of magic—protective, hate, love, defensive, destructive, healing, enticing, silencing, fertilizing, wealth, purifying—but nowhere does he dive down into the darkness of the pagan soul where many of us have seen stark fear enthroned beyond the reach, so it would seem, even of God's everlasting mercy—certainly beyond *our* reach.

A critic here comments:

> For some the spirits are practically 'hypostases' of God, as in the Old Testament (cf. The Spirit of God, The Wisdom of God, etc.), for others they are, practically speaking, independent. I do not think that any African God is purely malevolent. God is a person to be feared (cf. Yahweh in the Bible) and this fear is sometimes exaggerated and personified—a spirit that has to be propitiated. Sometimes the African's experience of evil is attributed to God, and is personified in a spirit or hypostasis. It is notable, however, that there has never been, traditionally, a 'Devil' in most African religions. Evil is more usually conceived as a human thing operating in witchcraft or sorcery. And there, you are right to say that some tribes are more concerned with magic than with religion. Magic is a common phenomenon and is mixed up with religious practice. Theoretically, it can be distinguished, and Africans themselves make the distinction. But some are more interested in one than in the other. (Magic, of course, is neutral in itself. The term is used by anthropologists to denote the ritual techniques for dealing with witchcraft, and with bad magic or sorcery as well as for ensuring

success in other fields in a harmless fashion.) Yes, I agree 'Shaitani' has been given a good introduction—though it would have been more effective if he had made use of previous African conceptions of evil, rather than introduce himself out of the blue!

An anthropologist, of course, has no brief to say whether or not sorcery is of the devil, he merely reports what people believe about sorcery. In general, Africans do not attribute occult evil powers to a personalized evil principle or devil. It is quite impersonal.

As a theologian, my opinion would be that sorcery is *not* of the devil, if by that you mean that it is an implicit invocation of the devil. But it *is* of the devil, just as *all sins* are of the devil, to the extent that its practitioners desire to harm their neighbours. Its degree of malice, therefore, depends on the degree of harm one intends to do. In theological language, sorcery is a 'vain observance' with an evil intention.

If the devil intervened directly with the phenomena of diabolical possession, or praeternatural phenomena of other kinds, there would be grounds in a particular case for positing that sorcery was 'of the devil' in the first sense.

Here, the anthropologist comes to the aid of the theologian to record 'occult' phenomena. To my knowledge there are no well-attested or scientifically examined occult phenomena associated with witch-craft, sorcery, or magic. On the contrary, as Prof. Evans-Pritchard has shown in his fine book on Azande Witchcraft, the 'wonders' and 'miracles' of the sorcerers and witch-doctors are all susceptible of a natural explanation. Many are simple conjuring tricks. None are wholly without explanation.

It remains theoretically possible that the Devil might intervene. The specialist who deals with a sorcerer is not exorcising a personal devil, he is counteracting the evil power of a human agent.

Where good and bad magic are concerned it is a question of nomenclature, as you say. Often the 'good' magic is designed to do considerable harm to the sorcerer. 'Good' is very definitely a euphemism here!

I think most anthropologists equate 'witch-doctor' and 'medicine man'. They usually refer thus to the 'good' ritual specialist, who is also a leech. 'Sorcerer' is reserved for the trafficker in bad magic. 'Witch' is the innately evil person with occult powers which can be exercised at mere will. A minor point though.

Into this closely knit tribal society, with its licence tempered by taboos, its practicalities of behaviour imparted to children from their earliest years, its close association with the living soil, its sacrificial prayers and its propitiatory offerings—into all this came crashing the European missionary, the European administrator, the settler and the business man, all alike proclaiming 'these men have just dropped off the tree—they are savages without God—we must mould them to a better way of life'.

It is the burden of Mr. Kenyatta's book that he stands up heedless of inaccuracy in matters implying a little more iniquity on the part of Europeans, in order to cry out something as follows: 'Our God is as good as your God, and it is you who have behaved like savages in our beautiful country, destroying all that was good and leaving us without any firm guiding star for our human destiny!' The words are mine but the thought seems to be Mr. Kenyatta's.

Here my critic writes:

I feel strong sympathy for Mr. Kenyatta when he says: 'Our God is as good as your God'. The African often had a profound experience of God expressed in symbolic thought and action, but his rationalization of this experience was faulty and imprecise. The tragedy is that we Europeans who have come to perfect and to make explicit the 'incohate Christianity' of African paganism by bringing the Gospel, have a too intellectual, too cerebral religion which is divorced from our daily life. Witness the materialism and laicism of Europe today.

Theologically speaking, grace was certainly active among pagan Africans. Their religions are expressions of a religious experience in which grace was active and their rites (the truly religious ones) contained a concealed indication of Christ's own action. This is the tradition of St. Thomas, and even of St. Augustine who goes so far as to speak of the 'Church of the devout pagan'.

4

THE WHITE HIGHLANDS OF KENYA

> As it is by driving him off his ancestral land,
> the Europeans have robbed him of the material
> foundations of his culture, and reduced him
> to a state of serfdom incompatible with human
> happiness.
>
> *Facing Mount Kenya,* by Jomo Kenyatta.

For a thousand years the forces of Islam, whether Arabs, Moors, Turks or their viceroys, had controlled the north African coast from Casablanca to the isthmus of Suez, and onwards to Palestine, Syria, Asia Minor, Greece and the Balkans; southwards, too, from Suez to Guardafui and from Akaba to Yemen.

From the sixteenth century the Ottoman Turks had begun to rule these lands, at first by reason of their military power and political authority, latterly in a scarcely more than nominal sense save that the Ottoman Sultan, as Caliph of all Islam, was their spiritual head.

The most serious cracks in the Ottoman Empire made their appearance in those conquered provinces where Christianity had maintained itself throughout the period of Ottoman rule— in Greece for instance during the first half of the nineteenth century, and in Servia during the second half. It was in support of Servia that Russia joined in the war of 1877–78.

At that time the Turks, in spite of their outward quiescence, were still redoubtable fighters; some say that with better leadership they might have won the war. Towards the end of it, however, their position everywhere had weakened: the revolt of their Christian subjects had been sustained against them, and their conscripting excursions into the neighbouring homelands of their Islamic subjects had made them detestable. The 'sick man of

Europe' was, however, still just in the field when the powers met for the Congress of Berlin under the 'honest broker' Bismarck.

Disraeli, concerned to safeguard the 'no warm-water port for Russia' doctrine of the Royal Navy, reached the Congress with the secret Cyprus Convention already in his brief case. His denial of having made any such secret treaty was unhappily shown to be untrue by its publication in a London newspaper. The French thereupon all but walked out of the Congress, but a breakdown was averted and the Foreign Ministers pursued their deliberations at the table and in the lobbies.

The 'sick man' was to be relieved of his Balkan estates—he had already been assured of Britain's support for his authority in the Middle East—while an understanding between some of the powers was reached over his North African estates. French influence was to predominate at the western end of the Mediterranean, British at the eastern end, while resurrected Italy, not yet ten years old, made a bid for colonial glory in the centre—a bid which the French took somewhat less than seriously. The sardonic broker probably smiled when Disraeli brought back to his people in Britain 'peace with honour'.

With the opening of the Suez Canal in 1868 the main weight of Britain's Mediterranean interests had moved from the western to the eastern end. Ten years of financial control of the canal had stimulated the desire for physical control, but first the rival powers must be kept at a distance.

Britain would do well to keep Germany counterbalancing Russia on land while Turkey was propped up to block any southward move of naval Russia into the warm waters of the Mediterranean and any eastward move of military Germany into India or south-eastwards to Suez or the Persian Gulf. The security of Britain's new sea-way could be consolidated by occupying or neutralizing the deserts which bordered it; Italy, who could never menace British power by land or sea, could safely, as Britain's protégé, be given a playground somewhere around the Horn of Africa to block French trans-African ambitions.

But just as Greeks had claimed their freedom from the sick man's sceptre so did Egypt dream that she too might yet be free.

In 1882 Ahmed Arabi, first indigenous leader of a truly Egyptian nationalism, raised a motley Fellahin army. It was a bloodless revolution against alien Turkish rule, and the army of

Arabi offered no external threat to anyone. Even the Sultan was prepared to recognize the new regime—how seldom indeed had the Sultan of late been master of anything or anybody in Egypt? Arabi Pasha was honoured by the Sultan, but a further Khedivial bankruptcy was not agreeable to the European moneylenders, nor was it believed possible that a simple Egyptian could handle the sixteen nations who had received 'capitulations' in Egypt from the Sultan.

So in the name of the Sultan the servants of Queen Victoria of Britain arrived to put order in place of chaos, to secure dividends from Egyptian taxpayers instead of losing dividends through the bankruptcy of Egypt's ruler. The Royal Navy bombarded Alexandria and the British Army invaded Egypt. Arabi might have been executed as a traitor but for the vigorous efforts to defend him made by my Blunt grandparents.

Occupation of the Nile delta was soon to lead to occupation of the Upper Nile. By 1898, after fourteen years of aggressions costing the Sudanese perhaps three hundred thousand premature deaths, all the Sudan was conquered to secure for Egypt the life-giving waters of the White Nile. In the nineties we secured the source of the White Nile itself by 'protecting' Uganda against predators less scrupulous than ourselves. To complete the circuit of essential communications we occupied Kenya as a corridor from the Indian Ocean to the source of the White Nile.

The 'good deeds' to be done were to make Suez solvent, to avert chaos in Egypt, to eliminate fanaticism from the Sudan, to fill a power vacuum in Uganda and to fill a population vacuum in Kenya. Of course, there were other and more moral themes: Suez must be kept open to the nations at all times—an artery so valuable to the whole world should not be exposed to the risk of being blocked by a rival power able to intimidate the unwarlike Egyptians. The Sudan must have its traffic in slaves suppressed. Further south, barbarians like King Mutesa of Uganda must be rendered obsolete. Finally those empty lands in Kenya were crying out aloud for the beneficial husbandman in a world hungry for raw materials.

Here a critic writes:

> I agree with you about the moral aims of the imperialists who partitioned Africa: prestige, strategy, economic development, en-lightened self-interest, humanitarian motives all played their part. However, there is considerable room for criticism of the methods

employed by the agents of imperialism. Stanley, Rhodes, Peters and many others were bloodthirsty ruffians who decimated whole populations without scruple and who lived on loot. I think this was indefensible, even granted their conviction of their own innate superiority over non-white peoples.

The British Government at Westminster decided for politico-strategic reasons to occupy the Kenya corridor, and did so with the slaughter of only a few thousand 'niggers' if we can accept the ruthless record of Colonel Meinertzhagen's diary. They then decided to build a railway—the Uganda Railway—from the ocean to the Nile's source. Forthwith they settled down to examine the economic problems arising from these decisions. The total length of the permanent way from Mombasa, on the coast, to Kisumu, on the Great Lake Victoria, was five hundred and eighty-four miles, the maximum altitude above sea level was to be just short of eight thousand feet or twice the height of Snowdon. There were to be numerous large viaducts, the largest being eight hundred and eighty-one feet long and one hundred and eleven feet above the floor of the ravine below.

The line during construction was exposed to drought, dust, landslides, floods, sabotage by the covetous, labour difficulties, pachyderms on the track and man-eating lions in the sleeping quarters. In 1922, when I first made the journey from Mombasa to Nairobi, the train even then was halted by a rhinoceros, and perhaps this is still one of the hazards.

It was an expensive capital undertaking which, if it were to remain an item of strategic expenditure devoid of revenue, would become increasingly exposed to the grumblings of the British taxpayer. Sooner of later some forerunner of Dr. Beeching might condemn it to extinction unless the drain on the home exchequer could be greatly reduced. But the prospect of attracting rail revenue from even the fertile sectors of this unproductive land seemed at first scrutiny very poor. It was sparsely populated, cultivations were of a low standard, the surplus if any was small and unsuitable for export, the only exportable item likely to yield railway revenue was ivory, and the railway could not expect to live by ivory alone. What then was the cause of this paradox? Africa was not an entirely empty continent, and even Uganda was well populated; no one could expect a dense population in a desert, but here were lush and fertile highlands free from malaria yet almost vacant of people!

Sir Charles Eliot, first Commissioner of the East Africa Protectorate, argued convincingly that conditions in the region
appeared more suitable for white settlement than black settlement, and that much of the region was wholly uninhabited, while
other parts were very sparsely populated or only intermittently
visited by nomadic pastoral tribes.

Comparing Uganda with Kenya, Sir Charles wrote that
Uganda 'has a sufficient and fairly thick population . . . climate
of the greater part is not such as to attract Europeans . . . a black
man's country.' Of Kenya: 'It may reasonably be asked, if the
highlands of Kenya are really a healthy and fertile country, how
does it come about that hitherto they have been scantily populated, miserably cultivated and almost totally unproductive?'

He answered his own question thus: 'The African tends to
frequent hot, low, luxuriant regions like the shores of Lake
Victoria. He can stand the climate and finds more easily the
plants or animals on which he subsists . . . the higher regions . . .
were especially accessible to the slave trade; they were devastated
by inter-tribal wars and raids . . .'.

Quite apart from the attractions of luxuriant regions and
repulsions of living in regions exposed to frequent raids, of which
there are copious records over the whole of my chosen region,
many virile Africans have always chosen to live in hot and even
malarious or semi-desert lowlands in preference to cool, salubrious
highlands. Forty years ago for instance some of us were trying to
recruit Turkana tribesmen for service in the King's African Rifles.
In their own lands on the Lodwar region the Turkana were willing
recruits, but when they were required to camp out on the high
Mau plateau on their way to Nairobi they disappeared in a body
during the night, and later explained that no matter how many
blankets they might be given to keep them warm they could not
sleep in such cold air. They preferred unanimously to return at
once to a region the reverse of luxuriant simply because it was hot.

Many Africans living in the highlands are prone to suffer from
bronchitis and pneumonia, which two afflictions may easily be a
greater danger to life and health than malaria. Be that as it may,
these highlands were in truth largely unoccupied by man. Ten
years before Sir Charles Eliot, Lord Lugard had reported of the
Mau in the following terms:

The area is uninhabited and of great extent . . . it offers unlimited
room for the location of agricultural settlements or stock-rearing farms.

At first it was not easy to attract white settlers, and in the first few years of the twentieth century the British Government even offered a six-thousand-square-mile territory in the Trans Nzoia region of Kenya to the Zionists, not in order to dispossess Africans but to bestow vacant, fertile land upon dispossessed and persecuted Jews from Eastern Europe—people who would be beneficial producers. The area offered to the Zionists at this time seems to be about the same as that which they subsequently occupied in Palestine.

Eliot gave very careful consideration to African interests, examining the problem of white settlement in that fairminded way of his which made all his work so useful:

> Closely connected with European colonisation is the question of native rights. This difficulty is lessened in East Africa by the paucity of native population, and I think that the obstacle which it has been supposed to present to European settlement exists in prejudiced imaginations rather than in reality. Natives must be secure from unjust aggression, and be secured sufficient lands for their wants, but with this proviso I think we should recognise that European interests are paramount.

Out of this and other careful assessments by Eliot, including the important passage which follows, Mr. Mboya chooses to quote in his book *Tom Mboya* only the passage 'white interests must be paramount'. He moreover dismisses the vacant land report of two first-class governors as 'a settler argument' and 'never accepted' by Africans.

Eliot continues:

> Nomad tribes must not be allowed to straggle over huge areas which they cannot utilise, nor ought the semi-settled natives to continue the wasteful and destructive practice of burning a clearing in the woods, using it for a few years and then moving on and doing the same elsewhere.

Again:

> There is no indication that for a measureable period it will be consistent with the welfare of the world to let the African races pass out of the state of tutelage.

Yet again:

> There is no real opposition between European and Native interests and no cause for hostility.

This was the very root of a doctrine that was soon to be established—that African as well as European interests depended and were to continue to depend on the successful establishment and subsequent preservation of a highland area dedicated to European managerial settlement. European dependence upon African labour for all the less skilled operations on farms and ranches was deemed a factor advantageous to the African who would thereby be introduced to good husbandry, good animal management, a monetary system and the marketing of surplus produce, thus contributing to the wealth of the community and to his own welfare. But the heart of the matter was that the white farmers should produce the essential surplus wealth of which the indigenous population was deemed totally incapable.

Half a century later a responsible verdict on the white farmers' efforts was made as follows:

Speaking in Legislative Council in November 1959, Mr. L. H. Brown, Acting Director of Agriculture, one of the colonial civil servants, said:

Of the land in Kenya which has a rainfall of over thirty inches per annum eight thousand five hundred square miles lies in European acres and thirty-two thousand three hundred and six square miles elsewhere in the colony, chiefly in African land units though some as Crown land. In other words, there is at best one acre in five in this category available to Europeans.

A large proportion of the European land is also cold, poorly drained or has shallow soil, and the area available for mixed farming is reckoned to be about four thousand seven hundred square miles in fact. Some of these same factors affect African lands in this category, but the proportion is smaller. There is, for instance, only a small proportion of African land badly drained, and little of it is cold, above eight thousand feet. Africans in fact concentrated in the past on those areas of the country enjoying an adequate rainfall to grow crops and where it was comparatively warm. Similar pictures emerge with ranching land. If you examine the areas of ranching land with a rainfall between twenty and thirty inches there are four thousand and twenty-five square miles of it available to Europeans and thirty-seven thousand six hundred and twenty-one square miles elsewhere, i.e., about one acre in ten is in European hands.

These are the basic facts of the division of agricultural land between the various racial groups at present. If we are to decide soundly on a future policy we must see what these groups have done with the land they have. To take the overall picture first, gross farming revenue on European and Asian land is of the order of thirty-three million pounds excluding subsistence of resident labourers living in the area, and represents about forty-six per cent of the Colony's total production of agricultural products. Of this nearly twenty million pounds' worth becomes available for export. That has been the average over the last two years. From the very much larger acreage of African land a total production of about forty millions worth is estimated, including all subsistence from the people living there. Of the total production in African areas some five million five hundred thousand worth is available for sale and not all of it goes for export. In other words, taking the Colony's figures for surplus production as a whole and neglecting land with less than twenty inches of rainfall, about twelve thousand five hundred square miles produces four-fifths of the surplus while the remaining seventy thousand square miles produces one-fifth. . . .

The picture, therefore, is that if all the land in Kenya were in African hands its productivity would be much lower than at present. In addition, the wage bill of over ten million pounds for Africans would not find its way into the pockets of Africans living (and working) in the present European highlands. I need not point out that this wage alone is nearly twice the total of surplus crops produced in African areas.

How far Africans are from accepting the settler contribution to Kenya's economy is illustrated by the following broadcast taken from the B.B.C. monitoring service 'The Voice of Free Africa', December 30, 1964, in Swahili:

If the imperialists had not come, the African continent would have been one of the great development areas of the world. . . . the imperialists have been using well-fertilised land to enrich themselves and keep Africans in poverty . . . but since independence in countries like Kenya Africans are now given land to farm. . . . Africans do not depend only on farming, they are building up industries . . . when this is accomplished Africans will be able to stand on their own feet and on an equal footing with other nations which have been free for centuries, and thus regain their glory.

A lot seems to have happened between December 12, 1963, when Kenya became independent and 30th of the next December when the broadcast in question was made. Although this broadcast was anonymous its chief untruth is the sentence which I have underlined: this repeats the main charge preferred by Mr. Kenyatta for a generation up to early 1962. Today, in 1965, Mr.

Kenyatta speaks with a different voice, but the land-hungry Frankenstein of his creation may be deaf to his new voice. A million or two acres of white farmland have already been deconsolidated at great expense to the British taxpayer in order to appease its voracious appetite. Some six thousand families of urban unemployed are reported to be squatting on the frontiers of another million acres. The best qualified Africans who were the white man's labourers are intimidated and pushed out and denounced as collaborators by an invading army with no qualifications at all.

In 1962 Mr. Kenyatta declared himself against big farms for Africans, and other Ministers followed his line, yet in 1963 a Minister in the same government tells the B.B.C. Television Interviewer in Nairobi that the next million acres are going to be farmed in their existing structure, and that holdings may even be amalgamated and run on a co-operative basis. In March, 1964, Mr. Kenyatta was himself reported to have bought a large farm. Whether Mr. Kenyatta likes it or not, however, the bias of his oratory has achieved the classic pattern of revolution on the land: first the skilled managers with capital are replaced by an incompetent peasantry; when existing holdings have thus been corrupted by fragmentation the agrarian economy is ripe for collective (co-operative if the word is more palatable) farming where the labourer in theory has no other master than the common good, but where in practice he tills (or loafs) at the bidding of a body of bureaucrats who call the tune.

The simplicity of the revolutionary tune is well described by Mr. Mboya where he gives his account of political rallies with their monotonous litany of slogans intended to wipe away, not the fact of incompetence, but the feeling of inferiority. There is no hint of exhortation to acquire skills, but only the inculcation of a passion to remove a label. In this campaign it is not the poor quality of 'Viazi Vya Kiafrika' (African potatoes) that calls for improvement, nor the superior quality of 'Mahindi Ya Kizungu' (European corn) that must be emulated, but simply that a label even where it correctly describes the facts of inferior quality, must be torn off and history rewritten (Mr. Kenyatta's phrase) to obliterate European superiorities in crops, houses, dogs, clothing, trees, etc. (items mentioned in the report of Mr. Kenyatta's address to the Teita tribe).

This is where African behaviour comes closest to meriting the traditional criticism of Negroes that when you have raised them with much effort to the practice of a higher standard you have only to remove the pressure and they will at once relapse into their past—a past of economic squalor, the antithesis of the golden age alleged by them to have been destroyed by Europeans. Indeed there has been some macabre licking of the lips at the prospect of indulging the new freedom to relapse. Mr. Odinga for instance is reported (Leg.Co., May 11, 1960):

If they (the African people) decide that savagery is the most fitting thing, then they will decide on it.

We may not have long to wait before African Negroes clamour for rescue from the menace of famine and massacre arising from relapses caused by their leaders' preference for 'savagery'! Happily, however, the voice of sense is heard in conflict with the voice of folly, as for example in the B.B.C. report from Nairobi in English on January 31, 1964:

The Kenya Finance Minister, Gichuru, left Nairobi for Washington on January 20 for talks in raising funds on the International money market for Kenya's development plan. He will be joined in Washington by the Agricultural Minister, McKenzie.

Again:

The government has plans for a major agricultural revolution which could result in the present critical unemployment situation being turned into a labour shortage in the next two years. The Minister for Agriculture, McKenzie, and the Minister for Finance, Gichuru, are to try to raise more than one hundred million pounds on the International money market for the financing of this project. Major and minor projects planned for different parts of the country would bring 'hundreds of thousands' of acres of unused land into agricultural production and would create vast employment opportunities. The main points of the plan include a halt to the fragmentation of large land units after the present million-acre scheme is completed. Government controlled co-operative societies would be set up, and in some cases farms will be amalgamated to make larger economic units.

If any of this goes through, Kenya will have escaped from the Kenyatta illusion that dispossession of the white farmer is the panacea for land hunger, and we shall be back to the common sense of Lennox-Boyd (now Lord Boyd of Merton) when he said (*Hansard*, February 22, 1952):

> It is not alienation of land that has led to land hunger amongst Africans. If the whole of the white highlands were handed over tomorrow to Africans it might lead to a small and temporary alleviation of the problem, but it would be the total loss of the whole economy of the country . . . the way to do that is not by futile recriminations over land settlements that have been accepted by all parties, but by looking towards the undeveloped areas and hoping that by precept and example we can lead the Africans to develop those areas in partnership with ourselves.

Anyone who has followed African utterances on the subject of land in Kenya will be likely to agree with Mr. Tom Mboya that 'an atmosphere was created over the land question in which it was no longer possible to reason', and many fair-minded people may be convinced that this atmosphere of emotional non-reason was intended by those who created it—notably by Mr. Kenyatta.

Today the long campaign of ill-will towards white farmers comes to its climax with a replacement of white by black in a manner that reeks so strongly of retrogression that even its sponsors seem disposed to revoke what they have done before they have gone too far.

Meanwhile, it may be a good moment to review the White Highlands episode in more detail. Evidence abounds that no African was 'driven from his ancestral land' but, on the contrary, Europeans were encouraged to settle by public policy in a highland area where some of the land was 'miserably cultivated', some of it was wastefully cultivated or wastefully ranched and some of it was neither cultivated nor ranched, nor was it within the competence of the indigenous population at the time to manage it at all even on the lowest standards of good husbandry.

The evidence as to vacant and available land was not produced by settlers with a vested interest in land acquisition but by the British Colonial Service. Settlement did not start by settlers acquiring land and then acquiring a governmental authority— it started with a governmental authority which thought that settlers, would be a 'good thing' and set to work acquiring them. So the 'vacant land' evidence, which Mr. Tom Mboya calls a 'settler argument' and which he says was 'never accepted' by Africans, is presented by them in one of those cart before the horse versions of history which does not stand up to critical examination.

The British Government, faced with an expensive railway from the ocean to the strategically vital source of the White Nile, adopted the settler idea because Kenya, unlike Uganda, was too sparsely populated and too miserably cultivated to offer the least hope of giving the railway a pay load.

In the event the settlers did all that was asked of them; it was not their task to enrich, educate, discipline, administer or control the indigenous African tribes; this sort of thing was the proper responsibility of the Colonial Service. But it was the task of the settlers to provide wealth, a pay load for the railway, an exportable surplus to pay for essential imports and taxable revenue to pay for order, health and communications. They did what was required of them in return for pledges of privilege in the small highland area allocated to them.

Before describing their difficult but ultimately victorious campaign to develop the land for efficient farming, it may be as well to describe the society itself which was established.

Only the smallest part of this society was white, and it started with that curious form of paternal despotism the British Colonial Service commonly called 'the Bureaucrats' and often in Kenya the 'bloody bureaucrats'.

The white farmer settlers, with pledges of perpetual privilege as their chief title deeds, started life with a strong aristocratic flavour which in time became less aristocratic but never less autocratic. Sometimes they were the 'bloody settlers' in the esteem of the bureaucrats, but in order to preserve a pithy jargon without epithets it seems fair to refer to them as the autocrats.

The autocrats and the bureaucrats alike had need of the professions such as doctors and priests, legal aid and dental aid, and in time the wealth-producing business man whom economists call the entrepreneur and modern jargon calls the tycoon. Thus the whites developed in these three main wings: the bureaucrats, the autocrats and the tycoons. None of these were in the technical sense wage-earning employees—they were salaried officials or professional men or self-employed persons employing non-white labour.

Now the East African economy was almost totally deficient in the skills needed to run a modern society. An administration, for instance, or a bank or a business of any size needed clerks. Everyone except an African also expected to live in a house of a higher standard than a Kikuyu round hut, but round huts were the limit of local building technique—you could have one of these in a day, but nothing more ambitious even in a year!

Then a barter economy was a tedious drag on the time of the average European who has long lost the art of trading his goats for pumpkins under the shade of a Baobab tree in the midday sun. So in order to replace barter by currency, at least in part of the field of trading, the settlement needed shopkeepers who were willing to pay money for goats and to sell such items as the following: lime juice, blankets, bicycles, pencils, wire, calico, matches, beads, saucepans, knives, pangas (choppers), jembes (hoes), sandals, trousers, shirts, shorts, trilby hats, nightdresses, cigarettes, cotton reels, needles, pins, buckets, pocket mirrors, razors, soap, scent, string, etc., in return for such other items as: money, goats, small monkeys, ostrich eggs, bananas, gourds, leopard skins, ivory, rhino horn, a tortoise, etc.—not really quite in the line of the average shopkeeper from Puddlecombe-on-the-Marsh!

So it came about that most of the *fundis* (building and other artisans), the *karanis* (clerks) and *duka-wallahs* (shopkeepers and itinerant traders) were neither white nor black, but brown.

The builders were Indians, often Sikhs. The clerks were Goans (Portuguese Indians who are Roman Catholics). The larger and static shopkeepers in the settled areas were Indians, while the mobile traders in unsettled areas were more often Somalis, probably from Aden.

Nearly all unskilled labour in the brown community was provided by the Indian or Goan or Somali family itself, but the entire body of unskilled labour in the white community was black. Most of the farm labourers in the coffee lands between Kiambu and Nyeri were Kikuyu Africans; those in the Machakos region were Kamba Africans. The ranchers more often employed Masai or Nandi Africans. The tycoons in town employed, in addition to Kikuyu and Kamba, a number of Kavirondo (formerly this included Luo) for heavy work.

Every white housewife had a household staff of at least four Africans (called 'boys') and probably a couple of *totos* (small boys) to peel potatoes and to de-tick the dogs. The police officers were all white, but the police askaris all African. The commissioned officers of the King's African Rifles were all British regular officers, while the 'other ranks' were all African. We did not recruit Masai because they did not want *us*, and we did not recruit Kikuyu because we did not want *them*.

This then was the set-up of the White Highlands: the autocrats, bureaucrats and tycoons at the head of the society reigned like Brahmins looking coldly (or overheatedly) at each other, while brown technocrats three times as numerous built their houses, typed their letters and established their currency.

At the bottom of the economy all unskilled, menial, heavy, dirty, or dangerous work was assigned to the African Negro who, mostly with great cheerfulness, did what he was told. But the numbers of Africans were immensely greater than the other two, perhaps in the ratio of thirty-three Africans to one Indian or one hundred Africans to every white man.

Every excellence from no matter what source was attributed to white, while cracks in the plaster were accorded to brown, and water in the petrol tank was unquestionably black. The girl to whom one did a good turn, perhaps mainly because she was pretty, would express herself in an ecstasy of gratitude: 'Thanks *so* much—you're a *white* man!' Indeed, the phrase has been Africanized, for not long ago a Somali language expert at the London School of Oriental and African Studies, telling me of his great disappointment at the black colonialism of Kenya, said: 'I thought Kenyatta was a white man but now I see he is just an imperialist!'

The autocrats were usually good with their labour, often feeding them better than the tribal standard, allowing them to 'squat' with their wives and children, giving them clothing, medicine and schooling for their children. The farmers' wives were matriarchs of the tribal employees, and the farmers, even when sometimes irascible, were tolerant of inefficiency and even sometimes of pilfering. Lord Delamere, for many years leader of the white settler community, was always willing to put up with the pilfering of his Masai herdsman; in the same sort of way one of my coffee friends suffered the pilfering of his posho (rations) by his Kikuyu 'boys'. He used to argue with me that 'we don't pay them very much and so long as they put it all inside their stomachs and don't flog it on the market I really don't mind. Of course I know just exactly what they take'. Elsewhere I have noted how my own cook when we served on the frontier (a Baganda in this case), on being taxed with helping himself to my sugar, replied, 'Of course I do when my own runs out!'

Perhaps there is something to be said for applying the scriptural maxim, 'Muzzle not the ox that treads out the corn,' to human relationships. However, when a Kikuyu boy in Nairobi stole my shirts, I put the police on to him and he was duly up before the magistrate and punished—that was in 1922. In 1961 things had got worse. For example rings, watches and money were taken from our bedside table in Mombasa as we slept. In the Nairobi car park police in loud-speaker cars regularly patrolled the area, warning all motorists to lock their cars and to remove their valuables from inside the car. House owners all over the country were also having in the 'fundi' to put expanded metal over their lower windows.

It was neither the aristocrat nor his habitat which had corrupted the African. The bureaucrat and the tycoon in town had, however, created a corrupting environment of squalor whose co-existence with their own affluence corrupted them in turn to the extent that the white man who was in no way his black brother's keeper could hardly plead, 'I did not know.'

Take, for example, the Kikuyu adolescent in the land of his fathers nutured in the strong collective atmosphere of the tribe as described in Chapter III. The time had come as it was bound to do when all land was in use. In the old days, so Mr. Kenyatta tells us in his book, a man needing land for his son would 'brew a little beer' and then go to a landed neighbour and negotiate for a strip of land for his son, as he might if the man had a daughter to wed. But we have persuaded the Kikuyu not to fragment their land in this way. It took fifty years of persuasion and the peril of Mau Mau to get action to consolidate their holdings, and now consolidation is an accomplished fact and there are villages for the landless. Of course there is also a shanty town in Nairobi, as there is in Bombay or in almost any other town you may care to visit.

So the young Kikuyu went to Nairobi to seek a non-farming job, and there he soon became jobless and homeless and tribeless as well as landless. There was not even firewood to keep a man warm during the rains in this city of concrete and glass.

There was also the irony of a sterile freedom, for there were no taboos, no solemn oathings, no watchful elders, no kiama, but there was no justice, and life itself wasted away whilst the superfluities of life flaunted their seductive presence behind every window and from the inside of every motor car. When the young African had been nine times round every rubbish dump in the city's outskirts, what was left to put in his belly—unless he robbed the rich?

Not long ago I came across a diary where Colonel Meinertz-hagen wrote vividly of a unique 'right and left', wherein he bagged with his right barrel a 'nigger' and with his left a lion. The choice of wording seemed to be symbolic and I doodled my feelings on the subject as follows:

> So here is a strange new society
> Of white men and brown and the clod
> And here is a new kind of piety
> Where black bears no image of God.

If this is a doodle with any relevance, it is certainly not a cap that fits the autocrats; though they have a great weakness, I must write first of their great strength—their skill in the use of land.

The newly introduced foundation crops of the White Highlands were coffee and sisal, followed later by tea. None of these were indigenous crops. None of them competed against indigenous crops. None of them displaced indigenous African labour. All of them created a new demand for indigenous farm labour. All of them gave rise to a secondary industry, and this in turn created a further demand for urban African labour. All of them brought into being exports which alone were able in the end to pay for the necessary imports.

Of additional importance as a model for Africans were such new things as the structure of holdings: large enough to make full use of fixed capital and equipment and to produce a marketable surplus; crop rotations in place of monoculture; maintenance of soil fertility; contour terracing to stop soil erosions; soil breaking by plough and other implements in place of the all-purpose tool the jembe (hoe); exclusion of the destructive goat; fencing in of own stock and fencing out of trespasser stock; water storage with distribution by pump and pipes; the introduction of shade trees for coffee and quick-growing trees such as mimosa, gums or cupressus macrocarpa for shelter belts; skilled pruning and use of chemical sprays and fertilizers; locust control (international); weekly dipping against rinderpest and other tick-borne diseases; inoculation against pleuro-pneumonia; quarantine for foot and mouth; the upgrading of indigenous cattle to improve beef and milk; the culling of inferior beasts; stock-breeding for a market instead of for prestige or bridewealth; shade-dried hides in place of sun-dried hides; introduction of wheat and other grains, and also grasses and lucerne and the hybridization of strains to obtain

F

suitable crops for the country; introduction of pyrethrum crops; hay-making, efficient storage, vermin control, organized marketing, packing and transportation, refrigeration and canning.

The report of Mr. L. H. Brown is a bare announcement of a great victory won, not against Africans nor at their expense nor by dispossessing them of their land, but against the fallen element in nature which Africans alone had not previously been able to master.

These great farmers, the autocrats, did what was asked of them; they did it well, and in the end they were betrayed by those who had asked them to do it and whose targets they had so admirably achieved. In the hour of their betrayal they were without friends, without sympathy, and without their former greatness, and it is interesting to trace out this remarkable case history.

The best elements amongst the autocrats were men and women of courage, vision and compassion. They knew their Africans and liked them, and their Africans liked them in return. I have seen it and I am certain of it. Lord Delamere, for many years their chosen leader, was a prototype of many: aristocratic, combative, enterprising, blood brother of the Masai by whom he was trusted and with whom he was always more of a brother than a master; a man who in the hunting field rode hard at his fences and in the club scrum put his head down and shoved! Many were like him. In the wilderness (porini) the pioneers encountered the dead weight of African fatalism 'shauri ya Mungu' (God wills) and tradition 'desthuri yetu' (this is our custom), while in town (mjini) the bureaucrats ever and awhile hung a millstone round the necks of the autocrats with their negative despotism of entrenched laisser faire and a different set of pledges that sometimes fitted ill with those made to the settlers.

Labour supply was often a controversial problem. Had not H.M. Government decreed that settlers should produce wealth in return for their privileges? How could settlers carry out their part of the bargain if no African came out to work for them?

The whole life of pioneering seemed to consist in overcoming one sort of opposition or another—opposition from the soil which was seldom 'just right'; from the sun which often put barely ten minutes between mud and dust; from the rains which in some seasons took away part of every man's farm and dumped it into the Indian Ocean.

The pioneer habitat was such that it bred men who jettisoned finesse and went to meet collisions head-on, even if they broke their necks, as Delamere did literally on two occasions and as all of the others did metaphorically in the end.

One of the characteristics of the country, in addition to breeding autocrats, was to insulate one autocrat from another. Partners quarrelled and separated more often than not; soldier settlers who had been brothers in arms and lifelong friends during the first half of their lives settled in Kenya together and became life-long enemies.

The insulated autocrats foregathered twice a year in Nairobi for racing and polo, a week before Christmas after the short rains and a week around July after the long rains. They danced all night at Muthaiga Country Club in convivial mood even when they were sober. Apart from them up on the hill the bureaucrats in Nairobi Club assembled there more regularly and habitually and less lightheartedly, even when they were not sober.

The first enemies marked down by the autocrats were Jews. Whether it was dislike of Zionism, which hung over the Trans-Zoia in 1904 and 1905, or whether it was dislike of 'Joburg Jews', whose profile and high stakes on board ship coming out provoked some of them, I cannot say. In Los Angeles and Vienna I have come across the same animosity directed against a 'huddle' of Jews; seeing that a huddle often implies a kind of closed shop, I can see the point of the resentment, but in Nairobi I never was able to uncover the point, yet up to 1961 both the bureaucrats and the tycoons on the hill and the autocrats of Muthaiga barred the Jews from membership of their club.

But the autocrats did not stop at barring Jews. The 'bloody bureaucrats' became at one stage so unpopular that the autocrats would not have any of them in Muthaiga. In my day (1922-26) I was member of both clubs, and my friend Sir Joseph Sheridan (Chief Justice) explained that the Governor, Sir Edward Northey, had recently healed this ancient feud. It seemed to me, however, that an entente cordiale with studied bonhomie at the top did not mean very much fraternity lower down.

It was in my time that the autocrats on their own made a further set of enemies far more numerous than the Jews and far more formidable than the bureaucrats. By this time the autocrats had long ceased to fear African competitive skills on the farm, and they were beginning to get all the farm labour they needed from

African sources. Suddenly they were faced with another threat to the security of their privileged paradise, and true to type they reacted with excessive passion and complete rigidity.

The threat this time came not from Kenyan Africans nor from any other part of Africa, but from India. The acuteness of the danger lay in the invocation by Indians of Lloyd George's wartime pledge of equal rights for Indians as British citizens within the Empire. Calcutta Indians were now insisting on equal rights with white settlers in that unique Tom Tiddler's ground the White Highlands.

The autocrats feared in part the size and scale of an Indian invasion of their highlands, an invasion which they correctly foresaw would displace African labour instead of, as in their case, making more jobs for Africans than ever before. But they also feared the undercutting of their way of life by a community living on a lower level than theirs.

In addition there were prejudices of a not entirely unreasonable sort in that many of the Kenya Indians were of low caste. In their own country even those other Indians who were demanding equal rights for them in the Kenya paradise would consider themselves contaminated even by their shadow! To the white settlers, amongst whom were a number who knew their India, this was preposterous cant! The autocrats, in fact, might have gained a political ally without serious economic risk if they had compromised on a willing buyer/willing seller basis, but they decided instead to resist by force any unfavourable decision that Westminster might make. Thus they offended the brown sub-community which had done so much for them and they virtually declared war upon the authors of their paradise, the government of the mother country.

The autocrats hoped by damaging the railway between Mombasa and Nairobi to secure a three-months delay before their insurrection could be forcibly repressed; meanwhile, 'anything might happen' and they thought, perhaps rashly, that the British electorate would come to their aid or even in some quarters that the Labour Party might rescue them from the Tories!

As evidence of this I print the letter in which the Commander-in-Chief of the Kenya rebel army reported his appointment to his father in England. I discussed the problem with him in Nairobi at the time and I have no doubt of his views, his serious resolve to fight if need be, and his integrity:

My dear ——   Norfolk Hotel,
                                                    28.2.23.

If affairs weren't so serious the present position would be the funniest thing recorded in English history. The present position is this. An Armistice was declared the day before yesterday. Devonshire wants Corydon to go home with two or three settlers and discuss the whole situation with D. and his colleagues. The C.O., however, is scared stiff at the prospect of what the Colony might do in Corydon's absence. Therefore they asked for an Armistice. We agreed to this and the terms are as follows. The C.O. undertake not to attempt to force any measures on us whilst Corydon is discussing the affair. We undertake not to take direct action until C. returns, but we reserve to ourselves the right at any time to turn against the Armistice should either side break off the discussion. Meantime, the military preparations are being quickly brought to completion and all steps taken to meet all eventualities. Such is the state of affairs as I write. It is quaint, isn't it? [There follows a description of a Race Meeting at Nanyuki.] So my invitation from the Governor to stay with him when the military situation allows of it must stand over for the time being. It is said that adversity makes one acquainted with strange bed-fellows. Certainly high politics and diplomacy does so. A man I am working with constantly is Ward, a Labour agitator from South Africa. In that country he has both done time and is also a deportee. A great friend of Tom Mann's. Well he is turning up the Labour Party at home in K.C.'s interests. The chief point he is making is that the Indian has a seventy-hour week. This, of course, is anathema to the Labour Party with its forty-four hour week. Also the Indians have no trade unions —so he calls a meeting of the white labour in Nairobi. This meeting cables home to Ramsay MacDonald, Sidney Webb & Co., pointing out the grave danger to the Labour Movement throughout the Empire that will be injured if the Indians are allowed to flood this country. He asked me to cable home copies of these resolutions so that the matter should not be allowed to drop. I asked him how much ice he thought all this would cut, and he said he considered quite a lot. He said the Labour Party at home had no idea how the principal keynotes of their faith were being assailed in K.C. and would be horrified when they did learn and that instead of backing the poor Indian through thick and thin, as has been their policy in the past, this knowledge would cool off their ardour very much indeed. It will be most interesting indeed to see if there is any result from all this. [Follows domestic news.] I have had the wonderful compliment paid me of being appointed Commander-in-Chief of the Forces of Kenya Colony. I can only hope and pray that I may

prove equal to the job. It is a big one, and the only claim to qualification for it that I can conscientiously advance is that I am convinced of the justice of our cause, and will endeavour to see it
through to a finish, cost what it may.

But it is an Empire business and I wish they could have found
a better man.

The letter is signed.

There was nothing disloyal in this movement and its motto was,
'For King and Kenya.' It was a movement intended to repel a
change of policy seen as injurious to the white settlers but represented by them as injurious to the Africans. Having given offence
to Jews and the bureaucrats, the autocrats in this new attitude
of theirs alienated the Indians and the House of Commons. Their
argument, however, was accepted by the government at home,
and the Devonshire Declaration of 1923 in one and the same
document affirmed the paramount right if indigenous interests
and re-affirmed the privileged status of white settlers in the White
Highlands. Putting these two things together, we can infer
properly that the judgment of H.M. Government on what was
best for Africans remained unchanged—that the best interests of
black Africans would be secured by the system of white settlement,
and that these African interests would be impaired by extending
such a settlement right from Europeans to Indians. Nobody at all
dreamt of the African being able to do without any of the settlers.

The present Duke of Devonshire seemed to argue during a
clash with me in the House of Lords in 1963 that the Devonshire
Declaration of 1923 (so named after his father) implied a charter
for Africans superseding the charter of white privilege, but the
evidence seems otherwise, as for instance paragraph 6 of the terms
of reference of the Commission of 1932:

> To define the area generally known as the highlands
> within which persons of European descent are to have a
> privileged position in accordance with the White Paper
> of 1923.* (That White Paper was the Devonshire Declara-
> tion.)

The position of the settlers still seemed impregnable thirty-
three years later when Sir Anthony Eden said (*Hansard*, July 12,
1956): 'For any period of time we can foresee European leadership and guidance will be essential.'

* Government Notice No. 418, from *The Official Gazette*, June 28, 1932.

A decision by Mr. Harold Macmillan four years later not only reversed the thinking and the pledges, but also converted half-a-century of administration without planning for African independence into a pledge of African independence forthwith. Of necessity the independence that followed in 1963 was unplanned, and the 'essential leadership and guidance' of Sir Anthony Eden's maxim were thrown overboard, heedless of the consequences. The promise of an African political majority (not necessarily one man, one vote) in thirty years would have been a sensible promise in 1950, but the undated promise of 1960, although in line with the resolution of the General Assembly of the United Nations, was a glaring folly.

Today the pledges can no longer be honoured, but in renouncing sovereignty to Africans, Her Majesty's Government cannot rid themselves of a moral duty to stand by the community brought into being by those pledges. Compensation for injury or loss from broken political pledges may not be a duty in a narrow legal sense, for the sovereignty of Parliaments seems to presuppose an unfettered right to break a Parliamentary pledge whenever it is deemed expedient to do so. Certainly, however, Her Majesty's Government has a duty of honour, not only to the autocrats who carried out so well the task with which they were charged but also to the bureaucrats who likewise carried out their difficult task; and also to the tycoons by whose energy labour had been found productive outlets away from the over-populated land. Many may hold as I do that the debt extends beyond these to the builders of the white men's houses, to the practical inaugurators of the white man's currency, and last of all to those of whom it is said 'the keys of all the white men's safes are in the pockets of the Goans'.

The fault of the autocrats had its roots in their acceptance of a pledge of privilege as a charter for all time as no doubt it was meant to be. Meanwhile other regions of strongly entrenched privilege had by 1960—the year of the betrayal of the autocrats—been crumbling for thirty-eight years. In 1922 the independence of Eire proved that not even Great Britain could preserve the unity of the United Kingdom against resolute demands for majority rule within a province—indeed the principle here had been conceded nearly ten years earlier. The granting of independence to India in 1947 was another warning signal, but the final and decisive warning came when the United Nations decreed that within ten years of 1950 even little Somalia should be independent.

The rigid temperament of the autocrats resembled a hardening of the arteries that may have been due to the fact that in the course of time the original pioneers became diluted in their greatness. The pioneers remained in the land albeit in dwindling numbers, but most of them went their way in pursuit of economic results and heedless of politics; some are still there to behold the ruin of their work, but like all pioneers things new did not appal them. Theirs was a temperament to meet every new challenge as it came; however recruits less worthy arrived to contaminate them. In the twenties a small flock of divorced persons from Britain, seeking escape from the attentions of the King's Proctor, joined with others in the 'Happy Valley' to introduce the 'crime passion-elle' and the satisfactions, as one lady put it, of being where you suffer no social handicap from living in open sin! Not that the polyandry of a few did any harm to Africans—indeed the most 'married' of them all lived on to become like Dorcas full of good works, so that when she died her passing was mourned by not a few of all races, yet the 'Happy Valley' was something a long way below the virile and austere standard of the pioneers.

Perhaps a contingent more injurious to Africans was the influx of Anglo-Indians (I use the term in its Victorian sense without implying mixed blood). These came with a more rigidly anti-colour prejudice than any of the pioneers—indeed that was perhaps the reason why some of them came at all. Was it not these and their ilk who voted recently against admission of African officers to Nanyuki Club at a time when the pioneers or their remnants voted in favour of their admission?

In the end the autocrats arranged for themselves a phased and subsidized exodus—that is the plain obverse of what was described as a subsidized re-settlement of Africans. In this subtle way the very word settler became Africanized and acceptable. In their going the autocrats said nothing on behalf of the Masai, who had helped them much in the early stages and whom they left dis-membered between Kenya and Tanganyika. They said nothing on behalf of the Somalis, who also helped them and whose Somali province had been allocated by Her Majesty's Government as a colony of Kenya instead of as part of the independent Somali Republic. They said nothing on behalf of the Fundis who built their houses, nothing on behalf of the tycoons, very little on behalf of the bureaucrats, and nothing at all on behalf of those keyholder Goans whose homelands in 1961 were forcibly annexed by the peace-loving government of Mr. Nehru with the virtual blessing of the peace-loving United Nations!

Thus the autocrats ended their reign in the 'Macleod of unknowing', and their last days showed little of their former pioneering greatness. Even so, and notwithstanding the United Nations resolution of making uninhibited plunges into independence, they did not merit from the mother country they had served so well the unheralded betrayal of all the pledges.

5

PASTORAL NOMADS

The word nomadic as applied to African farming does not usually carry a suggestion of vagrancy or uncertain wandering; nor does it imply a rootless gipsy life. It means simply that a clan or tribe moves between known dry season locations and known rainy season locations. Shifting on the other hand is a term usually applied only to the abandonment of an overworked clearing in favour of a fresh area to be cleared.

Both shifting and nomadic practices in agriculture were brought to an end in Kenya early in the colonial era, but in the case of nomadic ranching it was not so; although the boundaries of pastoral nomadism were fixed tribe by tribe approximately as we found them, the movement of pastoral nomads between dry and wet locations continued virtually unchanged to this day. At the risk of being told that I am out of date, I hazard a guess that four-fifths of the land surface of Kenya may be a pastoral nomadic area and that the same may be true of nine-tenths of the Somali Republic. Pastoral nomads occupy the lower-level provinces of the Habash colonial empire, but the Habash themselves, and by now most of the Galla, are settled agriculturalists. A curiosity of Habash history has been the shifting capital city, with a tendency to 'move on' when it had consumed all the firewood within reach.

The description of nomadism which follows is taken mainly from my own experience in the early 1920s. During my period to military service in Kenya I served two masters in the Northern Province. My military commanding officer was some hundreds of miles away in Nairobi, whilst I was responsible in matters of administration to the officer in charge of the Northern Frontier District (N.F.D.), about one hundred and fifteen miles away at Meru.

The Northern Province is more than twice the size of England and more than half of all Kenya—126,000 square miles or 56 per cent. Its population is probably no more than 300,000 compared with perhaps seven million in the smaller 'half'. It is a semi-desert region about as sparsely populated as Saudi Arabia, with two and half persons to the square mile. The Kenya Atlas has the following descriptions of various portions of it: Desert, bare lava rock, shrub desert, desert grass shrub, desert scrub.

The rainfall is everywhere under twenty inches, under ten in most of the Somali part, and in quite a number of places under five.

During my first assignment in the Northern Province I administered the whole of the Samburu district, during my second the Southern Turkana. The Samburu district is in the middle of the Northern Province; Turkana lies to the west and north-west of it, while the N.F.D. lies to the east, north-east and south-east of it.

Taking first the Samburu district, at Baragoi there was a small colony of Turkana whom we had put there for military reasons. At the south-eastern corner of Lake Rudolf lived the fish-eating El Molo tribe (less than one hundred persons), and in the Mathews Range to the eastward another small tribe which subsisted by hunting and collecting wild berries and wild honey—the Wandorobo. All except the Turkana were said to be offshoots of the Masai. The Samburu tribe may have numbered 30,000 or 40,000, although my own census was based on quite unreliable statistical samples. The tribe occupied a district then said to be about 10,000 square miles—it was much the same shape as England and about one-fifth of the size of England, and I was its sole white administrator. The Turkana tribe, apart from the small colony in the Samburu district, may have numbered about 80,000.

No settlers were allowed in the province without having business there and obtaining a pass. The entire province was under military administration and no wives were allowed to accompany their husbands. The only white woman in the province in my time was at Marsabit; she was the glamorous Osa, wife of Martin Johnson, the American film photographer.

In my time the Samburu district was the best African cattle-ranching area of the province, with grassy bush veldt, shrubless grass plains and two forested highland areas. It was largely free from malaria, unlike the rest of the province where there were malarial mosquitoes everywhere near water. There were known and troublesome belts of virulent animal tsetse which gradually killed off our wagon teams of oxen. Horse-sickness prevented the keeping of horses but not of donkeys or mules. Rinderpest and foot-and-mouth disease were endemic, and an epidemic of pleuro-pneumonia was raging through all the herds when I arrived. The district marched with the former Masai land of Laikipia, which by then had been alienated to, but was largely unoccupied by, white settlers. After my time the whole of the Samburu district was transferred administratively from the Northern Province to the Rift Valley Province, in which Laikipia was also situated; thus was facilitated the unified control of 'robbers' and 'robbed' at the cost of much statistical confusion which still persists.

Apart from the El Molo and Wandorobo, already mentioned, and a small agricultural settlement on the Tana River, all the tribes of the Northern Province (Somali, Boran, Wardeh, Rendille, Samburu and Turkana) were pastoral nomads—stockmen who neither tilled the soil nor spread any fertilizer nor sowed any seed—and there was nowhere any tradition of making hay.

In the better areas cattle predominated, in the most arid areas, camels. Lowly fat-tailed sheep and goats (the wealth of women and of the poorest) abounded in all inhabited regions except amongst the El Molo and Wandorobo. The El Molo in point of fact accepted my gift of sheep and goats at the same time as I re-established a military post at Loyangalani, on the lake, which protected them from Habash raiders. The Wandorobo consumed whatever I gave them and soon there was none of it left.

In only a few parts of the Northern Province would tillage have been possible under conditions as they then were. The pastoral nomads ranched as a way of life detached from money. When I first paid some of them in money, they spat on it and threw it on the ground to be gathered up by an honest interpreter and restored to them with a glowing exposition of its virtues. They did not ranch for a market—there was no market. The currency of exchange for their small-scale barter was goats and sheep. Cattle only changed hands as marriage insurance or bridewealth —or, in the language used by the boy friends, in conversation with me, the 'price' of a bride. With the Samburu this price was thirty head of cattle, which is some five to ten times the Kikuyu price mentioned by Mr. Kenyatta.

In the case of the Somalis the 'blood money' for a murdered man was one hundred camels, for a murdered woman fifty camels. I understand from Mr. Michael Mariano (Mogadishu 1963) that this fine remains unchanged, and the commuted value of a camel in cash for this purpose in 1963 was £8. Here again the figure seems five to ten times higher than the Kikuyu figure, and is one of many pointers implying the former superior wealth and power of pastoral nomads in semi-deserts compared with the poverty of tillers of the soil in luxuriant areas.

The pastoral herds were managed communally by clans or sub-clans or groups of families, and although selective breeding of cattle was obscured by the absence of culling and other factors, there were variations in the quality of beasts which did not appear to be wholly accidental. The practice of subsisting mainly on milk mixed with blood taken from the vein of a living bullock (Masai-Turkana-Samburu) kept down the slaughter of cattle for meat. The white settlers of the highlands had founded their grade herds of beef on the Boran cattle, and the Boran type in my day was to be found also amongst the best in the Samburu and Turkana districts. It was clearly much superior to anything kept by the Kikuyu.

Apart from these cattle traded to settlers, the only other exports I can remember from the Northern Province were ivory, rhinoceros horn, Somali shawls and Somali ponies. In Nairobi, where I had lately been honorary secretary of the polo club, it had just ceased to be good fun playing inexpensive polo on Somali ponies, for the height limit had been raised and millionaires with racehorses were beginning to invade the game, spoiling both players and play. Perhaps the new African officers of the K.A.R. will feel disposed to restore the more frugal game. In this connection I enjoyed introducing one of these during 1964 to riding on Exmoor; on his second day out on a horse he came fifteen miles with me almost as one born in the saddle. Here perhaps is my latest and last contribution to my old polo club in Nairobi.

One of the strange features of these primitive societies was the absence of wants and the apparent absence of serious ill-effects due to an unbalanced diet. The great majority of the pastoral nomads known to me lacked grain, vegetables and fruit in their diet. Few of them collected wild honey and few lived within reach of the great fish resources of Lake Rudolf. True, the fish-eating El Molo did suffer from an unpleasant-looking raw lower-lip, and they had malformed bones due to rickets. At intervals of a decade or so someone was sure to report that the El Molo were 'riddled' with V.D.; a doctor would be then sent to examine them and forthwith would find that they were quite free from any trace of the disease. The Wandorobo seemed stunted and pot-bellied, but my interpreter said that he and I would soon come to look like that if we lived on wild berries only. The Samburu and Turkana however were magnificent specimens, whilst for an experience of effortless endurance, just try to live three days on safari with Somalis following your pack camels hour after hour through the night and early morning led by these silent wraiths of men! In connection with my remark on the absence of wants, I can remember no household utensil except a gourd, no furniture except a small neck-rest, no feminine apparel except goat skins, no jewellery except beads and wire, no weapon or tool except spears and wrist knives and a knobkerry. There was of course the full-dress finery of the males such as baboon capes, ostrich plumes, oryx horns and perhaps some ivory knob fitted into the chin. There was no pencil, no book, no paper, no scribe. Some Turkana clearly felt the need of medicine whilst others were very pleased with a present of native tobacco; a red blanket was highly appreciated as a gift for a headman. So on my safaris I took a sack of tobacco (for chewing) and a sack of Epsom Salts, which was often 'paradise enow' for many a Turkana chief over forty. The Turkana used to supplement their diet by hunting, but the Samburu did not—indeed, as they once told me when they got to know me well, they regarded a liking for hunting and a taste for honey (my own weaknesses) as a mark of the poor of this world!

The nomads of my acquaintance built no houses but made mobile shelters of bent branches covered with goat skins or cattle hides. The Somali Muslims in the east were all well-swathed in loose cloth, both male and female, though the Somali women were not veiled as are other Muslim women. Amongst the pagan Turkana and Samburu the men, except when decked out in ceremonial 'full dress' capes and plumes, went naked, although the draping of American cotton cloth (Americani) or a red blanket over one shoulder was a growing habit. The little girls wore trivial triangles of leather in front, while the women wore 'topless' skirts of goat skins, some with beaded hems, folded over at the waist in front and intended mainly to cover the buttocks.

The 'villages' or 'manyattas' consisted of groups of shelters interspersed with compounds for stock, the whole surrounded by a high zariba of thorn-bush branches to keep out the ubiquitous hyena. The barrier had also to be high enough to keep a lion from jumping over it, and strong enough to resist a cattle stampede

from inside, which was what a hunting pride of lion would sometimes try to achieve—at any rate in the Samburu district. Numerous nondescript dogs helped in the work of guarding. Fires
were kept going all the time, but at each new encampment after
a move a new fire was restarted by rotating the point of a certain
hard wood in the pithy centre of a soft wood stick. The glowing
pith was then packed around with dry donkey manure, and
presently with care and gentle blowing a flame burst forth.

Good fires were needed at night to keep off predator beasts,
especially near donkey compounds, for the donkey was the
favourite meal of a lion just as a dog was the favourite meal of
a leopard.

The management of grazings (grass) and browsings (leaves of
bushes) was all important to the pastoral farmer, and in my time
in the Samburu district burning was a regular and necessary
feature of grazing control, just as it is where I now farm on
Exmoor. The burning was supposed to need the prior consent
of myself as officer-in-charge of the district, for in theory I 'knew
best' how to decide whether the burning was the routine burning
of traditional grazing areas or an attempt to extend the grazings
by forest fires which would damage the catchment areas of the
tribal water supply.

The case for burning had therefore to be made by the African
headmen before the young white official, to whom they expounded
the theory somewhat as follows: During the rainy season the
grass 'runs away' from the stock just as it does in England in June
and July. There is moreover no tradition of making hay, so the
grass grows long and coarse and becomes unpalatable. It is then
liable to be trampled and fouled by stock and game, especially
by the larger game. The worst fouling was alleged by the Samburu to be the expectorated residue of rhino chewings. These
often seemed to be the fibres of wild sisal. I regularly challenged
this allegation as an old wives' tale, but was always assured that,
while burning was needed everywhere to get rid of all types of
fouling, the rhino chew was poison to the rest of the herbage.
I suppose somewhat comparable allegations of fouling used to be
made against the rabbit population on British farms before the
coming of myxomatosis.

Burning is more difficult than it looks. On Exmoor we con-
gratulate one another on a 'good burn'. Here, if the ground is
too dry, the fire tends to 'creep' underground and to destroy the

top-soil. If there is too much wind it races along leaving woody stalks of heather and whortleberry and unburnt patches. If the sap is up or it is soggy with winter wet, it won't burn at all. The wild sedge ought to be burned annually, whereas the heather need only be burned every few years.

In any case, in the nomad country there was a deep respect for grazing control, and grass was accorded almost a sacramental reverence. The Masai seem to regard grass as 'holy' and to condemn any breaking of the soil as a 'sin'. This is but one or two steps back from the 'sacred' cow of the Hindus: In one case the 'mother' of man is the cow and in another she is grass and in a third she is the earth itself. In Africa, as in Somerset, the moment to burn is apt to be upon one for a few hours some morning, and the ranchers fear lest the opportunity may pass not to return during the current season. So it often happened that my Samburu did their burning first and afterwards came to me to ask for permission, especially if they thought that the glow of their fire in the night sky might attract my attention, or if the line of my projected safari was due to cross the charred plains where I should come across the evidence of their transgressions!

In *The Desert and the Green* I have referred to my special tasks in this district: One was to execute in public a Samburu murderer who had already escaped gravely wounded from one incompetent firing party. The purpose of this was to underline the Commandment, 'Thou shalt not kill.' Another and more important task was to re-establish as I have already mentioned a post on the Great Lake to intercept those murderous Habash raiding parties. A third task was to facilitate the work of stock inspectors who would be coming to inoculate the surviving herds against pleuropneumonia. Each of these tasks was directed towards the postponement of the hour of death and the prolongation of the life of man and beast.

Here I must underline a contrast between our impact on the African agricultural highlands (Kikuyu and others) and our impact on the pastoral lowlands (Samburu, Turkana, Somali and others).

In the highlands we performed a service which, incomplete though it was, laid the foundations of a lasting improvement in the old farming economy and made entirely new openings for Africans in a non-farming economy. The farmer settlers established a pattern of success for their husbandry, and by the pro-

5. *Somali religious leader: Sheykh Mohammed (Khadi of Sheykh).*

6. *Somali elder: the late Gerad Mohamoud Ali Shirreh, M.B.E.*

7. *In the floor of the Kerio valley, Kenya. The grass cover is still abundant.*

8. *Lower slopes of the Kamasia hills, Kenya; 4000 ft., 38 in. rainfall, 19.*
   Years of overgrazing have led to complete denudation of grass. Goats a.
   survive on seeds and pods of lowly thorn trees and shrubs.

ductivity of their methods created more jobs for Africans. Meanwhile the administration introduced for Africans land consolidation, soil conservation and a viable husbandry in place of the fragmentation, soil erosion and monoculture which had characterized much of indigenous African husbandry. In some of this work the administration were consistently opposed, especially in Kikuyuland and by such leaders as Mr. Kenyatta. Accordingly progress was always slow until the Mau Mau emergency, when satisfactory consolidation was achieved in agreement with the Kikuyu for the first time, and for once the tribe became far more responsive to other advances.

One of the additional effects of settler activity was the production of wealth in the form of an export surplus to pay for imports, and a taxable surplus with which to pay for at least some education in literacy and for improvements in health and hygiene everywhere. From this the Kikuyu gained most owing to their closer proximity to the main activities of the white settlers.

Mr. Mboya's suggestion that a 'spate' of improvements for Africans 'might never have taken place' had it not been for Mau Mau seems to miss the point: Mau Mau was the eruption that brought years of Kikuyu resistance to improvements to a head. This resistance then became in effect obsolete as soon as consolidation had been agreed upon. Thereafter enough Kikuyu tribesmen saw what was good and for the most part adopted it, even while some of their leaders continued to denounce it.

These were the fruits not of Mau Mau itself, but of the way in which we handled Mau Mau. In this we were more patient than, say, the Germans might have been (vide what they did in Tanganyika and Greece) or the Amharas (if we compare their massacres in Kaffa and Borana). It is not very difficult to put an end to resistance if you have superior armament and are prepared to apply collective punishments in the form of massacre to whole areas.

The conflict in Northern Algeria was between the French and the Arabs upon whom the French had made no cultural impact, while Mau Mau by contrast, as the casualties alone indicated, was a revolt by Kikuyu traditionalists against Kikuyu innovators who had stepped out of the tribal struggle on a scale threatening the survival of the old tribal structure.

Mr. Mboya's equation, condemning the violence of Mau Mau only if the violence of suppressing it is equally condemned, is

G

pacifism with a gun inside the trouser-leg. Every campaign to murder and mutilate civilians and stock ought to be stopped, and it can never be stopped without some violence. Of course it is possible to go too far. At Kalavryta (Greece) a local German Commander for instance avenged an ambush of his troops by armed civilians with excessive and misplaced violence shooting all males over twelve years of age in the village (some eight hundred). Not one of these villagers was even indirectly connected with the ambush. This sort of thing, and there were worse examples, is properly execrated, but it does not excuse the original ambush nor does it require us to condemn punitive reactions of all sorts.

The long revolt of the traditionalists culminating in Mau Mau was a highland tragedy which at first sight may seem to have little to do with the lowland nomads. In the nomadic lowlands by contrast we have allowed our civilization to make scarcely any impact upon the traditionalists, and the tension between new and old has yet in many cases to develop. In this we are not only more gravely at fault but we have handed on a more dangerous legacy to our African successors. Except in the matter of longer life for man and beast the nomadic way of life has been neither modified nor helped by British colonialism. Civilization intervened at one point, and only at one point, and because that one point was unaccompanied and unbalanced by the other prerequisites of civilized living it did tremendous harm. In seeking to preserve life it damaged the womb of life by greatly diminishing the fertility of mother earth. As evidence of this I give my impressions of a return visit to Kenya in 1961.

In 1961 I saw the reigning Provincial Commissioner of the Northern Province, and also spoke to a previous ruler of the province, Sir Richard Turnbull. Taking the nomad position generally, and eliminating minor exceptions, I understood the position to be, in 1961, as follows: there was still no regular market for any substantial number of the Samburu or Turkana cattle, and only a small market for those of the Masai. The Masai in Tanganyika and the Samburu in Kenya were declared to be rapidly destroying their habitat, while many of the Turkana were already on permanent famine relief.

With peace and good health, and better control over epidemics, the herds had increased since my day. All the districts had been heavily overgrazed. The bush and forests had been burnt to extend the grazings. The catchment areas had been denuded of their trees and shade. Much of the top soil had been exposed to the tropical sun and had been blown away by the winds, or carried away as the rains fell upon a bald pan, racing off unchecked by vegetation and scoring the earth's surface with gaping wounds. The rock beneath was becoming exposed in many places, and sand dunes had begun to form here and there. Grass in many places had ceased to grow. Thorn bushes and deep-rooted shrubs or weeds alone managed to spatter with green the russet surface of the land during the rains. The springs had been weakened, and some of them had disappeared, trodden in beneath the ungolden hooves of unnumbered and unwanted kine. Camels and goats could still browse on the thorn, and these survival animals had come to replace the kine and establish an economy on a lower level. Some of the river jungle still prospered, perhaps even improved from a deepening bed of silt, but all over the land there was less water and less grass, so that when drought arrived the remaining cattle wasted and wasted until they qualified for the current nickname bestowed upon them by the administration, 'hat racks'.

'Don't you ever try to control grazing and insist upon culling surplus stock and arrange to offer it in a market at a reasonable price?' I asked a leading administrator, somewhat impatiently.

'We did get the Samburu to agree to a controlled area in which only licensed animals might graze.'

'What happened then?'

'It was a complete success; that is, the controlled area was a complete success.'

'Did they cull?'

'They sold some.'

'What did they do with the money they got from selling their surplus stock?'

'They bought more stock.'

'What did they do with cattle which were redundant in the controlled area?'

'Moved them into the uncontrolled areas.'

'What about the beasts, then, in the uncontrolled area?'

'Oh, worse than ever, of course, over-grazing with transferred beasts superimposed on those that were surplus already.'

In 1923—forty years ago—we had established Somali 'dukas' (shops) in this area, and I had been sent with currency and urgent

instructions: 'Try to get the Samburu interested in buying something—persuade them to use money instead of goats—try and
get them interested in wanting articles which can be obtained
with money—put up a list of articles at controlled prices and
don't let the shopkeepers cheat the purchasers.' I asked myself
in 1961 if anything had happened during this past forty years,
and was able to assure myself that indeed it had: at first death
had retreated before us, then too much life had destroyed the
very source of life—mother earth had gone with the wind, the
green was already subsiding into the desert—oh yes, the Americans
have done the same sort of thing, too, with their dust bowls, but
here this is the fruit of white intervention with one over-riding
commandment, good in itself but unbalanced when in isolation
from others, 'Thou shalt not kill.'

I had already written the foregoing comments on the unhappy
consequences of over-stocking for forty years when a letter reached
me from a Kenya friend who prefers to remain anonymous. It
indicates the unhappy consequences of over-stocking in the
colonial period.

  While on leave in England two years ago I read with very great
  interest your book *The Desert and The Green*. This was of particular
  interest to me as we had been doing some pasture work in the
  Samburu area, including Baragoi district.
  Very briefly the position, and the query, is this; for a number of
  reasons the pastures of this area have become very poor indeed, and
  scarcely able to carry the livestock dependent on them; one feature
  of this deterioration is thought to be the rapid, and relatively recent
  spread of a small shrub, known locally as Sage Bush, and botanically
  as *Disperma sp.*: This plant now covers about four hundred and thirty
  square miles of the El Barta Plains, and adjacent areas, and has
  very largely suppressed and crowded out much more useful grasses.
  Local Baragoi opinion is that this has taken place since about 1939
  before which the Sage Bush only grew in the luggas or watercourses
  in any quantity, and where it grew on the open plains it only
  occurred as scattered plants.
  On page 130 of your book you have mentioned that 'at a place
  called el Barta just South of Mount Nyiro there are open rolling
  plains of grass forming a square of about twenty miles'.
  We should be most grateful to know if you have any recollections
  of this Sage Bush plant, and in particular the quantity of it in relation
  to general grass cover . . . although the Sage Bush is browsed lightly
  by cattle and camels, and other animals, it is considered undesirable

in such quantities. As it seems to have spread relatively quickly, it could spread even further. For this reason we are interested in getting precise information on just how, and when this spread began. Your book is one of the few with any information about this area at the time you were stationed there.

The writer enclosed three photographs showing various phases of this Sage Bush area, presenting a picture quite unrecognizable as the completely grass-covered plains I used to know. One of the consequences of allowing regions like this to perpetuate a false extension of a dead past is to distort their position in the contemporary economy to their great disadvantage.

Today everybody clamours for 'welfare'; the value of modern welfare may be debatable, but it is there and accepted, and where it is absent people want it. Peace and good order may in theory be no better than tribal warfare, but in practice we all ardently seek peace and do our utmost to avoid war. It is possible that even ambulances and hospitalization may theoretically be worse for the community than vultures and hyenas, but we hate in practice to leave our brothers to die like that. Continuing this theme, it is very likely indeed that education by tribal tradition so eloquently defended by Mr. Kenyatta may really be a fine thing, but it so happens that some juggernaut has gnashed its three R's at us and heaved us up into 'O' and 'A' levels and we cannot escape.

But to none of this can the primitive nomad aspire unless somebody makes him rich, develops his resources, shows him the secret of non-farming production and also the secret of multiplying farming productivity tenfold notwithstanding the law of diminishing returns. If we do not do this sort of thing—and in Kenya's Northern Frontier we did not do it—welfare has to be imported as a charity at the expense of some other set of workers or alternatively there is no welfare.

Welfare in the Northern Province since I was there has grown very, very slightly indeed. From information taken out of the Kenya Atlas, the Kenya Statistical Abstract and elsewhere I note that in the whole province there are no metalled roads and no bridges. There are no installations under the heading of industry, communications and power. In an area two and a half times the size of England there are only nine schools (one intermediate and eight primary) compared with five hundred and seventy-four secondary and four thousand and eighty-three primary for

Africans in the rest of Kenya. The 1958–60 Educational Survey
dismisses the Northern Province as follows: 'Except in remote
areas with scattered populations such as the Northern Province
and part of the Southern Province children attend primary
schools as day pupils'. The 'remote' Northern Province covers
fifty-six per cent of Kenya, and this percentage would be swollen
by 'part of the Southern Province' if only the Southern Province
were mentioned at all in the 1960 statistical survey, but it is not.
All reference to the Northern Province is omitted from the 1960
Report of the Department of Agriculture.

Turning to the newly designated and almost exclusively Somali
North-eastern Region (part of the old N.F.D.), which may be
about the size of England, there are in four places an administrative post, a postal agency and a district hospital.

In the reports sent to me of the 'Kenya We Want' Convention,
opened by Nairobi's African Mayor, Alderman Joseph Rubbia,
on the Feast of St. Grouse in 1962 with an exemplary address on
Freedom and Justice, there is no mention of the two or three
hundred thousand Somalis of the N.F.D., but only two or three
thousand Somali merchants in the urban centres of Kenya proper.
The 'Kenya We Want' activists displayed the customary indifference of Kenya to the N.F.D. And now they are interested only
in the old, old trick of promising the earth under their own alien
government, hoping to wean the province from loyalty to its
mother country, the Somali Republic. The bribes go hand in
hand with deportations, evictions, threats and a trigger happy
security service; this is the 'damnosa hereditas' which Her
Majesty's Government bequeaths as her daughter's dowry, and
which she sustains with British money and personnel.

Kenya has a tremendous task in bringing welfare to that part
of the desert which desires to remain with her—but the forcible
retention of the part which so naturally and logically desires
union with the Somali Republic is a great political folly.

In this connection and as a matter of general interest in the
future of nomadic peoples in the semi-desert stretching from
Uganda round the Horn of Africa it is important to have a true
picture of the problems. The first part of the problem is political.
The Habash have striven in vain for two thousand years to rule
the deserts that separate the Amharic highlands from the Red
Sea. The Kikuyu highlands have now, as I have just pointed out,
embarked upon the same kind of misadventure: they have no

prospect whatever of any lasting success—not even with British and American arms. The reason for the certainty of their failure is one of the simplest in the world: they do not want to live there and indeed they would regard it as a punishment to be made to live there. As evidence of this I cite once more Mr. Tom Mboya, who in New York on April 17, 1961, accused Her Majesty's Government not only of depriving Mr. Kenyatta of his liberty but of deliberately making him suffer. At once we have a picture of George III parading intolerably once more before the gullible Americans. Here are the particulars of Mr. Mboya's charge: 'Confined in areas which are unhealthy, extremely hot, mosquito-ridden and deserted.'

The place to which Mr. Mboya refers is Lodwar in Turkana—the headquarters of a district where I served in 1926 and from which I was indeed evacuated with severe recurring attacks of malaria. But that was long before the age of malaria control, and since then the disease of malaria has been eliminated as a serious menace from whole continents—from India for instance where, as I was assured by the Indian Minister of Health in Delhi in April 1963, a concerted effort has abolished the seriousness of malaria.

In any case the Turkana live there (80,000 of them) and they prefer it, as I have pointed out in Chapter IV. Certainly it is hot. Judging from memory it may have been as hot during the last two days I was there forty years ago as it was say in Benares when I was there last year. But it was a dry heat and there was quite a considerable drop in temperature at night. The climate at Aden seems to me very much more trying than the climate of Lodwar, and in any case Lodwar does not differ very greatly from the blazing Somali deserts which stretch from the Lorian Swamp to the Haud. Moreover they are not, as described by Mr. Mboya, 'deserted', for whenever in Africa there are mosquitoes there must also be water and shade, and wherever this is the case there are also people and stock.

A little fairy tale of cruelty to Mr. Kenyatta is no doubt good enough with a New York audience, notwithstanding Harlem, yet from my reading of Gordon Parks's article in the *Weekend Telegraph* of September 25, 1964, I feel sure that New Yorkers would have had been better served if Mr. Mboya had given his views on Harlem rather than some inept remarks about Lodwar. Be that as it may, I note that on November 15, 1962, a delegation

speaking for the Somali N.F.D. said, 'The Somalis are not prepared to be sold like goats to other people, they want self-determination. They want to join their brothers in Somalia.' However
Mr. Mboya is one of Kenya's adamant African imperialists
claiming for Kenya this hot, insalubrious *desert* similar to the one
where it was brutal to detain Mr. Kenyatta and where obviously
Mr. Mboya and his kin have no desire to live themselves. What
is the reason for this imperialism? Is it the corrupting whiff of
petroleum?

Since I am speaking of a semi-desert which is decidedly hot for
most of the year, it may be as well to make certain that there are
no misunderstandings about the effect of heat upon its inhabitants. In our northern climes we are habitually disposed to think
of the peoples of the warm Mediterranean as being less energetic
and virile than ourselves. This view we hold notwithstanding the
history of Greece and Rome and the Arabs and Moors and Spain. •

In the opinion of many keen observers it is not heat in the
regions about which I am writing which corrupts the virility of
man, but rather the steamy lakeside of Mr. Mboya's homeland
and the salubrious forests of the Kikuyu.

'The lake has corrupted all who live on its shores.' So said one
of our ablest administrators a year or two ago, and when I asked
him why he thought this, he replied, 'It is not good for man to
dwell where even his walking stick will sprout if he plants it in
the ground'.

Then I believe I remember Mrs. Elspeth Huxley commenting
in much the same sense on the debilitating effect on the output
of African energy on highlands, so fertile that two crops a year
arrive in return for a very small output of energy. Then to return
once more to Sir Charles Eliot: although he had good things to
say of Masai, Baganda and Somalis he was depressed by negroid
characteristics, finding the Bantu no better than other Negroes,
and indeed propounded the notion that the best thing for them,
including the relatively active and intelligent Kikuyu, would be
inter-breeding with Hamites. Searching for an explanation he
blamed partly inheritance and partly environment especially the
environment of the forest:

> He is the cleverest of beasts but he in no way dominates or
> ostensibly influences nature . . . it is the dense pall of vegetation
> exciting no emotions, offering no prospect of anything new, if one
> goes no further, which has so held in bondage the spirit of the

African and deprived him entirely of that inventiveness, energy and
mobility to which other races have attained.

Eliot in his term 'other races' had in mind, amongst others,
Asians.

The pastoral nomad of the region's hot deserts is by contrast
energetic and mobile. By mobility I mean mobility within the
confines of particular East African prairies, except in the case of
Somalis, who are to be found in small colonies in foreign parts,
including Aden, London, Cardiff, and New York.

Here is a kind of nomad diary of activities for the year: We
take it as the long rains come down and the tawny desert turns
green with grass and the green leaf on Acacia thorns or new
shoots on the evergreen Mswake (Tooth-brush bush) or other leaf.
At once the herds move to the areas where temporary pool water
restricts grazing (on grass) or browsing (on the leaves of bushes)
to a few weeks after the rains have come to an end. Life for once
is easy, save that after a long drought an excess of lush green
grass may cause the cattle to scour, and some of them who have
barely escaped death from starvation are apt to die from the
consequences of the sudden green purge.

Presently the rains are over, the rivers which have been running above ground for the last two weeks are back to sand and
water holes where they will remain underground for the next
fifty weeks, and the programme of conserving the herbage on the
basis of diminishing sources of water presents itself for planning
by the pastoral families. As to water supplies, some water is held
static in rocks, other water may have to be taken bucket by
bucket all day long from some slow spring in a small gorge, but
most of it has to be lifted from ever-deepening holes in the sandy
river beds.

Cattle, donkeys and sheep need water most often, goats less
often if they are not required to breed at the same time, and
camels least often. The cattle after watering move off at two
miles an hour, if they are not grazing as they go, to any point
which they can reach with the proviso that they must graze and
return to water on the third day. When things are bad the herds
even graze or browse at night if there is a moon, and in these
circumstances a constant watch has to be kept for the odd lion.
Young lions sometimes kill in the heat of the day, but if they do
they are soon disposed of by Masai or Turkana in whose country
no stock-raider ever goes unpunished.

As the season advances, so does the strain on man and beast increase. There is never enough herbage without going to extreme range, and the water needs a vast muscular effort to draw. In the case of camels—Somali camels, not Turkana camels—the range of browsing, unless it is salt bush, is immensely greater than it is with any other beast. As the pools dry up, this brooding master of the waterless bushveldt strides off at three miles an hour, swaying slightly until both he and his herd are far out of range of water. Up to a limit of as much as three months this unique survival animal can go without water, and can even breed under these conditions, while his human attendant abstains alike from food and water for the same period and subsists on the camel's milk. Here is a beast indeed which provides clothing, footwear, a roof over the head, transport and subsistence for those who accompany her.

Often Somalis who have left for the time being the nomadic life with all its strains and abstinences and have moved to foreign ports in great cities of the west are said to return to their homeland and to revert once more to the desert. This is a man's life, but the desert is flaming hot and there are mosquitoes and malaria in many places and to those without an eye for the desert it looks empty—deserted. Let those who can take it rule the desert without the burden of Kenyattas and emperors tinkering with the life they neither like nor understand.

Today there is a change in the remoteness of these desert regions. Imagine the herds sheltering from the grilling sun perhaps two hundred miles from the nearest water. If you are about, you may hear the sound of transistor radios, and if you understand the language spoken you will discover that the world's great powers old and new are wooing the desert nomad and his soul. Of late I am informed that the broadcasts from Peking are the clearest of them all, and no doubt they have something to say in line with Mr. Chou En-lai's dictum in Mogadishu in 1964 that the prospects of revolution are excellent.

At the end of the long dry season every creature is nearing the end of its endurance. The hump on the camel's back is lower. The hump on the withers of the kine has become nominal. The hides of the cattle seem stretched over protruding ribs like a drum. The tails of the fat-tailed sheep have become fatless. Even the donkeys are listless. Only the goats look more or less unchanged.

The old men and women are more lined and shrunken with

flies swarming along their eyelids. The young men speak but little, for all their energy is taken up in other ways. The girls are fetching firewood and water to the manyattas during most of the day. The totos are watching the flocks. The mind of those distant camel men is not possible to penetrate. If the herds have prospered under this grilling strain the young men may have earned part of the price of a bride: Who knows? Will she still be waiting?

All nature seems to be going dead. Then one evening the air thickens, the wind begins to whistle through the thorns, there is suddenly a delicious scent in the air, the scent of rain on the desert dust. The ordeal is over. The storm bursts. The lightning sizzles through the air, the thunder crashes. Almost at once the green herb begins to shoot. There will soon be social life and meat feasts and the laughter of girls. There will be the stories around the camp fire, stories of the desert and of attacks by wild beasts and rival tribes, and then there will be songs and boasting and courting. Presently even the dark rocks will flush with a soft green veil. Spring has come; the chromatic scale of the dawn bird summons young men no longer from the surliness of insufficient sleep. The mourning dove on the fringe of villages sings no longer of bereavement but of love.

Men of the desert often have to fight in order to survive, for there are constant choices between life and death as men and herds contend for the only grazing and the only water by which they can survive what remains of the drought. Nevertheless there is also a brotherhood, for this is not the empty desert but the inhabited desert. Anyone from distant and luxuriant highlands who tries to build an empire in the Somali deserts will first have all his substance sucked into it and then he will perish.

6

DISMEMBERED NATION

'De minimis non curat rex'

Africans accuse Europeans of having dismembered a United Africa. The charge is false.

When the European 'scramble' started about seventy years ago, most of Africa was a mosaic of small independent tribes speaking different languages and following different tribal rituals. The most up-to-date atlas still shows over fifty tribes in Kenya, and Budge lists over one hundred and fifty in Ethiopia, so it may not be unreasonable to suppose that in all Africa there were more than two thousand independent tribes, many of which were further subdivided into clans.

In Kenya men are still Kikuyu, Luo, Kamba or Masai, etc.; only lately and after much effort are men of Kenya becoming sufficiently nation-conscious to call themselves Kenyans; and this is happening within boundaries artificially contrived by Britain under a name invented by Britain. Some others of the nation's 'names' were replaced by fresh ones at the time of Independence, as for instance when Gold was turned into Ghana, and Nyasaland became Malawi; yet within the European-contrived boundaries barely seventy years old there now exists a remarkable degree of administrative unity; many tribes are well on the road to becoming a nation with one law, one legislature, one army, one police force, one currency, one Customs and Excise authority, one taxation authority, one postal authority, one communications authority and the extended use of a single language throughout the new nation state. A Kenya African cadet now at Sandhurst tells me that English is the only language in which he can communicate with a number of his fellow Africans. So it is that two thousand or more independent tribes have within the long lifetime of a single man coalesced into less than fifty nations. This is an achievement of the Europeans, and it is a work of unification not of dismemberment.

Africans talk glibly of African unity and of the forthcoming merging of many new nations into federations. It may turn out as they predict, and one hesitates to prophesy, but it looks very unlikely to happen quickly. The political unities contrived in Africa by Europe were strong as long as Europe remained. They are fragile on the morning of Europe's departure, and the strong focus of unity which brought them into being is replaced by a negative focus which subsists only by denouncing what has already gone and it is therefore unstable. In these conditions attempts to form larger unities may well produce disintegration rather than unity.

The case of the Somalis however is quite the reverse. They had been for centuries one nation, professing one religion, speaking one language and pursuing a single pattern of pastoral nomadic culture when the Europeans arrived and carved them up. Their sub-divisions are powerfully characterized and prone to schism, but are more accurately described as clans like the MacDonalds and Campbells rather than tribes like the Kikuyu and the Luo. The Somali clans all know themselves as Somalis and they do in fact occupy one large homogeneous region in Africa.

The Somalis were politically divided up between Britain, France, Italy and Ethiopia, and in this way the one Somali nation with one Islamic law was given a variety of overlays; an overlay of English law in the extreme north and the extreme south, of French law in the north-west, of Italian law in the middle-east and of Ethiopian lawlessness in the middle-west. The two English portions were many hundreds of miles apart, with the Italian portion in between them, and half way through the Colonial era the southern English portion was again split so as to transfer the province called Jubaland from England to Italy.

This dismemberment is unique in all Africa, and it was resisted for an unrivalled length of time—twenty-one years—by a Somali patriot and his followers, one Mohammed Abdille Hassan. It has been estimated that in the process of dismemberment by the intermittent and incompetent use of force probably some two hundred thousand Somalis ended their lives prematurely. Britain played a leading part in this process, mounting five massive expeditions against the ill-equipped Somalis whose resourceful leader we call the 'Mad Mullah' not so much for his folly of resisting the God-given rule of Britain, but for the impertinence of his successes.

Some of the Galla put up a briefer but no less gallant and death-despising resistance to the French-led and well-armed Habash forces of the Emperor Menelek II.

Of this period in our relations with the Somali Horn of Africa Sir Charles Eliot wrote sixty years ago:

> Our dealings with them not conspicuous for success . . . campaigns hastily undertaken . . . elaborate explanations . . . moral victory . . . achieved real object . . . quite different from what everybody had supposed from the beginning . . . The Englishman . . . has little sympathy for Somalis. He tolerates a black man who admits his inferiority and even those who show a good fight and give in . . . but he cannot tolerate dark colour with an intelligence in any way equal to his own . . . the Somalis are not willing to agree to the simple plan of having a fair fight and then shaking hands when defeated but constantly indicate that they think themselves equals or superiors and not infrequently prove it.

During the sixty years that have passed since this was written, our relations with Somalis have been punctuated by episodes wherein Somali interests have been treated as expendable minor assets. We have used them to appease the imperial appetite of Mussolini, Haile Selassie, and lastly Jomo Kenyatta.

The present state of the Somali nation is that they are still in four parts. One part is the free and independent Somali Republic consisting of some two hundred thousand square miles at ten persons to the square mile; another part is Ethiopian Somaliland —the Haud and Ogaden—perhaps half the size of the republic at fifteen persons to the square mile; a third part is Kenya Somaliland—part of the old N.F.D.—perhaps a quarter the size of the republic at five persons per square mile; the fourth part is French Somaliland, consisting of six thousand square miles with eighty thousand inhabitants.

If I am not precise over the size of territory and population, it is that Ethiopian and Kenyan Somalilands are not separately shown on any of the records except small-scale maps which leave the square mileage to be guessed. Population figures moreover are never up to date, and the Colonial Office inform me that they do not believe the latest census (British) for Kenya, and I do not seek statistics from Ethiopian sources for they are likely to deserve Disraeli's aphorism on the subject.

In Chapter II I have given an outline account of tribal and racial movements in the region I am considering. Even if the anthropologists manage to push Kush into a discarnate twilight of linguistic essence devoid of existence, it remains beyond dispute that movements have taken place; Galla have swung northward onto the Ethiopian plateau, Somalis have crossed three rivers on their south-westward journey, while the Masai, to mention only one of the moving Kush hybrids sallied out of the Sidama region and pranged their way far to the south.

Two movements survived into the British colonial era, the Somali, and the Habash. The Habash encroachment was an imperial one, unaccompanied by any need for additional living-room and devoid of any intention to settle in the conquered territories; by contrast the Somali encroachment was part of a struggle to survive; the whole purpose was settlement and it was devoid of any imperial intentions.

It so happens that in our time empires are on the way out, whereas charter after charter proclaims the rights of established occupiers. Here are some of the title deeds which Somalis can and do invoke.

THE TITLE DEEDS

1. *The Atlantic Charter, August 14, 1961. President of U.S.A. and Premier of H.M.G.*
   'Third, they respect the right of all people to choose the form of government under which they will live; and they wish to see sovereign rights and self-government restored to those who have been forcibly deprived of them.'

2. *The United Nations Charter, June 26, 1945. Preamble.*
   '. . . reaffirm faith in . . . the equal rights . . . of nations large and small.'
   '. . . to ensure by the acceptance of principles and the institution of methods that armed force shall not be used . . .'

   Article 1 Clause 2.
   'To develop friendly relations among nations based on respect for the principle of equal rights and self-determination of peoples . . .'

3. *Constitution of the Somali Republic.*
   (As approved by the United Nations, July 1, 1960.)
   'In the name of God the Compassionate the Merciful . . . the Somali people . . . Conscious of the sacred right of self-determination of peoples solemnly consecrated in the Charter of the United

Nations. . . . Firmly decided to consolidate and protect the independence of the Somali Nation and the right to liberty of its people,
in a democracy based on the Sovereignty of the people and of the
equality of rights and obligations of all its citizens.'

4. *Charter of the Organization of African Unity, May 25,* 1963.
   'We the Heads of African States and Governments assembled in
   the City of Addis Ababa, Ethiopia; Convinced that it is the inalienable right of all people to control their own destiny: . . .'

These general title deeds are strengthened and endorsed by
some of the statements of those concerned with granting or with-
holding Somali self-determination. Unfortunately they are also
weakened or contradicted by others of their statements or actions.
In order to produce a streamlined account of how Somali nationalism has been treated in the nineteenth and twentieth centuries
it is well to start at the beginning and work forward.

When the Horn was dismembered it was regarded by us British
as a useless and unwanted desert which had no merit as a colony
but which for politico-strategic reasons should not be allowed to
fall into the hands of France or Germany.

No part of the Horn was specifically partitioned with the
Habash, whose barbaric empire we assigned as a sphere of
civilizing influence to Italy; we did this even when in 1906 we
guaranteed in a treaty the political integrity of Ethiopia. Our
main arrangement direct with the Habash was the demarcation
on the map of respective spheres of influence.

Between 1899 and 1920 we were engaged in trying to enforce
the fact of dismemberment, but even then the desirability of
unification was being put forward by thoughtful observers, as
for example Sir Charles Eliot, who wrote in 1905 as follows:

> If it were possible to detach the districts inhabited by Somali, it
> would be an excellent thing to form them into a separate govern-
> ment, as they are different in population, economic and physical
> condition from the other provinces; but unfortunately, they are too
> small to form a separate administration, and the adjoining Somali
> territories are not British.

In 1924 we could have made a notable contribution to Somali
unity as well as to Anglo-Italian accord if we had been sufficiently
interested in either of these things. We could for example have
joined both the British Somaliland protectorate in the north and
all the Kenya Somalilands in the south to Italian Somaliland in

9. *Head of young Somali woman showing non-negroid features.*

10. *Head of middle-aged Somali woman showing non-negroid features.*

the middle. We could have invited the Ethiopians to add to this their part of Somaliland—Ogaden—over which up to that time they had not begun to exercise the smallest control. All we did, however, was to give Italy a part of the Kenya Somaliland called Jubaland as intimated above.

A quarter of a century after this baksheesh deal with the Italians, when we had reconquered for Habash rule not only the Habash homelands but also the mismanaged Habash empire, we did for the first and only time publicly proclaim our support for the unification of the Somali provinces.

In 1946 (*Hansard*, June 4th) Britain's Labour Foreign Secretary, Ernest Bevin, outlined a proposal he had made to the Peace Conference powers. He did so with a Bevin-like simplicity and a Bevin-like sense of fairness towards the inhabitants, and he used the following words:

> In all innocence therefore we propose that British Somaliland, Italian Somaliland and the adjacent part of Ethiopia, if Ethiopia agree, should be lumped together as a trust territory, so that the nomads should lead their frugal existence with the least possible hindrance and there might be a real chance of a decent economic life as understood in that territory . . .

For those who would have liked to insist upon justice for Somalis it was a disappointment when Bevin added:

> If the conference [the Peace Conference] do not like our proposal we will not be dogmatic about it.

During the course of his speech Bevin gave an outline history of the dismemberment of the Horn in the following words:

> In the latter part of the last century the Horn of Africa was divided between Great Britain, France and Italy. At about the time we occupied our part, the Ethiopians occupied an inland area which is the grazing ground for nearly half the nomads of British Somaliland for six months of the year. Similarly, the nomads of Italian Somaliland must cross the existing frontiers in search of grass.

In this simple, carefully worded survey in seventy words, the fact that we had not shared out the Horn with Ethiopia was made plain; the fact that Ethiopians had occupied parts of the Horn not previously in Ethiopian territory was also made plain, and if there is understatement about the extent of Ethiopian occupation, one can hardly expect everything in seventy words.

H

The whole of Bevin's statement is in marked and favourable contrast with the uncritical support of Ethiopian imperialism bestowed by Anthony Eden before Bevin's time and by Harold Macmillan after him. It also indicates a remarkable swing from the traditional indifference of the Foreign Office to the more perceptive views of the Colonial Office.

It was not to be, however. A decision was made that Somalia should be born; that much is satisfactory. But it was also decided that she should be born with four limbs missing, and of this Lord Rennell of Rodd in 1952, speaking of opportunities missed during the Peace Conference, concluded:

> The world was not sensible enough, and we were not sensible enough . . . and Somaliland will probably become a cock-pit of East Africa.

But before then the main opponent of any Somali independence had put his cards upon the table. Ethiopian myth-history was tabled at the United Nations in a memorandum of October 8, 1948. It embodies a crop of major inaccuracies but takes only a dozen or so more words than Mr. Bevin did to achieve this result:

> Prior to the race of the Europeans to divide up the Continent of Africa, Ethiopia included an extensive coastline along the Red Sea and Indian Ocean. It was only in the last fifteen years of the nineteenth century that Ethiopia had been deprived of access to the sea by the loss of Somaliland and Eritrea. The first step in this direction was the seizure of Massawa by the Italians in 1885. This was followed by a similar seizure of the Benadir and other areas of Somaliland. . . . [Benadir is a word used for Italian Somaliland.]

Here are some of the necessary corrections in this most inaccurate statement:

Ethiopia before Menelek II,* who died in 1913, was no more than a quarter of its present size. It had no coastline extensive or otherwise, and Massawa had been in the hands of the Turks since the sixteenth century. The Europeans, far from depriving Ethiopia of access to the sea, had built under French initiative Ethiopia's only railway from Djibouti on the coast in French Somaliland to Addis Ababa—the new capital of Ethiopia built in conquered Galla territory by Menelek II. This railway was opened in 1918, and so had been in use for thirty years at the time when the Ethiopians made this extraordinary statement. The

* Refer to the Emperor's letter of April 1891 in Appendix 3.

Financial Times of September 4, 1964, described the importance to the economy of Ethiopia of this railway and the port of Djibouti.

The claims of Ethiopia were based, without any attempt to conceal the matter, on Imperial Title. One might almost suppose that the Emperor was unaware of the numerous charters enshrining the rights of occupiers, and was out of touch with modern ideas of self-determination. Perhaps two thousand years of inward-looking had produced a people incapable of noticing that imperialism as a viable political idea is rapidly declining. Yet this is hardly possible; the Emperor is a much-travelled man who cannot have failed to inform himself about modern democratic ideas during his war-time sojourn in Bath in my county of Somerset. Moreover he does not flinch from reminding Her Majesty's colonial subjects of their rights to self-determination and Her Majesty's Government of their duty to bestow self-determination speedily. *The Times* of February 5, 1962, for instance carried a report dated February 4 of the Emperor's opening address to a conference of PAMFECA:

> It is incumbent upon Britain to apply the same wisdom that it has applied to its former colonies in Africa and Asia and speed up the political and constitutional advance of the African inhabitants of Bechuanaland, Swaziland and Basutoland and assure their early independence.

These three 'High Commission' territories are small inland enclaves of probably not more than one-third of a million inhabitants each. It was plain even at the moment when the Emperor was speaking that he had no similar plans to bestow independence upon the twelve to fifteen million colonial people who languish in his own empire.

It is on the whole surprising that Cape Town, after constant harrying from Addis Ababa on account of her white imperialism does not turn the tables and expose to the world not so much the Emperor's myopia, for he is not alone in this, as his black imperialism and the benighted state of some of his own colonial peoples.

The Emperor preserves and seems to believe in the old Victorian illusion that nobody not entirely mad could fail to take a loving pride in being a citizen of so noble a country as—Ethiopia. A speech recording sentiments of this sort appeared in the *British*

Survey in its issue of May 1957, which is devoted to the Somalilands and the passage reads:

> In August of last year, the Emperor during a tour of the Ogaden made a policy speech in Gabredare (*The Times*, August 31, 1956) in which he stated that he hoped that *Greater Somalia* would materialize because 'our country would thereby become yet stronger and larger'. He added 'we do not want what belongs to others and will not give up what is ours'.
>
> Many well-informed observers feel it is remarkable that at a time when Britain is still regarded with opprobrium because of her *Imperialism* and *Colonialism*, Ethiopia can, without much comment from any other nation, announce her desire to increase still further Menelik's empire which he has never yet been able to govern or develop properly.

The Emperor's last quoted sentence together with the record of Ethiopian myth-history as conveyed in the memorandum to the United Nations was embodied in a letter from the Ethiopian Embassy in New Delhi to an Indian newspaper as lately as April 1963—this was done with the object of contradicting a correct version of history—Mr. Bevin's sort—to which the leader of a Somali agricultural delegation to India had made reference during the course of his speech.

Those in touch with the Emperor believe he has in mind the 'Eritrean Solution' for the Somali Republic. Since he spoke on that occasion in 1956, we have had an opportunity of seeing Ethiopia's notions of federation put into practice in Eritrea—it looks very much like federation as understood by the boa-constrictor!

Mr. Mboya, Kenya's Minister of Justice, seems at first sight to have the right ideas about self-determination for he writes in his book *Tom Mboya*:

> In our Freedom Charter we declared . . . that the right of self-determination is God-given, and no man or nation is chosen by God to determine the destiny of others. . . .

And he seems also to have sound ideas on the destiny of unwanted federations because he also writes:

> We support in every way the efforts of Nyasaland and Northern Rhodesia to break up the Central African Federation and decide their own future as Independent States.

Yet on the matter of dismembered Somalia Mr. Mboya limply writes:

> Perhaps federation is the *only* solution for some of these boundary problems.

In other words Mr. Mboya accepts that the God-given right of self-determination is perhaps not available to the people of Somali provinces; that Haile Selassie and Kenyatta are perhaps dispensed from observing the Divine precepts!

The attitude of the French over French Somaliland is not known, but Somalis with whom I have spoken on this matter cannot believe that General de Gaulle who swallowed the camel of Algérie Algérienne will strain out the gnat of French Somaliland, though the peace-loving Emperor would probably arrive with three divisions to make certain of the loving pride of all Djiboutians in their Ethiopian citizenship—that is unless the Soviet Union or China were to help the Somalis to stop him, for it does not look as though anyone else would bother to do so. Since writing this the conference of non-aligned nations has resolved in Cairo in October 1964 to call upon France to grant immediate independence to French Somaliland.

In Ethiopian Somaliland all hope of freedom by negotiation with the Emperor has long ago faded, and in this connection I produce a well-informed special report printed in the *New York Times* of March 19, 1964, which describes what has been happening in the Somali provinces in Ethiopia;

> Ogaden Province in Ethiopia covers about three hundred and sixty-six thousand seven hundred square miles* bordering Somalia and inhabited by almost two million Somalis whose resistance began to crystallise with the 1936 Italian invasion.
>
> It hardened into an underground movement when the Four-Power United Nations Inquiry Commission visiting Mogadishu in 1948 ignored the request for self-determination presented by Ogaden Somali leaders. Open rebellion flared on June 16, 1963, following government efforts to 'Ethiopianise' the Ogaden Somalis and impose a livestock tax.
>
> Under the direction of a shadow government headed by Muktal Dahir, the Liberation Forces of about twelve thousand men have been waging guerrilla warfare against the Emperor's troops for the last five months. The third Division of the Ethiopian Army sent in last August to snuff out the revolt has since been reinforced. The

* Clearly an error.

guerrillas' surprising success is attributed to several factors. The hot, bare, bush country with clumps of thorn trees is ideal terrain for traditional guerrilla hit-and-run tactics, placing the mechanised troops at a great disadvantage. Since the only Ethiopians in Ogaden are military men they are in a position of an Army of Occupation surrounded by hostile civilians. Those who might have remained neutral have been alienated by the loss of relatives, herds, homes in Ethiopian reprisal raids on the border villages.

There is no way of ascertaining the number of casualties since June, but by now they must amount to thousands on each side.

No one who has closely followed the clashes at a dozen points along the thousand-mile frontier in February doubts the explosion was a direct consequence of the Ogaden rebellion. British, United States, French, German and Egyptian newsmen who visited the battle area on the Somali side were convinced that Ethiopia had attacked Somalia. Most diplomatic observers in Mogadishu believe the attacks were aimed at bringing pressure on the Somali Government to quash the revolution.

Yet neither Ethiopia nor Somalia has recognised the movement which is a severe embarrassment to both for different reasons.

The Ethiopians give the impression that armed bandits have been sent across the border by Somalia to harass her neighbour into ceding a large slice of Ethiopian territory. The Government has ignored repeated denials by Somalia's leaders that the Republic either inspired or fomented the troubles in Ogaden.

Ethiopia wants to minimise the scope and significance of the civil war, especially since it is assuming the character of a Moslem holy war and could spread to other Moslem minorities in Ethiopia.

While Somalia obliquely refers to the insurgents as 'oppressed people reacting against the Imperialistic yoke' the Government has remained officially aloof. President Aden Abdullah Osman has felt honour-bound to observe his agreement with Emperor Haile Selassie, undertaken after the first Organization of African Unity Conference to try to find a solution through direct discussion with the Emperor.

The Government is committed to a similar course by the 'Lagos Resolution'. The Somali Government cannot acknowledge that it has no control over the Ogaden Liberation Army, yet that is the fact. Much as the rebels desire recognition by Somalia, they are not willing to take orders from Mogadishu to achieve it. They feel they cannot risk losing momentum in what has been a successful operation so far, and will brook no interference no matter how well intended.

Western observers are concerned that Communist Nations may

use Somali Nationalism to try to drive Western influence from the strategic Horn of Africa; there already have been reports that Chinese communists have made approaches to the insurgents, but apparently the close relations of the Communist Nations to the Somali Government have prevented any direct Communist aid to the rebels.*

In connection with Kenya's Somali Province I have had occasion to take up its claim to self-determination personally, and of this I now give my account.

In the opening chapter I referred to the requests of a number of persons in Kenya late in 1961, that I should take up their problems when I got home and 'say what I thought'. Among the most pressing of these persons was a Somali who had reached Kenya half a century earlier as an orphaned refugee from the 'Mad Mullah' disturbances. 'You are a senator in Britain—you must go home and say publicly what you believe to be the truth about us', was the gist of his appeal.

At the behest of this Somali we first paid a visit to the Provincial Commissioner of the Northern Province at Isiolo. It was one of those torrential occasions when my wife and I took a chance and waded a swollen river which had washed a culvert away. Mr. Walters, the Commissioner, was helpful with information but, as I already knew, the heavy rains had made the rest of the N.F.D. inaccessible. We then flew to Dar-es-Salaam to discuss the Somali problem with that experienced administrator, Sir Richard Turnbull.

On returning to England I resumed correspondence on the Somali problem with that great authority of African desert dwellers, Sir Gerald Reece. Behind Sir Gerald is nearly half a century of experience of the N.F.D., Southern Ethiopia and our Somaliland Protectorate.

During the succeeding five months I refreshed my own out-of-date knowledge (I was in the Northern Province from 1923 to 1926) by reading some sixty books and reports and by probing for current information here and there. I received valuable help from Sir Arthur Kirby about East Africa in general, and from Ambassador to the Somali Republic, Mr. Arraleh, about the Somali people. Mr. Arraleh gave me that scholarly, readable and well expressed booklet, *The Somali Peninsula*.

From what I could ascertain in advance, the views of the White

* © 1964 by the New York Times Company. Reprinted by permission.

Highlands of Kenya were receiving powerful expression in the
House of Lords from the Marquess of Salisbury and several others,
including more than one peer with landed interests in Kenya.

By the time I was ready to make my maiden speech in May
1962 I felt that the Somali N.F.D. problem had been launched
towards a correct solution in the hands of Mr. Reginald Maudling.
Nevertheless, it seemed to me that, with independence from
white colonialism everywhere in the offing, the Somalis might be
left as victims of black colonialism if only because of British
ignorance about the imperialism of the Emperor of Ethiopia.

I refer specifically to the Emperor rather than to his government,
because in Ethiopia one-man Emperor rule is the only form of
central administration they know; to the Emperor also in preference to 'Ethiopia' because three-quarters of the Ethiopian Empire
is a heterogeneous collection of colonies acquired and retained
by force under the dominant Amharas, who number two million
out of the estimated total of eighteen to twenty millions. I hesitate
to associate even the Amharas with the Emperor's 'greater
Ethiopia' policy, for the Amharas have a strong tradition of
putting not their trust in Emperors. And I have no wish to lessen
the chances of fraternal relations between Galla, Amhara, Tigre,
Danakil and Somali when the last of the 'indefectible' Emperors
comes to be replaced by an administration more worthy of the
Queen of Sheba's children.

My first speech on May 15, 1962, was well received as are all
'maidens'. My references to the Somalis were underlined by more
eminent speakers. I imagined that I had made my first and last
speech in a chamber where I had long known that nothing of
consequence is ever decided. I spoke from the cross-benches to
which I had gravitated after what I had deemed to be the dangerous and foolish adventures of Suez in 1956.

Shortly after this occasion I received via the B.B.C. a letter of
thanks from the Somali community in Aden. Then from the
Prime Minister of the Somali Republic another letter of thanks
charmingly expressed and ending with an invitation to visit
Somalia as his guest. Later there reached me via the B.B.C.
further messages of thanks from Somali leaders in the N.F.D.
The Somali who had sought my support in Kenya did not fail
to add his thanks to the others.

At this time I learnt from *The Times* and later from our ambassador in Addis Ababa that my speech had been accorded

headline abuse in the Ethiopian Government newspaper. At
this time I did not suppose that disapproval from the world's most
unenlightened empire could possibly deflect Her Majesty's
Government from the course of justice. My Muslim statesman
friend in New Delhi, Dr. Syed Mahmud, wrote his appreciation,
and when the Somali Premier visited this country the Foreign
Secretary (then Lord Home) invited me to sit beside him at an
official luncheon.

So it was that I had all but taken it for granted that the N.F.D.
Somalis were certain to win their case, when by chance Lord
Dundee astounded me by saying during an encounter in one of the
House of Lords corridors, 'I am not sure that we are going to let
them have it'.

The issue was one of the simplest of its kind, namely the appli-
cation of a principle of self-determination to the desert half of
Kenya, which includes the Somali N.F.D. The main impulse
came and still comes from the Somalis who live there. These
British subjects made a case for separate representation at the
Kenya Constitutional Conference in London in the spring of 1962.
The two political leaders of Kenya, Mr. Kenyatta and Mr.
Ngala, objected to this separate representation, but Mr. Maudling
with his quick instinct for the right and proper course gave his
consent.

At the conclusion of the conference Mr. Maudling, notwithstanding the objections of Mr. Kenyatta and Mr. Ngala, issued a
pledge which I summarize from the White Paper (Cmnd. 1700,
Paragraph 26):

1. To appoint an independent commission to ascertain the wishes
of the people of the N.F.D. regarding their future.
2. To make a decision *on the findings* of this commission.
3. To complete 1 and 2 before the introduction of internal self-
government for Kenya.
4. To refrain from changing the existing status of the N.F.D.
before a decision had been made.

This was understood by all who read it, supporters and critics
alike, to pledge Her Majesty's Government to apply the principle
of self-determination to the N.F.D. The Kenya leaders, Kenyatta
and Ngala, understood it in this sense, and Kenyatta threatened
war to recover any part of Kenya that might be ceded by Her
Majesty's Government.

The N.F.D. Somalis, knowing their immense numerical preponderance in the area, prepared to meet the commission with enthusiasm. Dr. Shermarke, the Prime Minister of the Somali Republic, entertained in turn Mr. Kenyatta and Mr. Ngala in Mogadishu, where these two Kenya leaders were accorded an enthusiastic reception. It was at that time the strong wish of Somalia to work towards joining the projected East African Federation.

During Mr. Kenyatta's visit, Dr. Shermarke declared his support for impartial self-determination for the N.F.D. in the following words, 'If they want to remain in Kenya we shall raise no objection.' Both Kenyatta and Ngala refused to agree that if the N.F.D. should express a wish to join Somalia they would raise no objection. Kenyatta based himself rigidly on the imperialistic principle of Kenya's territorial integrity. Dr. Shermarke sent me transcripts of the various speeches, and the main features of the two visits were printed in September 1962 in a Somali Government official publication 20681/22962 called 'The Somali Republic and African Unity'. This is the answer to those persons —and they include some of our Cabinet Ministers—who allege that the Somali Government have refused to discuss the N.F.D. issue with Kenya African leaders.

Incidentally it had been clear to me since November 1961 that Mr. Kenyatta in the matter of Somali aspirations was already pledged against them to the Emperor of Ethiopia, and that his hands had been firmly tied about nine months before his visit to Mogadishu. Reading between the lines, and having regard to hostile reactions in the Ethiopian Press, it seemed certain that the Emperor of Ethiopia, to whom self-determination spells the dissolution of his Colonial Empire, intervened to insist with Mr. Macmillan that Mr. Maudling's White Paper pledge was a violation of another pledge by Mr. Macmillan (*Hansard* April 11, 1960), which reads: 'Her Majesty's Government do not, and will not, encourage or support any claim affecting the territorial integrity of French Somaliland, Kenya or Ethiopia. This is a matter which could only be considered if that were the wish of the governments and peoples concerned'.

Dr. Shermarke had already brought this statement to my notice, giving it as his view that, with the creation of independent Somalia due on July 1 of the same year in accordance with the proclaimed principle of self-determination, any statement basing

itself on the imperial principle of territorial integrity was a political
anachronism and, in this particular context, improper. I must
acknowledge that I failed to recognize the danger. Mr. Macmillan's statement had been made under the heading of 'Written
Answers' at the end of a long day's business after eleven o'clock at
night, and in answer to a question addressed, not to the Prime
Minister nor from the Opposition, but to the Colonial Secretary
and from a member of his own Party. Taken all round it seemed a
statement of policy three years out of date, devoid even at the
time of any hard-and-fast pledge to anybody. It had been made
on an occasion of the lowest political importance in answer to a
questioner of the least political significance. Moreover, Mr.
Maudling in a White Paper issued by the Government was
apparently taking most deliberate steps to ascertain the 'wish of
the people' in his capacity as a fully competent member of 'the
government concerned'. He had already over-ruled the objections
of the Kenya African leaders, and it was inconceivable to me that
this was being done as a kind of exercise *in vacuo* with no intention
whatever of granting the aspirations of the people.

In December 1962 the N.F.D. Commission made their report.
In terms of political topography they found three areas in the
N.F.D.: first, the Somali and pro-Somali area where the people
almost unanimously wished separation from Kenya in order to
join in an act of union with the Somali Republic on the other side
of their 350-mile frontier; second, an area mainly pro-Kenya or
indifferent; third, an area where the leaders of one tribe (the
Rendille) had expressed pro-Somali views which the commission
considered were not truly representative of the tribe.

A second commission, the Regional Boundaries Commission
(Command 1899), taking it for granted that a decision to allow
the Somali part to secede was a foregone conclusion, suggested a
region which could be lopped off without confusion or administrative difficulty from the rest of Kenya. They too were convinced of the wishes of the people in this region. This is now the
north-eastern region of Kenya.

When the report was published Mr. Kenyatta again declared
'not an inch' and threatened war to recover any portion of Kenya
which Her Majesty's Government might permit to secede. The
Somalis of the N.F.D. were at this time, however, absolutely certain of British justice under the clear pledges of Mr. Maudling,
who had made an outstandingly good impression on all races in

Kenya after the depression brought about by the 'Macleod of Unknowing'.

Then on March 8, 1963, Her Majesty's Government 'dropped the bomb'. Mr. Duncan Sandys in Nairobi inaugurated internal self-government for Kenya within its existing boundaries, which incorporated the Somali areas inside Kenya. On March 12 Mr. Sandys told the House of Commons that even if Her Majesty's Government had wished to act otherwise they could not have done so owing to the *prospect of violence* and political non-co-operation in Kenya. He seemed totally unconcerned with any possible re-actions in the N.F.D. or in Somalia. Thus did Her Majesty's Government make a decision in the tradition of Pontius Pilate, placing a miserable expediency ahead of what they saw and knew to be just. It was not pleasant to watch a Minister of the Crown bowing to menaces from Mr. Kenyatta.

The shock of Mr. Duncan Sandys's brutal and even flippant treatment of the Somali N.F.D. in his Nairobi speech of March 8, 1962—'The wrong decision announced by the wrong Minister in the wrong place' as I said in the House of Lords—put a heavy strain upon the Somali Republic. With scarce a break for more than a week the Assembly debated the issue of breaking off diplomatic relations with Britain. Before going to bed after they had decided to do so the Prime Minister wrote me a letter of explanation—regret moderately expressed. *The Times* commented on the dignity, on the Somali side, of this diplomatic breach.

In May 1963 the whole circumstances of this affair were set out in a Somali White Paper called 'The issue of the Northern Frontier District'.

During a motion of censure which I moved on May 3, 1963, a Labour peer, Lord Huntingdon, spoke openly in support. He was the only peer of any party to do so on that occasion. It was late in the day and the House was almost deserted. I spoke for an hour. The government spokesman, the Marquess of Lansdowne, apart from a few impromptu words, read a prepared speech which did not in any way tie-up with the points in my own. Both he and the Opposition spokesman, the Earl of Listowel, acknowledged that my claim for the N.F.D. Somalis was based on justice. Neither they nor any other speaker in four further debates on this subject was to question the justice of the case, but on that night the noble marquess implied that justice was too difficult while the noble earl implied that it was too dangerous. The precise words used by both may be read in the context of their full speeches in *Hansard*. Lord Listowel held out a ray of hope, suggesting that this was an 'interim' decision, and the noble marquess looked as if he nodded his assent. There was, however, nothing in either statement of Mr. Sandys which hinted in any way at an interim decision, and there was at least one sentence which implied finality.

Owing to the lateness of the hour, or more probably because of the unimportance of the speaker and his subject, little of my speech got into the English newspapers, but a half-hour version of it was broadcast several times from Mogadishu radio.

As opportunities presented themselves in Parliament I sought to reverse this evil decision: Twice more (June 26 and July 15) before Her Majesty's Government acknowledged their interim decision as final—this time in Rome!, and twice afterwards (November 28 and December 2).

On November 28 I gave notice of an amendment to the Kenya Indpendence Bill seeking to remove the North-eastern region (Somali) from the Kenya to be transferred to the Nairobi Government of Mr. Kenyatta. On December 2 I moved the amendment which was negatived. One peer on the Labour benches, notwithstanding the forlorn eleventh hour effort, spoke in support. Lord Faringdon thus concluded his short but effective speech:

> I share the anxieties of the noble earl who has moved this amend-ment and I believe that Her Majesty's Government would have done a much better job by the people of Kenya had they excluded this province until such time as agreement satisfactory to all parties could be reached. I hope that Her Majesty's Government will re-consider this matter.

In a letter to me afterwards Lord Faringdon referred to the N.F.D. as Kenya's 'damnosa hereditas'. Lord Somers had intend-ed to speak in support of my amendment from the Government benches, as he had done in a forthright manner on an earlier occasion, but another engagement prevented him from doing so. No Liberal peer at any time spoke in support of Somali self-determination, but Lord Ogmore, Chairman of the Party, speak-ing from the Liberal benches opposed the lopping-off of portions of Kenya. I cannot find that any member of the House of Com-mons uttered a single squeak on behalf of the Somalis.

My kinsman, the Earl of Enniskillen, who is a Kenya rancher

and who spoke in the Kenya Independence debate, had nothing
to say about the Somalis in the Chamber although in the lobbies
I understood him to say of Somali secession, 'I don't think it's
possible.' It was, curiously enough, his mother who had introduced me to the Somali, whose appeal for 'British justice' I had
been assiduously supporting.

Why was it 'too difficult', 'too dangerous', 'too late' or 'impossible' to do justice to the Somalis of the N.F.D.? I have discussed the matter with many an eminent colonial administrator
of our Somali territories without finding one who agrees with the
decision of Her Majesty's Government.

For a full, scholarly, temperate, most able but too polite
account of this and other injuries inflicted upon the Somali
nation, Mr. John Drysdale's book, *The Somali Dispute*, is on the
high level of dignified debate which has been a singular characteristic of the Somali Republic's dealings with the black and white
colonial powers. Mr. Drysdale was until lately political adviser
to the Prime Minister of the Somali Republic.

What has happened to those fair pledges of Mr. Maudling? In
correspondence with me in the summer of 1963 Mr. Maudling
intimated that Her Majesty's Government were throughout
guided by the pledge of Mr. Macmillan on June 11, 1960. Does
this mean that Mr. Maudling deliberately induced the Somali
N.F.D. to declare its allegiance to the Republic of Somalia,
knowing and intending that Her Majesty's Government should
make a gift of the district to Independent Kenya where such views
would become treason? I find it difficult to believe this of Mr.
Maudling, but if it is true of Mr. Macmillan, and that certainly
seems to be the case, I must end this part of my review by citing
a judgment chosen from Mr. Macmillan's own words.

It will be remembered that during the summer of 1962 the
serious business of government in Britain was almost wholly
suspended by the intense interest aroused in a sex scandal. During
the course of a debate on June 17, 1963, Mr. Macmillan passed
judgment on one of his colleague. The colleagues in question,
after protracted harrying by the Press on the matter of his
relations with a girl who was not his wife, had gone to bed one
night in his home dog-tired and after taking sleeping pills. Then
after the nidnight hour he was roused by a team of Mr. Macmillan's other colleagues who bade him hasten to get dressed and
come to make a personal statement in the House that the girl

in question, by then thought to have been somewhat promiscuous, had been his friend but one with whom he had never shared the bed. Tired out, bemused by sleeping pills, his back to the wall, his good name and that of his family at stake on an intimately private and by this time long-dead relationship unreasonably and inexcusably raised to the level of high security—this was the state of the victim when he told the House that he had not been to bed with this girl—as if the bed part made any real difference. It was a lie told to preserve the sanctuary of his family life—a lie richly deserved by the gullible simpletons who drove him to utter it.

What did Mr. Macmillan say of this? 'For what greater moral crime can there be to deceive those naturally inclined to trust one . . . ?'

Will Mr. Macmillan come with me to Mogadishu and repeat to my Somali friends what he said a column later during the course of this debate? 'I know that I have acted honourably; I believe that I have acted justly—?'

Is it honourable to jettison the rights of small nations? Is it just to practise deceptions upon them in matters more precious to them than life itself?

It remains that America and Britain continue to provide for Ethiopia and Kenya respectively many of the sinews of peace and war whereby the rulers of these two states are able to preserve and extend the evils of black colonialism. The final overthrow of this imperialism is absolutely certain, but it may take another generation of disorders, and at present at any rate it looks as though matters will have to grow very much worse before they can begin to get better. The John Redmond of the captive Somali provinces has been rebuffed and in his place over the next twenty years the violence of Michael Collins will probably take over to pull the noses of imperialists. There may be neither peace nor prosperity nor federation in this part of Africa now that a phoenix has risen, black and blazing from the embers of Europe's vanished empires. As I write (January 1965) the 6th World Muslim Conference sitting in the Somali capital has proclaimed its unanimous support for Somali unity—the writing is on the wall for the Emperor to read.

7

NOAH'S CURSE

> 'Well! I've often seen a cat without
> a grin,' thought Alice, 'but a grin
> without a cat! It's the most curious
> thing I ever saw in my life.'
>
> —*Alice's Adventures in Wonderland* by Lewis Carroll.

In Chapter II I referred to much evidence supporting the presence, the impetus and the halting of Kush—or Ham. I will now examine the credentials of Noah's Curse and its impact upon his descendants, if any, in North-eastern Africa. It will be necessary to examine the plight or condition of Negroes as well as of black non-Negroes because there was a time when *Hamite* was a term of approbrium applied to African Negroes and not a term used by anthropologists and applied to black non-Negro races or language groups.

Starting with the Negroes of my chosen region, Budge the historian tells us that the aboriginal population of Abyssinia was Negro. By this he clearly means us to understand that Negroes were there before the Agau who were and are Hamites, and before the Habash whose provenance has been explained in Chapter II.

The experienced British Consul in Southern Abyssinia, Sir Arnold Hodson, confirms this in his book *Seven Years in Southern Abyssinia* as a piece of common historical knowledge, and goes on to add from his own observations in Abyssinia that, far from being honoured as founder members of the multi-racial Abyssinian society, Negroes are to be found everywhere at the bottom of it, and even the name for them is identified with servitude.

> The aboriginal population was Negro, and more or less pure remnants of negroid tribes are to be found at the bottom of the social scale everywhere, although they are most numerous in the

118

west and south-west. The Abyssinian word for these people, Shangalla, is practically equivalent to slave. . . .

The *Encyclopedia Britannica* 1929 edition refers to the Negro as 'one of the most primitive of the African stocks', thus adding yet further confirmation that *Negro* is a racial term and that Negroes in Africa are firstcomers, foundation peoples or aboriginals. The reference goes on to give a description of Negro physical characteristics, much as I have already done in Chapter II, and then states that with these physical characteristics 'there go certain cultural characteristics'. This sentence implies the belief of the writer that Negro cultural characteristics are a factor of race—of being a Negro by physical inheritance—so that a particular culture is something 'in the blood'.

Sir Charles Eliot not only saw these cultural characteristics as factors of race, but bluntly and repeatedly described them as 'disabilities' and 'limitations'. In this sense he wrote:

> . . . I am not sanguine as to the future of the African race nor do I see any ground for hoping that it will attain to the same level as European or Asiatics.

Clearly Sir Charles, like most thinkers of his day and like many observers of the present day, believed that the fact of African Negroes as he saw them having raised themselves so little above the level of the beasts in the control of nature was due to 'something in the blood', even where this something was strongly reinforced by environment. In this he could see no great difference between Bantu with a supposedly non-Negro strain in the blood and pure Negroes.

Sir Charles referred to the much more advanced West African, who has been the main source of the American Negro population but who has nevertheless gone to the bottom of the social scale in that continent:

> The example of America shows that they have great limitations. In the Northern States the Negroes, though they speak the same language and enjoy the same political rights as white men, though they are objects of no social or commercial persecution, still manifestly remain on a lower plane than the whites, not only in such matters as art, science and literature, but in business. Their powers of organization, management and controlling other men seem too deficient to allow them to conduct any but the simplest concerns . . . the most effective talent they possess is eloquence.

I

He foresaw their progress but could see nothing to suggest an escape from these limitations: '. . . That the African races will greatly improve under a civilised and beneficient rule is clear; but . . .'

Eliot believed that the Kikuyu tribe were a recent hybrid formed by inter-marriage between Bantu and Masai, and expressed himself in favour of such inter-marriage. All this, though for different reasons, is very much in line with some of Mr. Kenyatta's writing, although whether Mr. Kenyatta shares Eliot's view that his Masai grandmother was of 'superior stock', and that Negroes in general would be improved by crossbreeding with this and other superior stock such as Somali, is questionable. All I can say is that in these days when I repeat to my friends that Mr. Kenyatta had a Masai grandmother, my hearers are apt to say at once 'Ah! that accounts for the iron in his soul!'

Eliot was a great linguist and a man closely associated with so many races on this planet that his comparisons cannot fail to be interesting. He seems resolved to uncover what is most promising and he records a bright ray of promise in the Baganda of his day:

'Incomparably the most intelligent and progressive' who may 'rival the Japanese in their power of assimilating European culture, and become a factor of the highest importance in the future history of the African continent.'

But he does not believe in the lasting power of the improvement which he acknowledges in the Baganda. He has seen similar bright promise in many African children and watched it wither away and retrogress after a comparatively short time:

'But it may prove that what happens in the individual will also happen in the race:'

An illustration perhaps of organic evolution in reverse where philogeny recapitulates ontogeny!

That as the African child after showing great quickness and power to learn suddenly reaches a limit where development ceases . . . so that the Baganda will find themselves unable to endure the strain of continual progress, and will stop or recede.

Having completed a brief survey of the Negro in and out of his own continent, I turn now to examine the position of the black non-Negro peoples of the region. First a summary to focus the existence and impulse of Kush—or Ham—throughout the region including Abyssinia. Here is the *Encyclopedia Britannica* 1929:

The history of East Africa is the history of the Hamites, for the various groups are differentiated by the degree and nature of their Hamitization.

Apparently the Hamites with Caucasian characteristics had been moving down from the north-east for a long time, with oscillations of fortune but a continuing probing advance towards the south:

> Southern Abyssinia and regions round Lake Rudolf have during the last four hundred years witnessed a perpetual ebb and flow of immigrant peoples, more and more Hamitized, who were deflected by the Nile valley and moved southwards to populate the highlands of Kenya colony and Tanganyika until gradually the whole area from these highlands to the Horn of Africa was filled up with mainly pastoral peoples of Hamitic ancestry . . . only checked by the intervention of Western Powers in whose absence the process would undoubtedly have continued despite temporary checks such as the defeat of the Masai at the hands of the Bantu Hehe.

This sums up my Chapter II and while it does nothing to suggest any all round superiority of Kush—Hamite—over negroid it does suggest a consistent Hamitic superiority of authority over Negro. Wherever the two clashed the Hamitic prevailed over the Negro. Wherever the two fused it was the Hamite culture which predominated over that of the Negro. According to some the fusion has not gone very far in many cases and, for example, here is the Foreign Office report of 1920 on Ethiopia stating:

> The Hamitic race which inhabits almost the whole of North and North-eastern Africa is always distinguishable from the Negro peoples by its comparatively European type of face though the colour varies greatly.

The *Encyclopedia Britannica* 1929 is beginning to find *Hamitic* a confusing term but under *Hamitic races* it gives:

> The definition of the term Hamitic as an anthropological description is still a type of brown people with frizzy hair, of lean and sinewy physique, with slender but muscular limbs, a thin, straight or even aquiline nose with delicate nostrils, thin lips and utter absence of prognathism.

So up till then Hamitic races were still holding their own with Hamitic languages, and we could still speak of the Abyssinians as belonging to the Eastern Hamitic race together with 'Nubians, Bejas, Gallas, Somalis and Masais' though speaking a Semitic language—the only one in the group to do so. We still had also a vivid pen picture of the visual impact of Hamites 'in the flesh'.

I hope I have now said enough to show that the Negro is reported by many to occupy the lowest position in his own continent, of which he is a founder-occupier, and the lowest position when he emigrates into other continents. On this there is a general measure of agreement. On the causes there are divergent views. Up to and including my own period it was generally thought to be 'something in the blood'. Latterly it is more commonly thought to be 'everything in the environment', perhaps summed up in the word 'culture'. So it is an argument mainly between culture and corpuscles. But there is at least one more theory and that is the theory of a curse.

Those who are familiar with the doctrine of original sin will readily follow the curse theory. Two 'flaws' were transmitted to mankind in consequence of Adam's sin and one of these flaws was extended to the non-human part of organic nature: all mankind became heirs to the *guilt* of the first sin and they also inherited a proneness to sin on their own account. The natural world apart from man inherited a proneness to retrogress far below its potential best unless the hand and mind of man were incessantly put to work to sustain a higher standard.

A curse *might* have started a similar inheritance line of disabilities—for example was it owing to Christ's curse that the Jewish race became dispossessed? Was it owing to Noah's curse that Negroes became the slaves of others? In the course of looking up the terms Hamitic and Semitic one comes across pointed references to Genesis, and at first it looks as though ethnologists must have regarded the Hebrew table of Nations as a contribution to history.

The Ethiopian Chronicles accept that the seed of Ham was cursed, and this puts them in a difficulty seeing that one of their strongest traditions traces the Habash descent through Ham and a curse is unbecoming in a 'chosen' people! However that may be, a study of the curse must leave open the question of what, if any, peoples of today are inheritors of such a curse. If we accept that Negro peoples are to be found in so many places at the bottom of the social scale, dominated by all other races, persecuted by some, afflicting one another most grievously in their own land, we might guess that they if anyone might lie under such a curse: to Genesis then we should go.

Genesis informs us that Noah, emerging from the Ark when he was six hundred years old 'began to be an husbandman and he planted a vineyard'. From this it looks as though Noah may have been a pastoral nomad until the new fertility derived from Euphrates silt induced him to become a cultivator for the first time. Then it happened that Noah became drunk on the fermented grape. The fathers of the Church excuse him on the ground of his ignorance—an excuse which would hardly have been available if he had been cultivating the grape for six hundred years.

On this occasion of Noah's inebriation one of his sons Ham was guilty of an act of impiety, if not of some unmentionable crime, perhaps telling the brethren 'you ought to have a look at Dad, he's as drunk as a lord'. The two other sons then went into their father and respectfully covered the old man, making him comfortable.

The consequences of the impiety of the one son and of the piety of the two others appear in both cases out of proportion: the punishment does not fit the crime nor does the reward fit the act of virtue; both punishment and reward have the appearance of misproportionate excesses. Be that as it may, all of Ham's seed appear to have incurred the consequences of Noah's curse although the curse itself was administered not to Ham but to his youngest son Chanaan—the son apparently being held responsible for the delinquency of his parent—or did he perhaps take the lead in disrespectful ridicule?

There followed in Genesis, Chapter X, a table of the Nations all founded from Noah's three sons: 'And of them was the whole earth overspread.'

The sons of Ham were Kush (= Nubia), Mizraim (= Egypt), Phut (= Somali/Danakil Coast?), and Chanaan (= Palestine). These are the Hamitic peoples, and it seems that all were tainted with Noah's curse, yet if the ethnologists are correct none of them were negroid. In any case, is this history? Is it to be a contribution to ethnological fact? We note the story telling us of a new moral handicap superimposed on Adam's sin and transmitted by inheritance to a large portion of mankind—is this a correct inference and do the consequences survive today after some six thousand years? Did Ham's issue move into North-eastern Africa, and if it did not do so why have ethnologists who are specialists in the truth about human movements grab hold of unhistorical passages in Genesis in order to teach us history and anthropology?

In seeking an answer I first had recourse to the *Catholic Dictionary* of 1929—an American publication—and I find this under *Cham:*

'. . . Noe . . . pronounced a curse upon Chanaan, the son of Cham and foretold the characteristic of Cham's descendants, and the debasement that would follow (Genesis IX). The descendants of Chanaan have proved morally corrupt and are in subjection to the rule of Sem.'

It does look as though the *Catholic Dictionary* took the episode as history making pronouncements on both ethnology and theology.

Reference to the *Catholic Commentary on Holy Scripture*, 1952—a scholarly British product—still suggests that the curse is something historical rather than an invented story. But the *Catholic Commentary* is rather unhappy about it and recommends other reading, perhaps hoping thereby to escape from a dilemma.

Let us review then the disabilities under which Ham's descendants may be supposed to have suffered. As human beings they were heirs to Adam's sin which an ungallant male chronicler attributes to female influence 'the woman tempted me'. Guilt and weakness were the inheritable consequences, the guilt to be removed in the course of time by a Redeemer but the weakness to be irreversible. Having regard to the inherited weakness, it need not surprise the reader to find another generation of proud and ungallant males, glorious in their election as the 'sons of God' coming in 'unto the daughters of men' and being so corrupted by these glamorous but carnal creatures that 'it repented the Lord that He had made men upon the earth'. The deluge was then sent to obliterate all the 'sons of God' with the exception of a single family, the family of Noah, and of course not including unspecified communities coming under the heading 'sons and daughters of men'.

Then a fresh start was made with Noah, but almost at once a further section of God's chosen peoples merited another inheritance of moral calamity. By this time we have before us the curse on Adam, the curse on Cain and the curse on Ham all inheritable. Modern Jews should not take it amiss that the Hebrew authors of the Christian gospels following a well-marked tradition, recorded a fourth guilt inheritance—the self-invoked curse of the Jewish crowd before Pilate: 'His blood be upon us and upon our children'.

But here I am concerned to dig out whatever there may be of history in Noah and his curse, in Ham and Ham's descendants. Seeing that I do not count myself a person qualified to interpret Holy Writ, I have referred to a Scriptural scholar who is also a qualified anthropologist and a missionary, inviting his criticism on my first draft of this book. Here is a part of his reply:

The Bible:

It is very regrettable that physical anthropologists and ethnologists should have taken the Biblical scheme to describe the races and languages of North East Africa. In actual fact, Genesis ch. 10 is *absolutely irrelevant* to the whole question! The author of this chapter knew nothing about the ethnic affinities of the peoples he grouped together and cared even less. His aim was to give a schematic enumeration of the various peoples known to the Jews at the time. The southern peoples were the enemies of the Jews and therefore they were classed together and a story was told to their discredit. Egypt, and its colony, Kush, were put together and even Canaan was added to the list because it had formerly been under the rule of Egypt. The scheme was genealogical in form—a very frequent device, but the grouping was more geographical than ethnic. We are in the realm of myth-history. Ham's impiety towards his father, Noah, and the curse put upon him and his descendants, means that Israel will prevail over her enemies through God's intervention on behalf of his chosen people. The aim of the passage is theological, not historical or scientific. It is natural that there should be some ethnic affinity between peoples juxtaposed geographically, but the group includes Semites, Hamitic Egyptians and Kushites, as well, presumably, as Negro 'Kushites' (from the Sudan). Kush in the Hebrew Bible meant the same as the Egyptian Kush. In the Septuagint it was translated into 'Ethiopia'. Ethiopia quite clearly refers to Nubia as well as Abyssinia (contrary to the opinion of the translators of the Ethiopic Bible) cf. the 'Ethiopian' baptized by Philip in Acts, who hailed from the country of the Candace, now known for certain to be Meroe.

It follows that any historical hypotheses which speak of an historic personage called Ham, or Kush, or Misraim, invading and establishing an extended family in North Africa, is not only contrary to the current hypothesis concerning the Hamito-Semitic speech community in North Africa, but also quite unrealistic, since the Biblical evidence is not to be taken seriously as history at all. Misraim and Kush are eponymous ancestors, invented to symbolize a whole people in the myth which the Bible employs to transmit its theological teaching.

The reason, of course, why the curse falls on Chanaan, and not on Ham or the other southern enemies represented by the genealogical fiction of the sons of Ham, is because the Chanaanites are the principal enemies at the time of writing. You simply cannot talk of 'Ham's blood line'.

Clearly the table of Nations is anthropologically, ethnologically and historically irrelevant, so out goes Genesis X from the files of history, and it seems that even if there is a curse somewhere there is no Ham. Mindful of a theory of successive waves of Hamitic peoples from Arabia or the Caucasus beginning more than seventy centuries ago I ask my critic if something of this kind is not still accepted to account for our visual experience of European features in North eastern Africa. My critic continues:

> I would not agree that the main outlines of our knowledge about the peopling of Africa have remained intact during this century (as you say). Seligman's theory of 'waves' or 'invasions' of Hamites or others (usually conceived by the writers as culturally superior) succeeding one another, is now largely abandoned by ethnologists and social anthropologists.

What then is the favoured theory of today? Are there not racial differences in Africa as great as those between a Briton and a Chinaman? How are they accounted for at the present time?

My critic replies as follows:

> The hypothesis favoured by ethnologists today is this: There was originally one speech community, which we call Hamito-Semitic, living in North-East Africa. From this group are derived the following language groups: Semitic, Berber, Kushitic, Ancient Egyptian, Chad languages. The original group was probably in North-East Africa from 10,000 to 12,000 years ago. From there, the Semites 'invaded' Arabia. The only 'invasions' back into Africa of this group were the Semitic Abyssinians from Arabia, and the later Muslim Arabs. This is purely a language classification. It is quite impossible to make any sensible physical classification of the peoples who speak Semitic and Hamitic languages. Semites are strongly Caucasian in appearance; of the other four branches known generally as Hamites, the Berbers and Ancient Egyptians were also very Caucasian. The Chad Hamites are complete Negroes in appearance, and the Kushites are strongly negroid, not merely in colour but in other physical characters as well. I grant that the visual impact of a Kushite presents affinities to the European type, colour apart. His linear physique, however, he shares with Nilotes; this appears to be a physical adaptation to regions of intense heat.

The language classification is therefore the only workable one for Hamite. You point out that a Semitic language is spoken by people of differing ethnic composition. This is equally true of the Hamitic languages spoken by people of differing races. Race has very little to do with culture, as the Victorians used to think it had. The Hamitic languages may owe much to people of Negro blood, therefore, at the origin.

I would not say that the differences between Africans of differing cultures are in the same ratio as those between a Briton and a Chinaman! The differences are there, agreed, but there is a basic similarity of mental functions in these pre-literate societies of Africa, coupled with a widespread exchange of cultural elements which have been shuttled to and fro between these fragile and flexible cultures, which have co-existed in this continent for so long. There is a danger in thinking that every cultural import must be accompanied by an 'invasion' or a racial 'overlay'.

So the term Hamito-Semitic has no blood connotation at all, but is applied to a 'speech community living in North-East Africa' some 6,000 to 8,000 years before Ham and Sem were born—or invented! And Ham has been banished altogether as a racial term. This seems to leave a disembodied curse like the vanished smile of the Cheshire cat.

In further correspondence with my critic I challenged the use of the term 'negroid' as applied to the Kushitic speaking Galla and Somali. My critic defends his use of the term:

I would defend my phrase 'strongly negroid' when used of the Somali and Galla, if I were comparing them with the 'white' Hamites, e.g. Berbers and Touaregs. The North-Eastern Hamites have widespread negroid characters: e.g. a very dark pigmentation, everted lips (to a greater or lesser degree), kinky hair (often of the same type as the Negro, though it grows to greater length). Personally, I remember some very negroid Somalis from my K.A.R. days! Trevor, in his generally accepted classification, places the North-Eastern Hamites (or Erythriotes) as 'intermediate' between Negriforms and Caucasiforms, and I think that is quite fair.

I suggest to my critic that much of the trouble seems to arise not so much from differences of opinion over physical characteristics as incompetence in classifying them. The critic does not wholly agree with me:

The difficulty of classification is partly due to inefficient description, as you rightly say. But all the indications are that a more efficient description only blurs the distinctions between the races even more. Obviously, visual impressions and crude anthropometry are highly inefficient techniques, but when one descends to blood-groups and other important genetic factors, the picture is much more confused. The fact is that African races are among the most mixed in the world.

In any case, race is far less important than culture, which over-rides the barriers of race. It is surely significant that linguistic criteria have had to be used to classify African groupings, rather than physical criteria?

So my Victorian views arise from 'crude anthropometry' and 'visual impressions'! Still I must continue to the bitter end of this argument, and I tax my critic with the word Negro, wondering if perhaps Negro has ceased to be aboriginal! My critic replies as follows:

Points:

1. Is Negro foundation of all Africa? More or less. The Negro is the base for the greater part of African physical types.
2. 'Negroid' is a sensible physical classification. It means a type which is related to the true Negro type. 'Non-Negroid', though a purely negative term, is obviously correct when applied to physical types which have nothing in common with the true Negro, e.g., the northern European. If it is applied to people who have some physical characters in common with the true Negro but not the majority, it is less exact, but does correspond to an established differentiation. c.f. North-Eastern Hamitic speakers.

So far so good, but the Kenya tribes other than those labelled 'Hamitic' or 'Nilo-Hamitic' are with one exception called 'Bantu' and the odd one out is called 'Nilotic'. Can I safely refer to both Bantu and Nilotic peoples as Negro? My critic replies:

Bantu and *Nilote* are linguistic terms. Physically they are both negroid. Both have non-negroid elements in their make up. The Nilotic group of languages is not Hamitic. Nilo-Hamitic is another language group with an extremely unfortunate name. It suggests a mixture of Hamitic and Nilotic elements, and it seems that the Hamitic element in some of the so-called 'Nilo-Hamitic' languages is very doubtful indeed. The Nilo-Hamites (of whom the Masai are the most well-known and the most photogenic) probably have little to do with Hamites. They are linguistically much more closely related to Nilotes, as also culturally. They have always been in the area, at least from early times, probably, but they seeped down from the Sidama region in the seventeenth-eighteenth centuries. The Nilotes are the great cattle specialists. It is they who have created the pattern of pastoral life in the swampy flats of Southern Sudan. No objection to the use of 'Negroid' for Bantu, Nilote and Nilo-Hamite. These peoples obviously have a predominant Negro strain in their make-up.

Where do the Caucasian features come from, I ask my critic? He replies:

I don't see any problem over the Caucasian features of your North-Eastern Hamites. This physical anthropology business has not been worked out by any means yet. Archaeology, however, gives the best clues to origins of physical types. The archaeologists tell us that there were 'Homo Sapiens' men of Caucasian type living in East Africa in the early Stone Age. The Negro type does not appear until much later, in the Mesolithic, and then over in West Africa. It seems to be increasingly clear that Negroes spread over much of the Southern Sahara in the Neolithic, the Sahara being considerably more fertile then than now. I do not see any difficulty in the two types, or their descendants, coalescing in the North-Eastern area. It is not possible to say whether one or other type, or the mixture, characterized the populations that formed the parent Hamito-Semitic language group of modern Hamitic and Semitic speakers. Bones cannot tell us anything about language, unfortunately.

Now it seems to me either that there is a Caucasian who has no connection with the Caucasus or that there is a Caucasus somewhere west of Khartoum! And what has happened to those superior qualities of the Hamites? Encouraged by the views of the authorities whom I have quoted earlier in this book, I enlarge on this to my critic, who again replies:

I detect an unjustified romanticism, if you will forgive me, about the pastoral nomads of East Africa.
Archaeological and documentary evidence (such as it is) together with the analysis of oral histories gives us already an increasingly clear picture of what happened in East Africa.
In the fourth century East Africa is inhabited by a Bushmanoid people, probably hunters and collectors. Intermingled with them are the 'X' group, an advanced Stone-Age people with dolicho-cephalic skulls. (They may have been Hamites or Nilo-Hamites, but we cannot tell from skeletal evidence what language they spoke!) On the coast were other strains, probably Indonesian in

origin. The Black Bantu (the 'man-eating Ethiopians' of the Periplus) lived to the south of the Rufiji delta.

By the eighth-ninth centuries, East Africa had become the land of 'Zanj', the land of the blacks. These Bantu people brought the knowledge of iron with them and probably also the use of domesticated animals, cattle. They filtered up from their dispersal area, the Zambezi-Congo watershed, lapping round the other northern peoples and swallowing up the Bushmen (the pygmies or 'Agumba' of Kikuyu tradition). Some pockets remain.

The Hamitic peoples are, and probably were, mainly agriculturalists. They acquired the cattle complex from Negroes or Nilotes in all probability. They have not shown the same ingenuity and response to environment. Whereas the great Nilotic Luo migrations have made innumerable adaptations possible, and have produced the great conquest-states of the Lacustrine Kingdoms, the Nilo-Hamites never exploited the potential of their land. They clung to the pastoral way of life in a habitat which offered excellent hunting, and facilities for agriculture. (Their predecessors had often been agriculturalists as archaeological evidence shows.) They were predatory, terrorizing the negroid Bantu with their continual raids, and preventing them from developing a more precocious technology. The Bantu are obviously capable of great things when not harassed, witness the Metropolitan kingdom-cultures of West Africa erected by Bantu and Negroes. The Nilo-Hamites proved incapable of forming conquest states, instead, they never fused, but merely preyed on their neighbours. Pastoralists are usually noted for a streak of militarism. Their mobility gives them a tactical advantage. They do not take slaves, as this means extra mouths to feed. They are technically the inferiors of the settled cultivator. They do not need many tools, and depend for the manufacture of weapons, either upon their agricultural neighbours, or upon a despised stranger caste of specialists and smiths.

I would not, therefore, call the Nilo-Hamitic nomads of East Africa, the leaders; they are the chief factor in the debasing of the Negro to their own level. Without them, the Negro of East Africa might have achieved what the Hamitic agriculturalists achieved and what the Negro in so many other parts of the continent achieved.

I admire the forthright defence of Negroes, but in places I feel moved to quarrel with my critic. In line with him I deplore the military streak which I have noticed in many pastoral tribes, but I have noticed also a horrifying over-preoccupation with military conquest on the part of the agricultural Habash and their emperors. It is amongst the Habash in particular in this region that there are the despised crafts and smiths such as the Falasha, to whom epidemics and other natural visitations have by tradition been attributed, and they have been denounced as sorcerers. Again, too, in defence of the pastoralists I readily concede that the Masai have been wasteful exploiters of land and deprivers of land use, but most of the desert tribes of my acquaintance have been masters of their arid environment and they are undoubtably beneficial users of the land they occupy. Finally the conquest state of the Habash seems to me a dark blot of savagery in a savage continent!

Following the verdict of Sir Charles Eliot, I suggest to my critic that the tribal African who cultivates a forest clearing is often a man of narrow vision quick to imagine and harbour grievances, 'earthing' his gods in mountains and trees, multiplying taboos and elaborate superstitions. To this my critic replies perceptively:

> The 'narrow vision and elaborate superstitions' of negroid peoples. This is unfair, I submit. 'Superstition' is a loaded word. The Negro peoples have some very valuable religious and moral insights. Their arts of song and dance and speech are by no means to be despised. Culturally they are rich when compared to other so-called 'primitive' peoples. It is true the pastoralist often appears to possess a Deistic religion with a subtle theology of God's spiritual presence, while the Negro tends to imprison his theological concepts in the more earthy symbols of the settled life. But I would maintain that his world is as spiritual as that of the nomad, and that superstition and magic are the common property of both.
>
> I think it an extremely good idea to get the S.O.A.S. at London to look at the revised version, they will be able to give you the very latest twist on all these theories. I must frankly admit that African studies move almost as fast as Biblical studies these days—and it is all rather bewildering!

8

UNWORTHY CAUSES

When Italy joined us against the Central Powers in 1915, she had been 'United Italy' for no more than forty-five years. Her unification had been achieved by military operations trivial in scale and amateurish in character. Her unity had not been tested in warfare with other European powers, and her powerful neighbours, Austria and France, had been laid low in quick succession by Prussia around the time of her own rebirth. She had not proved herself as a military nation on the battlefield, and she was still devoid of those sources of industrial wealth which had begun to transform the poverty of peoples elsewhere.

During the 1914-18 war Italy received a hammering. She had as yet neither the aptitude for war like the Germans nor the sinews with which to wage it like the British. At the end of the war she was ripe for revolution and might have followed the Russian pattern of 1917 with a Bolshevik rising of her own. From this she was saved by Mussolini, who raised her to a position of importance in the affairs of Europe during an era when Germany, the greatest military nation in Europe, lay prostrate and despoiled, even her posterity saddled with an impossible burden of so-called reparations.

There was a time when the great Winston S. Churchill described Mussolini as the saviour of his country. Some years after that, we all thought Mussolini a fine fellow for draining the Pontine marshes, mopping up the Mafia in Sicily, and marching to the Brenner to save Austria from the Nazi python. Then almost immediately we quarrelled with Mussolini in circumstances which drove him into the arms of the Hitler whom he hated; in so doing we also exposed our own weaknesses to both Hitler and Mussolini without in any way alleviating the grievances of their peoples. It all arose out of a quarrel over the 'sick man's' estate.

Once more I revert to the Tripartite Treaty of 1906 between

Britain, France and Italy—the selfish treaty whereby the three of us guaranteed the integrity of both the Habash empires, the historic empire north of the Blue Nile and the colonial 'looting grounds' south of it. The treaty embodied a pledge given by each of the three high contracting parties to the other two concerning the property of a fourth party whose interests were not mentioned in the treaty, and whose ruler was not even consulted about it. From the time when France had grabbed Italy's intended African booty, Tunis, in 1891, France and Italy had been in collision, and Italy had joined Germany and Austria in the Triple Alliance. Since the repulse of French ambitions on the Nile, Britain and France had collided in Ethiopia and France had been the *eminence grise* behind the power of Menelek II. What then had happened to change the pattern of rivalries in 1906? The explanation is to be found partly in the ambitions of the new German giant and in the fact of a powerful German Navy.

In 1904 King Edward the Peacemaker of Britain made good use of the new atmosphere of apprehension of German ambitions; under his auspices the Entente Cordiale was achieved and sealed by an agreed division of African spoils between France and Britain; France was to have a free hand in Morocco, while Britain was to have a free hand on the Nile. Then, with an eye to a possible naval conflict with Germany, the two partners resolved to detach Italy from Germany if they could: but Italy still deemed herself among the poor in the matter of European colonies in Africa, and there was not much left to divide. However, the Anglo-Italian Treaty of 1891 had recognized almost all Ethiopia as within an Italian sphere of interest; development of this interest had been thwarted by the intrigues of France, and also by the military ineptitude of Italy herself as I describe in another chapter. Many observers, however, held that Menelek's victory over the Italians had only served to postpone the blessings of civilization for the Habash and their colonial subjects! Outside the Emperor's own circle there was a widespread and confident belief that the days of dark mischief in the Habash highlands were already numbered.

With this as the background, the two parties to the Entente Cordiale were in 1905 sharply reminded of their danger when France and Germany came into a head-on collision over Morocco, and by then the First World War was barely nine years ahead. So in 1906 they patched up French points of friction with Italy, intending to reaffirm their designation of Italy as their candidate for civilizing Ethiopia, and thus to frustrate the penetration of German influence into the catchment area of the Blue Nile.

Thereafter it would be up to Italy to choose her methods of spreading civilisation so long as she scrupulously respected French interests in Abyssinian railways, Anglo-Egyptian interests in the waters of the Blue Nile and certain grazing rights of British-protected Somali nomads. The treaty embodied the hopes of the three signatories that the methods chosen would be those of peaceful penetration rather than military conquest, and to this end the negotiators guaranteed the territorial integrity of the Ethiopian empire and its political independence from outside control. In order to provide for a possible breakdown of peaceful intentions they inserted a clause, clause 4, whereby in a changed situation either of the signatories who might wish to make some change should consult the interests of the other two before doing so.

By 1934 no less than forty-three years had passed since we had first, in the treaty of 1891, accorded to Italy our recognition of Ethiopia as her sphere of influence, and meanwhile much had happened. When the treaty itself was signed Menelek II was at the height of his power, and yet the limitations of that power to control those of his subjects who treated Ethiopian colonies as looting grounds were notorious.

Menelek was informed of the Tripartite Treaty of 1906 after its ratification, and although he was incensed at the drawing up of such a document without his knowledge or consent, he restricted himself by way of protest to insisting that nothing therein should be cited as an infringement of the sovereignty of Ethiopia.

In the year following the signing of this treaty, that is in 1907, Menelek had a stroke from which he was never fully to recover; for six more years, until his death in 1913, and then for another ten years after his death until 1923, all Ethiopia south of the capital was in a state of disorder quite outside the control of the imperial government.

One might have expected the Italians to intrude into Ethiopia soon after Menelek's death, but this was a period of maximum German influence in Addis Ababa and the first great war itself was already imminent. During the course of that war Italy was to join the Allies in 1915, and to find that her share of the booty was restricted to a belated 'strip of desert with a few palm trees'.

This was perhaps the last great victory where the victors set about dividing the booty between themselves regardless of the repercussions, not only upon the vanquished but upon themselves. They left Italy out until she received Jubaland from Britain in 1925.

By 1934 Italy had proved herself a good colonizing power and a good colonial neighbour to others. By 1934 Ras Tafari—the present Emperor Haile Selassie—after eleven years at the helm, had barely restored a precarious unity to the old Habash Empire, and had quite failed to effect any substantial or permanent improvement in the maladministered or non-administered colonial empire.

Far from accepting peaceful penetration from Italy, however, the Ethiopian authorities began speaking of the whole Horn of Africa as historically Ethiopian territory; incursions across the frontier by Ethiopian government forces began to be interspersed with tribal raids and shifta lootings, while the memory of Adowa added a note of arrogance to the intolerable incompetence of Ethiopian border administration.

The 'shame of Adowa', as D'Annunzio called it, was never far below the surface of Italian popular feeling, but there is much to suggest that the spirit of revenge was suppressed in Italy for a whole generation while a dichotomy developed between a treaty-bound Italian Foreign Office and colonial administrators on the spot who were becoming more and more exasperated by Ethiopian border irregularities.

Much of this sort of thing happened in our case too. It is curious that in the course of thirty years British and Italian Foreign Services had both somehow managed to transform the guarantee of Ethiopian integrity of 1906 from its true status, as a vested interest of their own to secure European peace, into something necessary to ensure well-being in the Horn of Africa.

Consequently many of our distinguished colonial civil servants in the Horn have felt that the interests of the Somalis of the Horn were recurrently sacrificed to the Foreign Office maxim of always appeasing the Habash. 'The Foreign Office always let you down' is an expression that I have heard, and of late a distingui-shed official having retired from the Horn was re-employed in the Foreign Office, and when confessing this fact to me he added, 'Yes, I have embraced the enemy'.

Even as late as September 1934 Italian foreign policy was still just ahead of its colonial resentments, but in December a pitched battle between Ethiopian and Italian escort troops at Wal Wal

K

put the Italian colonial lobby on to the front bench, and the
period of restraint finally ended, to be succeeded very soon by a
war psychosis so unbridled that even some of Italy's sympathizers
began to fall away from her.

Within a month of the Wal Wal incident, however, the Italians
had peacefully settled their post-world-war African grievances
against France in a secret agreement wherein France gave Italy a
free hand in Ethiopia or at least implied her willingness not to
obstruct. The Italians had appealed to France under clause 4 of
the 1906 Tripartite Treaty, asking in effect, 'What are your
interests in Ethiopia if we should occupy either a part or the
whole of that territory?'

No sooner had the Italians received satisfaction from France
than they approached Britain with the same question and under
the same clause of the 1906 treaty, informing us at the same time
of their secret agreement with France. Unless the British Foreign
Office were mad, they must have seen that a 'showdown' between
Italy and Ethiopia was then very likely to come about and that
the danger was not far off but imminent. I am personally quite
certain that the British Foreign Office were not mad, and that
they did not see this, and that the action which they took under
Sir Samual Hoare (later Lord Templewood) was taken in the
context of seeing clearly what was most likely to come to pass.

Our Foreign Office might have considered saying, in reply to
Italy's inquiry: 'Spheres of influence acknowledged in 1906 are
today subject to the over-riding provisions of peace-keeping
machinery embodied in the Covenant of the League of Civilized
Nations. We agree with you that there are civilized standards to
which Ethiopia may not have attained, but it was owing to your
support of Ethiopia's application that she was admitted to the
League of Civilized Nations in 1923, and today, after a further
eleven years, she is a little less of an intolerable anachronism than
she was at that time'.

They might have added something on the following lines: 'In
addition to the Covenant of the League we are all signatories of
the Kellogg-Briand Pact renouncing war as an instrument of
policy; finally, in September last you yourselves renewed your
pact of amity with Ethiopia, and that pact provides for the settlement of disputes by arbitration. Subject to all this we will review
our interests and let you know further what they are'.

Having drafted something on these lines we might then, before communicating our answer to Italy, have considered the action to be taken if Italy should decide to ignore our warnings and occupy a part or the whole of Ethiopia by force, notwithstanding our refusal to support such action. Italy would, in such an event, become a delinquent member of the League and lay herself open to sanctions on the part of her fellow members. There were three tiers of sanctions: diplomatic, economic and military.

All sorts of questions should have been thrashed out in advance: for instance was the barbaric Ethiopian colonial empire a good enough case upon which to make a stand involving sanctions? With America, Germany and Japan none of them members of the League, what chance would there be of effective economic sanctions? If economic sanctions did become effective would Italy be likely to turn violently upon some of those who were seeking to apply them, and if she did were the prospective policing states all prepared for the consequences? Would there be widespread support or widespread opposition in connection with taking steps that might involve us in war with Italy? What were the views of British leaders such as Lloyd George, or Commonwealth leaders, or members of the Little Entente in Europe? Would America be likely to take any action under the Kellogg-Briand Pact? Seeing that only total exclusion from all sources of oil would be capable of stopping a resolute Italy, would the great American Oil Companies join in or cash in?

If we were not going to examine these things exhaustively, and were not prepared to go to the point of sanctions, we could still have complied with the Italian request by drawing up a considered statement of our interests in Ethiopia, and informing the Italians. This third course of action, however, unless accompanied by very clear warnings against the use of force by Italy, would unquestionably have implied our acquiescence in her use of force in case she deemed it necessary.

In actual fact we took the third course, not only without giving any warning against the use of force, but in such circumstances as could not fail to imply a considered indifference to its use.

In January, 1934, the Italians asked the question; in March, 1934, we set up a high-powered commission to report on our interests in Ethiopia in the light of an Italian occupation of a part or the whole of that territory; in May, 1934, at the Stresa Conference we sought Italy's vitally necessary co-operation in Europe to contain Hitler; during that conference we mentioned nothing

whatever about African matters which we knew Mussolini
considered vital to Italy; in June, 1934, the Commission of
Inquiry reported that an Italian occupation of a part or the whole
of Ethiopia would be advantageous from every point of view; at
some later date the Italians, whom we had led to await the outcome of this report, managed to photograph a copy of it in our
Rome Embassy; on February 20, 1936, the *Giornale D'Italia* printed
it.

Under the fifty-year rule the report has still a Foreign Office
security label on it (till 1985); had the report been circulated in
Britain we might have been spared involvement in the first of the
adventures of Mr. Eden in Africa (Wal Wal 1935), and perhaps
the second as well (Suez 1956).

As a peer of the realm I have a right to read this report, but no
right to make public use of its contents, although there is no
official objection to my using the version printed in Italian in the
Giornale D'Italia, and it is this version which now lies before me.
I have not compared it with the original and there may be
discrepancies, but this is what the Italian people read.

The paper carries the following headlines on the subject of the
Maffey Report:

> *La relazione della commissione interministeriale Maffey. Il rapporto dice
> che con l'accordo tripartito il governo inglese 'ha riconosciuto come pertinente
> alla siera d'influenza italiana la quasi totalita dell'etiopia' e che 'non
> esistono vitali interessi britannici nell'etiopia e nelle sue vicinanze, tali da
> imporre al governo di S.M. la resistenza ad una conquista dell'etiopia da
> parte dell'italia'.*

Here is my translation of the foregoing:

> *The report of the inter-departmental Maffey Commission. The report says
> that with the Tripartite Agreement the English Government 'has recognized
> as pertinent to the Italian sphere of influence virtually the whole of Ethiopia'
> and that 'there exist no vital British interests in Ethiopia and her adjacent
> territories of a kind to oblige His Majesty's Government to resist an Italian
> conquest of Ethiopia'.*

The paper quotes Sir John Maffey's covering letter, and follows
up with a summary of the introduction to the report. A letter of
March 6, 1935, brought the commission into being, and they were
told of Signor Vitetti's approach of the previous January, this
approach having followed immediately upon the secret agreement between France and Italy of the 7th of that month. In the

first part of the report the following words are used to describe the unstable character of Ethiopia.

Vi e un'assenza die omogeneita che colpisce e le ambizioni discordanti delle varie razze—inasprite in taluni casi dal rude trattamento riservato agli altri dai cufiti dominanti—costituiscono un altro fattore dell'instabilita etiopica.

There is a striking absence of homogeneity and the conflicting ambitions of the various Rases—sharpened in some cases by rough treatment which the dominant Kushites reserve for other races—constitute another unstable factor in Ethiopia.

Here the use of the term 'Kushites' is curious. If it is intended as a linguistic term then it is incorrect of the Semitic-speaking dominant Amharas. If it is intended as a racial term then it belongs equally to the Galla and Somali who are the victims of rough treatment.

The report goes on to quote a second time the reference to the Tripartite Treaty contained in the headlines.

There is a reference to Ethiopian unwillingness to accept peaceful penetration in the following words:

Gli abissini non hanno dimostrato di voler consentire alle domande italiane perche non hanno affatto paura della potenza militare italiana.

My translation of this is:

The Abyssinians have shown no willingness to accept Italian requests because they have in fact no respect for Italian military power.

The newspaper comments acidly:

A quest'ora, forse, gli abissini hanno cambiato opinione!

At the present moment possibly the Abyssinians have changed their opinion on this point.

The paper's quotation from part 3 of the report demonstrates in absolutely unmistakable terms the *raison d'être* of the report:

La parte III del rapporto e dedicata ad esaminare 'in quale misura gli interessi britannici sarebbero preguidicati: (a) de una occupazione italiana dell'Ogaden fino alle colline di Harrar o con Harrar inclusa; (b) da una conquista di tutta l'Etiopia da parte dell'Italia'.

Part III of the report is devoted to examining 'to what extent British interests would be prejudiced (a) by an Italian occupation

of the Ogaden, either to the foot of the Harar Hills or including
Harar; (b) by a total Italian conquest of Ethiopia'.

This unmistakably reveals what the Foreign Office believed to
be Italian intentions for the immediate future. The report refers
to existing disorders in the Ethiopian border areas in terms with
which we have been familiar throughout the twentieth century:

Vi sono ancora tribu della periferia, come per esempio quelle
dell'Ogaden, sulle quali il controllo etiopico e soltanto intermittente
ed incerto. Questa regione e una specie de Alsazia ed e fonte di
continuo imbarazzo per le amministrazioni vicine. Razzie di bes-
tiame non accennano a diminuire ed e sempre difficile ottenere
la punizione dei colpevoli che spesso sono anche rei di omicidio.
Ogni incidente da luogo ad una lunga procedura che fa capo ad
Addis Abeba e non e raro il caso che governatori locali recalcitranti,
disobbediscano alle istruzioni del governo centrale. I criminali
continuano a trovare rifugio in territorio etiopico e permane latente
il rischio che le condizioni di disorganizzazione dei distretti di
frontiera cadono in uno stato di completa confusione come successe
negli anni dell'immediato dopo-guerra: cio importerebbe speciali
e forse costose misure atte a proteggere le tribu britanniche.

In English:

There are also border tribes, for instance those of the Ogaden,
over whom Ethiopian control is at best fluctuating and uncertain.
This region is a kind of Alsace and is the source of constant embarrassment to neighbouring administrations. Stock-raiding practices
show no signs of falling off, and it is difficult to secure the punishment
of those guilty of perpetrating them. The raiders are commonly
guilty of homicide as well.

Every incident gives rise to lengthy procedures which all culminate
in Addis Ababa where the central government are not infrequently
unable to ensure that recalcitrant Rases comply with their instructions. Criminals find a convenient refuge in Ethiopian territory, and
there is always a latent risk that lack of control over the frontier
districts may bring about a reversion to the utter chaos of the
immediate post-war years. This would give rise to special and very
expensive measures for the effective protection of British tribes.

The next paragraph compares Italian administration with that
of the Abyssinians:

Malgrado le difficolta di cui piu sopra si e fatto parola, le condizioni
della frontiera fra i territori italiani e quelli britannici in Africa
sono piacevoli e in contrasto con le condizioni delle frontiere che
noi abbiamo in comune con l'Etiopia.

In spite of the difficulty to which reference is made above, frontier conditions between Italian and British territories in Africa are peaceful and in contrast with conditions on the frontiers which we share with Ethiopia.

This part concludes with a nine-point summary of which the following is a partial quotation, together with the necessary translation by myself:

(1) L'Italia certamente durante i prossimi anni fara di tutto per assicurarsi il controlio dell'Etiopia, anche se nel momento attuale essa abbia intenzione di limitare la sua azione alla conquista dei bassipiani che confinano con la Somalia italiana.

(2) Non esistono vitali interessi britannici, nell'Etiopia e nelle sue vicinanze, tali da imporre al Governo di S.M. la resistenza ad una conquista dell'Etiopia da parte dell'Italia. Il controllo italiano dell'Etiopia da alcuni lati sarebbe per noi vantaggioso (per esempio per quel che riguarda la sicurezza delle sone di frontiera) per altri non lo sarebbe (per esempio nei riguardi del commercio). Parlando in linea generale, per quel che riguarda i locali interessi britannici, sarebbe indifferente che l'Etiopia rimanga indipendente o che venga assorbita dall'Italia.

(3) Dal punto di vista della difesa imperiale una Etiopia indipendente sarebbe preferibile ad una Etiopia italiane, ma la minaccia agli interessi britannici sembra essere lontana e dipenderebbe soltanto da una guerra tra noi e l'Italia, guerra che sembra per ora assai improbabile.

(4) L'interesse britannico principale in Etiopia e costituito dal Lago Tana e dal bacino del Nilo. Cio costituisce anche un interesse dell'Egitto che il Governo di S.M. e tenuto a proteggere. Nel caso in cui l'Etiopia come Stato indipendente dovesse scomparire, il Governo S.M. dovrebbe tendere ad assicurarsi il controllo territoriale del Lago Tana e di un corridoio adeguato che congiunga il Lago al Sudan.

Analogamente, nell'ipotesi che gli italiani si stabiliscano in Etiopia, il Governo di S.M. dovrebbe fare i passi necessari per salvaguardere gli interessi britannici relativi ad altri tributari del Nilo, provenienti dall'Etiopia (per esempio il Sobat) mediante un impegno preciso circa la costruzione di opere lungo questi fiumi, le quali, se provocanti l'interruzione o la diminuzione della loro portata, non potrebbero venire intraprese senza il concorso del Governo di S.M. e di quello egiziano.

(1) Undoubtedly during the forthcoming years Italy will do her utmost to achieve control of Ethiopia, even if at the present moment

her intentions are limited to the conquest of the lowlands adjacent
to Italian Somalia.

(2) There exist no vital British interests in Ethiopia and her neigh-
bouring territories of a kind to oblige the Government of His
Majesty to resist an Italian conquest of Ethiopia. Italian control of
Ethiopia would be advantageous for us from every point of view
(for example in regard to matters connected with the security of
the frontier zone) . . . speaking generally in matters regarding local
British interests it would be a matter of indifference whether
Ethiopia remained independent or came to be absorbed by Italy.

(3) From the point of view of Imperial defence an independent
Ethiopia would be preferable to an Italian Ethiopia, but the threat
to British interests seems to be remote and would arise only in the
case of war between ourselves and Italy, a war which seems to be
quite improbable.

(4) Principal British interests in Ethiopia lie in Lake Tana and the
Nile basin. These interests are also those of Egypt, which His
Majesty's Government is under obligation to protect. In the event
of Ethiopia ceasing to exist as an independent State, His Majesty's
Government should endeavour to secure control of the Lake Tana
area and of an adequate corridor joining the lake with the Sudan.

In like manner, on the supposition that the Italians establish
themselves in Ethiopia, His Majesty's Government should take the
necessary steps to safeguard relative British interests in others of
the Nile tributaries rising in Ethiopia (for example the Sobat)
calling for a definite veto on the construction of works along these
rivers of a kind to stop or reduce their deliveries of water without
first obtaining the consent of His Majesty's Government and that
of Egypt.

Sir John Maffey signed this report together with two officials
representing the British Foreign Office and one each from the
Dominions Office, the War Office, the Admiralty and the Air
Ministry. The Secretary came from the Colonial Office.

At last, then, after all these years we had the Foreign Office
marching in step with the realities of the situation so long apparent
to the Colonial Office. The tripartite doctrine equating 'integrity'
with 'equilibrium' had received its death blow. British refusal to
acknowledge this truth was soon to have catastrophic consequences.

The date of the report is June 18, 1935. In September of 1935
Italy produced some of her most damaging evidence of Ethiopian
aggressions and maladministration and atrocity, perhaps in order
to confirm the verdict of the Maffey Report, but obviously too

late to have any effect on the situation which she had every right
to suppose would have been resolved in line with the Maffey
Report.

The war with Ethiopia started on October 3.

December 7–9 the Hoare-Laval Plan to partition Ethiopia
was prematurely printed in the French Press. The plan was in
general a sensible one, albeit far too late. The publication of the
plan produced public protests in England, possibly, if we follow
the memoirs of Lord Templewood, based on an incorrect supposition that British Somali territory was to be transferred to Italy.
In any event Hoare resigned as Foreign Minister to be succeeded
by Anthony Eden. Mr. Eden was prepared to transfer Somali
territory as a 'British sacrifice' to Ethiopia, while being unwilling
to see the maladministered Ethiopian colonies transferred from
Ethiopia's incompetent administration to Italy.

The effect of British intervention in the matter of sanctions was
insufficient to deter Mussolini, but adequately effective to compel
him to withdraw his protection from Austria, and to throw in his
lot with Hitler. The whole episode stands out as one of those
instances where bad cases break good law.

The Eden memoirs recount the efforts of Sir Anthony to drag
into a policy of sanctions involving the possibility of belligerency
an unwilling France, an unwilling United States, an unwilling
League of Nations, an unwilling Commonwealth and an unprepared Britain. He summed up with a conclusion that we had built
Mussolini into a great power and that he awaited debunking by
the Greeks. It is clear, therefore, that Mr. Eden did not intervene
on the ground that he was concerned at the menace of Italy to our
imperial security in Africa. Those who believe that the Suez
affair in 1956 was another of our bad causes will notice a
resemblance.

Thirty years later in this area today we have the same Habash,
the same aggressive maladministration, the same Emperor, the
same undesirable integrities applied to an even larger Ethiopian
Empire, the same 'Eden tradition' towards Somalis, the same
declension towards wider disturbances, and a massive under-
pinning of black colonialism by Britain and U.S.A. The cause of
Ethiopian integrity is even less worthy in 1964 than it was in 1934,
by which time it had already worn through the veil of respecta-
bility in which we had draped it in 1906.

9

EMPEROR AMBA

The Habash imperial power was extinct from the sixteenth to the nineteenth centuries, and by the end of the eighteenth century imperial ambitions had been so far exorcised that the powerful Rases ('Ras' is Abyssinian for 'chieftain'), having a great distaste for all that imperialism could mean in the way of tribute and rapacious armies without official issues of food, clothing or pay, incarcerated all candidates for the imperial throne on a selected amba; in so doing they made certain that the emperor would be chosen by themselves from among the more elderly candidates who could be counted upon to die soon, or alternatively from among children who could be managed by a regent and easily dethroned before they grew up. In the year 1800, for instance, there are said to have been no fewer than six emperors living.

Habash distrust of their own imperial traditions is all the more remarkable that they do not share our Western distrust of kings in general—they love kings, and their kings are never constitutional sovereigns or democrats. Government by the Kikuyu 'kiama' bears no resemblance to the rule of a Habash 'negus', nor has negus-rule much in common with the pastoral democracy of the Somalis as described by Dr. I. Lewis. Each nation loves its own system best and the Habash love kings, but they are suspicious, and with reason, of their negus negast or king of kings.

In this chapter I shall set out to study the outlines of Habash culture and the background in Hebrew and other traditions against which the supreme negus has developed his remarkable claims. Here I am in some difficulty, for I can find no Habash Kenyatta to enable me with indigenous literary distinction to withstand the indigenous critics who will challenge what I say. Quite a crop of Europeans have written, and written well, many with the *imprimatur* or at least the blessing of the present emperor. . . . This fact however implies a contract of courtesy which tends to blunt the nib of criticism when dealing with matters royal.

Habash Christianity, like Hinduism, is a way of life with great cultural authority even where the practice of virtue is weak and where much of the prescribed ritual is ignored. Like Hinduism it has an eclectic history in the matter of ritual, but unlike Hinduism it is tenacious of its doctrine. In this it resembles the Orthodox Church. An Orthodox Christian who may never confess his sins will nevertheless reject as preposterous any notion of including the 'filioque' clause in the creed. In like manner a Habash more familiar with arak than theology may reject in disgust the doctrine of two natures in Christ— at least that is my inference from various literary and other sources.

Eclectic practices include circumcision, the addition of the Jewish Sabbath and some fifty annual Saints' days to the Christian Sunday where total abstinence from all work is prescribed. The vision of St. Peter does not dispense the Habash Christian from avoiding the unclean animals mentioned in Leviticus. The 'eye for an eye' of the lex talionis still holds good. The Islamic and pagan superstition of the 'evil eye' is widespread. The Habash hold that slavery is justified by Leviticus: 'Let your bondmen and your bondwomen be of the nations about you' (Leviticus 25:44) and that a particularly obscene form of mutilation is justified by the bride-price paid by King David for his wife Michol (one hundred foreskins of the Philistines). These last two practices have made the Habash abhorred by all their neighbours.

Having regard to the clear affinity between Jewish practices in the Old Testament and Habash application of the New Testament, we may find some useful sidelights on the notion of negus negast by examining the notions of kingship in Israel.

Kings came into being curiously in Israel, not as good institutions in themselves but as a Divine concession to Jewish ingratitude and envy. The Israelites, if I have read the story correctly, were assured of peace and prosperity—sustained where needful by miraculous manna, or water from a rock—the only condition being that they should remain strong in faith and obedient in fulfilling to the letter the detailed Commandments of Jahweh.

There was no need for them to imitate the 'heathen' nations around them in the matter of kings, who were in any case a burden on the people, levying taxes to pay their servants, conscripting young men to fight their battles, commandeering workers of both sexes to staff their productive enterprises and their manufacture of weapons, requisitioning their subjects' best land, and even murdering rightful owners to get that which they coveted as in the case of Uriah's Bathsheba and Naboth's vineyard.

All these drawbacks were pointed out by Samuel when the Jews, disgusted with the corruption and bribery of Samuel's two sons, demanded a king so that they might have a captain in war to defeat some of the neighbours whom they disliked most. Samuel, instead of providing them with just judges in replacement of his unjust sons, chided them for their ingratitude, painted a grim picture of kings at their worst and invited them to concur in a negative confession reminiscent of ancient Egypt, expounding his own blameless life. Having readily concurred in this negative confession, but perhaps mindful of the blameworthiness of Samuel's sons, the people renewed their demand for a king.

At this moment Jahweh intervened to overcome the scruples of Samuel. He approved a king in principle for His chosen people, and in fact chose the candidate Himself. That is how Saul was chosen to be king of all the tribes of Israel. That is how a king is chosen to be king of all the kingdoms of Abyssinia. He is God-chosen.

The God-chosen Saul was to be king of a God-chosen people. Equally the Habash count themselves a God-chosen people.

King Saul had pre-eminent personal qualifications, standing physically and metaphorically 'head and shoulders' above all the people. But he had an inherited handicap which proved to be a millstone round his neck just as it has done in the case of a Habash emperor, he was neither of ancient lineage nor a member of one of the greater tribes; he was an ordinary man from the smallest tribe—a Benjaminite—a Vespasian in a sense. With the Habash, merely to have a 'pedigree from Alfred the Great' is not nearly ancient enough to command respect, nor is the 'grandeur' we associate with General de Gaulle sufficient to magnify a negus negast.

King Saul was anointed and crowned Head of State by Samuel, Head of the 'Church'. The Habash negus negast is anointed and crowned by an Abuna who, although Head of the Abyssinian Church, is not like Samuel in relation to Saul nor like the Pope in relation to Charlemagne but rather like a contemporary Archbishop of Canterbury and Queen Elizabeth II. Our queen is

Head of the Protestant Church by law established. The negus negast is in like manner supreme in matters spiritual.

After his consecration the 'Lord's anointed' in Israel was a being unlike other men. He was not a Levite or priest but he was 'sacral'—he was God's representative on earth in matters temporal. Regicide for instance seems to have connoted sacrilege even when done at the bidding of the sovereign himself! It still seems to carry a stigma of its own even in our own day, and one which homicide does not and which assassination of presidents does not, though perhaps it should.

With the Israelites the king was not indefectible—he made mistakes and they were brought home to him, for instance, 'At the turn of the year when kings go forth to war David sent Joab . . .', where it is clearly implied that David was too lazy to go to war himself at a season when it was his duty to do so. The king was not impeccable, for again and again prophets at the risk of their lives proclaimed such hometruths as 'Thou art the man' as the prophet Nathan said to guilty David. The king was not infallible, and indeed the instructions of Jahweh as well as His censures were commonly conveyed by a prophet to the king and not direct by Jahweh to the king himself.

But here the Habash negus negast appears to deviate from the Jewish notion of kingship into the notion of a 'Divine Right of Kings', which was a doctrine held variably in England from the Tudors to the Stuarts. 'The King can do no wrong'; 'Duty is from the subject to the sovereign not the other way round'. The Jews had no illusions of this sort. Jeroboam, for instance, king of Israel, great-grandson of Saul, is among the many whom Jahweh 'repented' having made a king and he is chided by the chroniclers for refusing the advice of the elders to make himself the gracious servant of those who would be his servants. He is censured for adopting instead the advice of the young men and for addressing his people, 'My father chastised you with whips but I will chastise you with scorpions'. Habash emperors often have recourse to 'scorpions', and they might conceivably consult God before chastising their subjects but it is difficult to imagine most of them being guided by any section of their people old or young.

The 'Divine Right of Kings' seems to be a doctrine implicit in the office of supreme negus whose sacral status is further heavily fortified whenever he can, as he should, trace his descent from Solomon and the Queen of Sheba. The Solomonid pedigree makes him not only royal, ancient in lineage, the Lord's anointed, emperor by divine right, supreme in Church and State, but also a kinsman of Christ and a member of the Holy Family. The invocation merely of his sacral name is an instrument of immediate and absolute privilege in the hands of his servants. Examining the doctrine of Egyptian Coptic Christianity which holds to the proposition of Eutyches, I began to question whether this claim to be a kinsman of Christ according to the flesh might not also imply a claim to participate in Christ's Divinity.

Accordingly I wrote to a theologian who has studied the question and I included in my letter something on the following lines: The significant words recited in every Coptic Mass imply an attenuation of Christ's humanity, so that it is swallowed up in His one Divine Nature and the carnal counts for little more than a vesture. If Christ has two perfect natures He is fully God and fully man, as Athanasius proclaimed. If He has only one nature He is either human but not Divine, as proclaimed by the Arians, or He is Divine but not human which is the claim of Eutyches. It follows from Eutyches that Mary the Mother of Christ became divinized not only in herself but also in her progenitors so that Solomon and his descendants are not merely ancestors of Christ's humanity but kinsmen of Christ's Divinity.

Thus the Habash are not only a 'chosen race, but their Solomonid dynasty is in a significant sense 'divine'. The 'humble' priest-king Prester John has become in later centuries a quasi-divine Emperor assuming the titles of Christ Himself, 'King of Kings' (Timothy, 1, 6 and Apocalypse, 17, 14) and 'Lion of the Tribe of Judah' (Apocalypse, 5, 5).

All justice is the emperor's. A title of the Chief Justice is, so I am assured, 'The emperor's breath'. The emperor is not responsible to the people. He is neither their father nor their servant. It is they who are responsible to him through the council of ministers. The emperor, like Charles I of Britain, is answerable to God alone if indeed, as kinsman of God, he is not already on a Divine amba responsible to nobody.

My theological critic comments:

I find your explanation of the quasi-divine kingship of the Ethiopian emperors extremely interesting, but I am inclined to think that you are wrong in attributing this phenomenon to Monophysism. Much more important is the Solomonic tradition by which the emperor is the kinsman of Christ according to the flesh. Is there any evidence that the Ethiopians believe that the emperor shares in the Divine nature itself? I do not think that the evidence you adduce proves this.

I think you are wrong about the Monophysism for the following reason, which I base on my reading of Fr. Coulbeaux. Ethiopian Monophysism is not the same as Egyptian Coptic Monophysism or Eutychianism. It adopts the opinion of Severus of Antioch. This is that the 'nature-hypostasis' of the Word and the 'nature-hypostasis' of the humanity of Christ were joined together to form an individual substance. This substance was consubstantial to the Father and to the Mother, but, as subsequent Ethiopian synods and holy men have repeated, the substance of Christ's body is a special substance. This substance unites the two nature-hypostases in one, just as soul and body are united in the human composite.

You will see that the carnal element is not swallowed up in the Divine here. On the contrary, Fr. Coulbeaux concludes that really the Ethiopians wish to preserve the separation between the two natures as we do, but they do it by means of incompatible com binations and comparisons. Consubstantiality with Christ's progenitors does not, therefore, mean that Divine quality is conferred on the House of Juda. If that were the case the Incarnation would have been repeated in every generation of the House of Juda! No. Christ's substance is unique for the Ethiopians.

It is significant that at the Council of Florence at which two Ethiopian delegates attended and a plan for reunion drawn up, the Ethiopian doctrine was not condemned though the Jacobite doctrine was.

'King of Kings' is an ancient imperial title used by both the Persian and the Byzantine emperors, and is not exclusively reserved to Christ. 'Lion of Juda' refers to the blessing of Jacob upon Juda, rather than to St. John's use of the term. St. John was showing that Christ was both lion and lamb. The Abyssinian use of the title is probably more Solomonic. (And, after all, people are called Emmanuel and Jesus in European countries.)

I have always been of the opinion that 'Prester John' was founded on the Nubian Christian kings of Dongola, Makurrah and Alwah, who were, according to Monneret de Villard, ordained priests. Ethiopian emperors were not.

These valuable comments shed a strong light upon the relations between the Abuna, who must be an Egyptian copt (Eutychian), and the Habash monophysite clergy, who, it now seems, are not Eutychian. Quite apart from the anomalous tradition of an alien Abuna, the doctrinal anomaly is something more serious; it is therefore fully understandable not only on narrow nationalistic grounds that the Habash Church should begin to want a Habash Abuna in place of an Egyptian.

Ethiopianism is something in which Mr. Kenyatta professes to be interested. Dr. Nkrumah is a great admirer—so I gather from his autobiography. Miss Margery Perham has somewhere said that Ethiopia is Zion to many African nationalists or something of the kind. There are many excellent reasons why this should be so. The Habash can point to their unrivalled and almost un-broken story of independence on the pages of history. They may try to extend their two thousand years of authentic history back to Solomon or even to Adam and to represent their ancient territory as something several times larger than it ever was, but with these excesses lopped off their story is still immensely old and immensely exciting.

The Habash have had their eras of sloth and administrative corruption, their kings have had their absurd vanities and many have been extremely cruel. Their crafts have always been lowly and their husbandry very modest, but somehow they have 'held the fort' for two thousand years. Their cruelty alternates with kindness and compassion. They may get drunk but they also fast. Like the Hebrew scribes, they are always at war reviling those whom they dislike in a spirit of intense hatred but they also pray. Their temperament like their territory is a collection of ambas separated by gorges and torn by torrents. The tension of their extremism moves in an instant from suavity to hysteria. Their way of life resembles a circulating tombola of contradictions that make no pretence of being paradoxes. They are a world unto themselves, indeed several worlds in the same person, none of them ever meeting.

Very few of the Habash have ever been traders or travellers or explorers. For the most part they have left their continent only as pilgrims or as slaves, and they have sallied from their impreg-nable fortress into neighbouring territories only as local raiders for tribute, slaves or stock. Islam, for instance, circulates around the world, and the tiny world population of Jews seems to be represented everywhere; but I seem only to have encountered Habash Christians outside Ethiopia on the roof of the Church of the Holy Sepulchre in Jerusalem. The Habash are a nation where the early promise of development was arrested more by their own introversions than by any barrier put up by enemies.

Habash Christianity may well have atrophied in these circum-stances, but if so it has atrophied in an environment which

11. *West African nursing sister showing negroid features.*

12. *Successful Bantu 'settler' in Kenya's 'white' highlands (Mrs. David Tole at work on her husband's 13 acre holding).*

included an austere Islamic culture and a sometimes lofty pagan monotheism and a Jewish culture developed by Africans who are not Hebrews.

Even if Habash Christianity has suffered as a lonely island lapped by these alien cultures, it has at least come to terms with them all. This may end up to its advantage if it should cease to try and dominate the others. Were the Habash Church to reunite with Papal Christianity, it would remain an African expression of Christ's Gospel owing little to European inspiration, and being so steeped in the practices of the nations around that its under-standing of them might even enrich the Church in all Africa. The great impediment to all this is Habash imperialism.

There can be few of those able to stand a little way off who can wish that the Habash should perish, or that twenty centuries of kings should enter the limbo of obsolete institutions. But the evil that all Africans now recognize in imperialism and colonialism has been with the Habash all their days—when they were weak as well as when they were strong.

The Israelites looked for a Messiah who would be a king and restore the kingdom; by contrast with this modest nationalism the Habash emperors have yearned to rule the whole world. This yearning has become a menacing and intolerable nuisance since the Habash at the turn of the century began to spread their unenlightened rule over Galla and Somali provinces and other nations as well. The emperor today claims the love and loyalty of his colonial subjects towards their God-chosen ruler. Queen Victoria, for much sounder reasons, had the same beliefs. She believed that her people ruled the Indian Empire by 'droit de race' added to *droit de conquête* as my grandfather, without I believe intending to flatter, wrote to her from India. As well might Saul have claimed the 'love' and 'loyalty' of the Philistines and the Chanaanites!

My copy of the *Statesman's Year Book* describes the Amhara as the 'most important race' in Ethiopia, numbering two million in a population of eighteen to twenty millions. Presumably the Ethiopian authorities, like others, have supplied this particular information. So then the Amhara are claimed as a separate *race* with 'most important' as the contemporary equivalent of 'chosen'. That is what the Amhara *think* they are. This claim of an indolent tribe can hardly please the Somalis, who in the sixteenth century were made less important by Portuguese seapower, or the Galla,

L

who in the nineteenth century were displaced from a position of greater importance by French-led and French-equipped Habash armies. It may not even please the Tigre.

Here I must recapitulate the story of how a triangular balance of power—Habash, Galla, Somali—came to be so unpleasantly unbalanced in favour of the supreme negus at the end of the nineteenth century.

First, a hundred years before, Napoleon sounded the imperial trumpet in Egypt. It was heard first by the miscellaneous collection of Turks and Levantines who ruled Egypt and who then set about to conquer the Sudan. Then the Egyptian viceroys in the name of the Turkish sultan occupied ports and towns in Eritrea and Somaliland where there were Muslim populations—places not in Habash occupation nor ruled by the Habash.

The sound of the trumpet was then heard by the indigenous Egyptians, an unwarlike people, and by the indigenous Sudanese, a warlike people, as also by the slumbering Habash, who were then an unknown quantity resting in an equilibrium of power for the past three hundred years or so.

Then a young man of the Amhara called Kassa awakened to the sound of Napoleon's trumpet in the land of the Habash themselves.

Kassa constantly puts us in mind of Saul, from his brilliant beginnings to his tragic end. He was an attractive and impressive young man who when young acquired renown as athlete, horseman and marksman with gun and spear. In these pentathlon-like activities as well as in education and qualities of leadership there came a moment when, like Saul, Kassa stood 'head and shoulders' above his contemporaries.

Kassa, like Saul, came of humble, not patrician, stock—a sort of Benjaminite. Like Saul, he was derided by some of the powerful on account of his *petit bourgeois* origins, so that when he had risen swiftly to national eminence jealous Rases may have muttered scornfully, 'What, is Kassa too among the prophets?'

Kassa was given a literary education in a monastery, but in the course of time the monastery happened to be looted by a band of robbers. The monks were dispossessed and Kassa, taking the lesson to heart, himself became the leader of a robber band. Some say that in following this less-exalted vocation he acquired something of a Robin Hood reputation by plundering the rich and protecting the poor. Possibly his activities did not endear him to the powerful nobility.

Kassa, in the fullness of time, becoming aware of his great and growing influence and having defeated all rivals, came to believe himself or was convinced by others that he was God-chosen to fulfil an old Habash prophecy; this foretold that an emperor called Theodore would rule justly, destroy Islam, capture Jerusalem and reign over a world entirely Christian in peace, happiness and plenty to last for a thousand years.

In every supreme negus—with one notable and unsuccessful exception—there is a mixture of crusading Richard the Lion Heart, Charlemagne, Alexander the Great and Attila. It is difficult to imagine most of them without the passion of a living vendetta against Islam even when, for centuries on end, their more powerful enemies were not Muslims but pagans.

In the year 1855, at the age of thirty-seven, Kassa was crowned and anointed Negus Negast by the Abuna taking the prophetic name of Theodore—the third. He was to rule for thirteen years until his death in 1868 at the age of fifty.

Kassa achieved greatness, as most other Habash emperors have done, by military successes in which his own personal leadership counted for much. He seems not to have held with garrisons the provinces he subdued, as Menelek was to do a few years later. When he was in the field all submitted; when he decreed from afar his decrees were ignored and he was then obliged to return with a punitive force. Starting from a position of unchallenged strength he set about making great reforms in a great hurry, more as a soldier conquering enemies than as a statesman winning support from friends. He started with a humanitarian reform which affected his own position: instead of executing his captured rivals he put them in prison—from prison there was always hope of escape and some, including Menelek, did escape.

Kassa was the first to pay his soldiers so that they had no need to rob the poor of food in order to live. This should have endeared him to soldiers and farmers alike, although once it is the custom to loot, soldiers need something more than a little pay to deter them from continuing the practice.

Kassa is said to have reduced the number of internal Customs barriers to three. In so doing he may have secured by better control a larger part of Customs revenue for the imperial treasury, but one may suspect that unsubdued vested interests were antagonized by being suddenly deprived of their customary revenue.

Drastic changes of this kind have an impact not only upon the rich, who can stand it, but upon the many they employ who are forthwith rendered jobless.

Kassa's greatest reforming aim was to abolish not only the slave trade but the institution of slavery itself, and to accompany his decree with efforts to enforce it; but the Christian Habash economy was partly founded upon slavery. At least three days a week were the equivalent of a Calvinistic Sabbath when no work was supposed to be done by Christians. Fasting was prescribed for many days in the year, and on a fast day hard work is not very congenial. A monetary system existed, but it did not replace the barter of goods and services nor the reward of services with accommodation, squatting privileges, firewood, milk and the like —a feudal arrangement that gave much to the poor though neither money to spend nor freedom to quit.

Theodore was an academic soldier, handling great economic issues in the spirit of a short campaign between the season of mud and the season of dust.

The 'men of Belial' who long before had resisted Saul were once again present to thwart an upstart self-made Kassa sitting on the Queen of Sheba's throne, and they soon had every sort of additional reason for their dissatisfaction.

Theodore might have rallied the Abuna in his support but his wife, beautiful, companionable and normally prudent, managed to rally the Abuna against him. A theological dispute arose between the Egyptian Abuna and the Habash clergy—how understandable that such a thing should develop between rival upholders of two distinct and conflicting doctrines about our Lord! The empress sided with the Habash clergy.

When Theodore's beloved wife died, much of the moderation went out of his life leaving only the natural ruthlessness to grow and intensify under the impact of mounting opposition. His second wife, another beautiful woman and a princess of royal blood, made him aware that she was giving much and receiving little in bestowing herself upon the son of an undistinguished little headman. When he slapped her as she no doubt well deserved, she abandoned him and then added herself to the list of his enemies, leaving Theodore in deeper isolation than ever and alone to seek in bitterness the consolation of women who could not share his imperial thinking.

A successful war might have saved Theodore from a more

general falling away of his supporters, but in his war against the Galla he was successful only at the beginning. Theodore did not hold conquered territory or govern conquered people, so the defeated Galla got to their feet again and fought back under their Queen Warkit, whose lovely name as a Galla Boadicea sounds almost too good to be true.

Theodore seemed fated to antagonize all who could help him, even those who had long looked to him for protection. In the puritanical spirit of those Americans who passed the Eighteenth Amendment to the Constitution (the Volstead Act), Theodore prohibited smoking and snuff taking. Offenders were liable to have their lips cut off for the crime of smoking and their noses cut off for snuff taking. Even the tipplers who enjoyed their arak and tej must have begun to wonder when their tongues were going to be cut out.

Revolt followed revolt, and each was savagely avenged; even the murder of Theodore's English friend by bandits was avenged by the massacre and mutilation of two thousand people. Did Theodore read in the first book of Samuel how Saul had merited the wrath of Jahweh? 'Thus saith the Lord of Hosts—now go and smite Amalek and destroy all that they have and spare them not; but slay both man and woman, infant and suckling, oxen and sheep, camel and ass'.

All this did Saul and his people perform save that the people retained the best beasts and Saul retained the captured king. For this transgression, which Saul admitted with lame excuses to Samuel, the first king of Israel merited the 'repentance' of Jahweh that he had made Saul king. Saul pleaded that he had 'feared the people' when he should have compelled them to slaughter their loot. Theodore however feared nobody. He had made up his mind to destroy the predatory power of the Rases, to curtail their levy of Customs duties, to free their slaves and to purify the whole community of its enervating vices. God would stand by him if he stood firm, and if he destroyed Amalek root and branch. Such was undoubtedly the temperament if not the precise thinking of Theodore.

It is just possible that some of the worst excesses attributed to Theodore may have been invented. The eye-witnesses were Habash, and the information comes from their chroniclers. There are no bounds to the imaginative revilings of the Habash against those whom they come to hate—no enormity is too preposterous to emerge from their fertile vindictiveness, and it need not have even a grain of truth as its foundation. But with this reservation I take the accounts as they stand with mass decapitations, burnings, torturings, starvings and mutilations which transformed the admirable Kassa into the monster Theodore.

Theodore may well have reflected that the American Civil War was being fought at this time to abolish slavery by force, so why should not he abolish slavery by force in his own land?

Yet dimly Theodore seems to have seen himself as a man of vision in a brutal and unstable community. As was the case with all other Habash intellectuals, the main stream of world civilized thinking was closed to him and he sensed it. The great renown of Europe had come to his ears, but no Habash had ever seen it. Theodore seems to have craved to make a viable contact with more mature Christian nations and there was at least one precedent for so doing. Lebna Dengel had appealed to Portugal for help against Islam in the sixteenth century, so perhaps Theodore could go further and establish a permanent official relationship with the world's leading Christian powers. He had English friends, and they spoke with reverence of their sovereign whom perhaps he imagined as an authoritarian ruler like himself. He resolved to get into touch with this great queen. A letter should be sent by a safe channel, and by all the traditions of Habash courtesy a prompt reply was incumbent upon the addressee. Failure to reply would be a mark of contempt. In November 1862 Theodore sent this letter to Queen Victoria by the hand of Consul Cameron, requesting safe conduct for his 'Ambassadors' to her Imperial British Majesty because 'I was prevented by the Turks occupying the sea coast from sending you an Embassy'. The letter was duly laid before Parliament, but was mislaid in the Foreign Office and it was never answered.

Brooding over what he deemed to be a slight, Theodore took his revenge upon a handful of British subjects and threw them into prison. This was, of course, a dangerous thing to do in Victoria's England, where the misfortunes of a single British citizen, even a somewhat disreputable British citizen, like the Maltese Don Pacifico in Greece, might bring about wholly disproportionate military gestures on the part of the imperial authority. It did so in this case, for Theodore was soon labelled both bad and mad, and a great British force invaded him all the way from India with infantry and cavalry and cannon and hospital ships and elephants and all the trappings of an important expedition of war.

The invasion was meticulously planned and carried out over a period of twelve months with wonderful military efficiency. It ended in a new and again unexpected misunderstanding between the commander of the force and the threatened emperor. Thereupon the emperor's gallant army was destroyed in a single battle at Magdala. The emperor who had tried to become Victoria's friend gave way to despair; like Saul he took his own life when he saw that all was lost. There followed the release of the British captives, the 'liberation' of the imperial gold crown and other loot, the orderly departure of the British invaders without any attempt to intervene in the political succession and the relapse of Abyssinia into the chaos from which it had risen, a relapse which lasted four more years.

Thus ended the first revival phase from 1853 to 1868, the year of the opening of the Suez Canal.

Theodore, the would-be friend of Britain, was, by one of the most irrelevant absurdities in our nineteenth-century diplomacy, invaded and destroyed by Britain.

During his last hours Theodore sat down to write:

> Out of what I have done of evil towards my people may God bring good. His Will be done. I had intended, if God had so decreed, to conquer the whole world; and it was my desire to die if my purpose could not be fulfilled.*

The 'might have beens' are interesting to speculate upon. Supposing we had exchanged embassies and sent one of our diplomatic men of culture. There could with tact have been an exchange of missions, the Habash mission entering the great and developing western world while the British mission opened up the many lessons of world history to a nation three thousand years behind the times. But no, the thing was impossible, and so Theodore joins the Sudanese Mahdi and the 'Mad Mullah' of Somaliland as one of those damn fools of Victorian history who dared to lay hands on a British subject. One of the Habash weaknesses is an immense deficiency in a true sense of proportion but this—this elephantine British expedition to Magdala—does it not reek of a punishment totally misfitting the crime?

The sudden death of Theodore left the governors of the three

* *The Blue Nile* by Alan Moorehead.

provinces Tigre, Amhara and Shoa struggling for the throne. Menelek of Shoa, formerly prisoner of Theodore and one whom Theodore had treated with kindness, at once proclaimed himself king with acceptable credentials as a member of the Holy Solomonid family. Soon afterwards the ras of Amhara also proclaimed himself king, but in 1872 another Kassa, ras of Tigre, defeated him and was crowned John IV at Aksum. So there were two Habash kings at the same moment, neither of whom as yet exercised any authority over the Galla nor any authority over the Turks on the coast and neither of whom indeed reigned over all Abyssinia.

In 1878, John, taking advantage of a revolt stirred up against Menelek by his own wife, forced him to abandon his claim to be negus negast, and Menelek was content to call himself king of Shoa. Early in John's reign the unwarlike Egyptians under the Khedive Ismail with the sultan's consent took over from the Turks in Massawa and other places, including Harar. They then launched from Massawa several attacks against the Habash, who under the valiant John defeated them with tremendous slaughter.

With the arrival of Britain in Egypt in 1882 both the unwarlike Egyptians and the warlike Turks were removed from the maritime regions of the Horn of Africa. Britain also provided the Habash negus with an ally against the Mahdi albeit not a very effective ally during John's lifetime. Very soon the entire balance of power in the Horn was to be transformed by the total elimination of Islam as a threat to the Habash from north and east.

During the course of a Press Conference in Mogadishu in 1962 I happened to refer to the growth of the association between the British in Egypt and the negus of the Habash in suppressing the Sudanese Mahdi. Hereupon a Habash diplomat took umbrage and shortly afterwards wrote me a letter in which he took me sharply to task for trying to impair the existing good relations between the Ethiopia of Haile Selassie and the Sudanese Republic of General Aboud! The Habash, so it seems, are as ready to delete from authentic history as they are to add to it.

Reverting to John, in 1879 the Khedive Ismail sent Colonel Gordon to negotiate peace with John. Here John expresses himself in a letter to Colonel Gordon replying to the Khedive of Egypt, October 27, 1879, at Debra Tabor.

> You want peace. Well, I want retrocession of Metemna, Changallos, and Bogos, cession of Zeila and Amphilla (ports), an Abouna and sum of money from one to two million pounds; or if His High-

ness likes better than paying money, then I will take Bogos, Massawa and the Abouna. I could claim Congola, Berbera, Nubia and Senaar, but will not do so. Also I want certain territory at Harar.

This is the language of a conqueror who still has not got all that he wants and who in particular has not got any ports on the Red Sea or the Gulf of Aden. It is clear that Massawa, which had been in Turkish hands from the sixteenth century up to and including Theodore's time, had lately passed together with Harar into the hands of the semi-independent Khedive of Egypt. The purpose of underlining these known facts of history from contemporary Habash imperial sources is to refute contrary claims made by the present emperor and recapitulated in Chapter VI.

In 1889, John IV, at the conclusion of a victorious encounter with the Mahdists, was himself killed, whereupon the defeated Sudanese, discerning the demoralization of their Habash foes, returned to rout them. By that time, however, the unwarlike Egyptians in Massawa had been replaced by the unwarlike Italians with the full knowledge and consent of Britain, notwithstanding Britain's claim to be trustee for the sultan in Egypt and in Egypt's colonies.

Seeing his opportunity Menelek had already occupied Harar and added it to his kingdom. It had never been part of Abyssinia.

The death of John produced the customary period of anarchy in Abyssinia. He died having failed in 1874 to achieve decisive victory over the Galla but having, however, thrashed the Egyptians and repulsed the Mahdists. Suddenly he had found himself face to face with an advancing European power and at that moment he died. John, like Theodore, is accused of extreme cruelty.

Menelek II succeeded John, although not without having to mobilize his forces to meet a challenge from Ras Mangasha, and having also immediately to negotiate with an unknown factor of power in the shape of Italians advancing from Massawa.

On March 9, 1889, John was shot dead; in May, even before his coronation, Menelek had signed the Treaty of Ucciali with the Italians, allowing Ethiopia to become an Italian protectorate. On October 1 a supplementary treaty provided Menelek with a substantial loan, and he also received a present of 38,000 rifles and some cannon. The Italians informed the powers of their protectorate. By 1891 Menelek, after freeing himself from the

Italian spider's web, addressed a circular letter to the European powers on April 10.

> En indiquant aujourd'hui les limites actuelles de mon Empire je tâcherai si le bon Dieu veut bien m'accorder la vie et la force de rétablir les anciennes frontières d'Ethiopie jusqù à Khartoum et jusqù au lac Nyanza avec les pays Gallas.*

Queen Victoria had ideas of a similar sort and must have smiled when she read this letter.

The Emperor Menelek in his letter proclaimed, as all emperors must have done for a thousand years, his hostility to Islam, but his target was the Muslim nation to the north rather than the Muslim nation to the east. Desirable communications were, to the north, with Egypt, for there were no maritime traditions, and a negus from Shoa at this time would not see any great advantage in acquiring Massawa.

Menelek's ambitions in the north and those of France as well were thwarted by Kitchener, whose oriental notions of treating captured enemy leaders and prisoners-of-war are honestly and starkly dealt with by Sir Philip Magnus in his biography. By Christian standards of the West they are far from edifying.

Against the Galla, Menelek seems to have operated with French technicians, French map-makers, French advice on the management of a standing army and more French advice as to holding captured provinces with permanent garrisons of conscripted colonial troops. The French also armed his troops with firearms, and did much else to organize his campaigns. Menelek was at work on these adventures as King of Shoa during John's lifetime, adding to his revenues and conscripting the Galla into his armed forces. The Galla were thus conquered by the Habash for the first time in recorded history during the last thirteen years of the nineteenth century. Without massive European help the Galla would not have been conquered at all.

Accounts seem to differ as to whether Menelek followed his two predecessors in abolishing slavery or only in abolishing the slave trade. It matters little, for he allowed that prisoners-of-war could be used as slaves and he took more of these than any other emperor. He may even share with Mohammed Ali the title of the greatest African enslaver of African people. In this alone he insured himself handsomely against the dissatisfaction of his rases

* See Appendix 3.

—to Menelek then goes a tribute of worldly prudence from the Rases, but Theodore must have the greater honour amongst slaves.

Menelek added a colonial empire of non-Habash people to the old metropolitan empire consisting of several small Habash kingdoms. The ratio of the old empire to the new in territory and population was probably as one is to three. Modern Ethiopia is about four times as big as the Abyssinia prior to Menelek II. The new colonies include the Somalis of the Ogaden province who, like the Galla, had never been under Habash rule or part of Habash territory. Subjugation of the Somalis was achieved almost entirely by British arms.

Sir Charles Eliot wrote of the Habash methods of colonization and military occupation of new provinces in its later phases near the southern limit of Menelek's proclaimed target: 'The southward movement of the Abyssinians is a serious matter'. He referred to the appearance of the Habash at El Wak in the east, and near Lodwar on the west, both places being situated some five hundred miles from the Habash homelands north of the Blue Nile gorge. He went on to give the classic reactions of the Menelek dynasty to complaints about the raids of their unruly subjects:

King Menelek and his government disclaim all responsibility and knowledge of these raids, but the superior chiefs do not keep the smaller chiefs quiet and the advance continues.

Mentioning the two main purposes of the raiders, 'loot' and 'slaves', Eliot says of the first:

The Abyssinians, though not nomadic, are like the Turks very destructive and soon strip a country bare; and as their southern districts are occupied chiefly by military bands the process of exhaustion is accomplished with unusual activity, and a new looting ground is soon required . . . there is no mistaking the rapidity and significance of this southward advance. If it continues at the same rate which it has maintained during the last six years the Abyssinians will, in another six years, be on the Uasin Gishu plateau and the slopes of Mount Kenya.

Of the second purpose Eliot wrote:

The only slave raids in recent years have been made by the Abyssinians who, according to report, have carried off many, both of the Turkana and the Boran, as slaves. I do not think that any tribes in East Africa have this reputation.

Lord Lugard in *The Dual Mandate* quotes a Major Darley of a British Official Mission reporting that when an Abyssinian Chief is removed,

> it is the invariable custom for him to seize all those natives on whom he can lay hands, and carry them off en masse for sale to keep him in cash until he gets another province. In 1911 I saw a chief moving from his district. The natives he carried off were so numerous they took four days to pass my camp—certainly ten thousand. I counted seven thousand and then got tired. The arrival at the capital of the Chief of Baccu with the whole population of that district is another instance.

By the end of the First World War the only people who still enslaved and mutilated in our part of East Africa were the Habash. The Habash, too, were the only people still able to massacre and loot without fear of punishment from their own authorities.

For the period which followed the war Sir Arnold Hodson (*Seven Years in Southern Abyssinia*, 1927) refers to his experiences up to 1922. Hodson confirmed the fact of Ethiopian slavery and the slave trade, notwithstanding the so-called abolition of one or both of these practices by more than one Ethiopian emperor. Of Ethiopia in general he wrote:

> Jimma is one of the headquarters of the slave trade in Abyssinia. Formerly slaves used to be sold only in the markets, and although this has now been stopped the traffic is still carried on more or less secretly. On the road we passed several hundred slaves going up to Shoa from Kaffa, and as usual the outgoing official was taking away as much as he could in goods and slaves.

On the universality of slavery:

> Even a common soldier will nearly always have his slave running behind him carrying his rifle.

On the matter of looting, Hodson described an Abyssinian raid on a village inside British territory:

> The village presented a scene of wild confusion. Bowls, sticks chairs, wooden spoons and all kinds of household utensils were lying about everywhere. The huts had been ransacked and everything of value removed, but the raiders had not troubled to set fire to the place. It was now deserted, but among the debris we discovered seven complete skulls besides many broken species of the

skulls of women and children. Altogether I collected the remains of at least ten persons who had lost their lives. How many other victims there were of whom all trace had been removed by the depredations of hyenas and vultures it was impossible to estimate. The survivors who escaped to us have reported fourteen casualties in their village. The raiders got away with seven kraals of cattle and eighty sheep and goats from Sura, while they looted eight more kraals of sheep and goats from Gala close by.

The author then tells that close to this village was another village of British subjects who started to flee in fear of what might happen to them, but they were caught near the Abyssinian frontier and twenty-four of them were murdered by the Habash raiders, three kraals of cattle and eight of sheep and goats were taken.

Of attempts to get compensation for British victims of raids conducted by Ethiopians, Hodson wrote:

Whenever a complaint about these forays was laid before an Abyssinian official he would repeat the parrot cry of 'Tigre'. . . . It was true that there were bands of hunters scattered about, perhaps in larger numbers than usual at this time owing to the unsettled state of the country, but in most cases their activities were winked at by the Abyssinian soldiery. Moreover, the latter did not scruple to take the same liberty themselves when opportunity offered. Ill-fed and underpaid as they were, the men would have been saints to resist the temptation to loot and raid whenever they had the chance of doing so without being found out. . . . The majority of the common soldiers were in sympathy, if not in actual alliance, with the Tigre. From the government they got only a miserable pittance of twelve dollars (about one pound four shillings) a year, and the local chiefs were too thoroughly selfish to trouble about food and clothing for their men. The latter, therefore, took whatever they could get from the Tigre, who paid handsomely for all services rendered. . . . From these and many similar incidents it was clear that the Abyssinian government had no control whatever on that part of Boran to the east of Moyale, while even in the rest of the province its authority was scarcely more than nominal.

Of the Abyssinian habit of robbing and outraging natives on British territory, Hodson adds:

The list of outrages during the past six years for which no satis-faction has been obtained ran well into over one hundred items. The chaos and anarchy which prevailed in Boran during 1920 were not peculiar to that province. Similar conditions existed over the whole of Southern Abyssinia—practically everywhere south of the capital.

Of the attitude of Abyssinia's colonial subjects to their Amharic masters, Hodson wrote:

All along the road the Boran were kind and helpful, but they detest the Abyssinians and I had to be most careful in what I said.

The following paragraph shows how the sacral name was made a substitute for orderly administration.

According to Abyssinian law any one person can stop another from doing anything with the formula 'baa Menelik'—'in the name of Menelik.'

Sir Arnold mentions that there are penalties for frivolous use, but much more severe penalties for disregarding it.

For the period which followed—that is from 1929 onwards—I refer to a colonial civil servant who authorized me to quote him but not to mention his name when he wrote to me on March 7, 1964.

In reply to your letter dated February 26th. Yes, by all means use my words, but I should prefer not to be quoted by name. . . . The Tigre have always quarrelled with the Amhara-dominated Ethiopian government. In Menelek's time many Tigre fled to the south after an uprising and lived on the frontier as shifta or bandits. For some years, therefore, shifta were usually called (and usually were) Tigre.

In my time . . . the raids were usually made by tribesmen, and in that area they were usually connected with the pagan-Islam feuds. For example, the Boran in Ethiopia used to raid the Gurreh and Adjuran and vice versa. The Gelubba or Merille raided (and still do) the Gabbra and Rendille in the Marsabit district.

Shifta, or real brigands, did not in my time cause much trouble on the frontier. But during the Italian invasion of Ethiopia, and after Oeta were suddenly withdrawn during the Second World War, all sorts of lawless types including Ethiopian soldiers came over and caused trouble.

The enclosed photo is of the corpse of a small boy from the Gurreh tribe (Muslims) who had been murdered (and mutilated by the removal of the genitals) together with about forty other people of the village during the latter period. They were British tax-payers in Kenya, and the raiders were a mixed lot of Ethiopian civilians and soldiers. Compensation for this was eventually paid, by the British tax-payer.

After the British Mission under Banks reorganised the police, Borana and Sidamo were better policed, but nothing much was ever done to better the situation near Lake Rudolf, and the Gelubba continued to raid into Kenya from the Bako and Maji provinces.

On these occasions what almost invariably happened was that our own F.O. declined to raise or press the matter—usually stating that other more important matters were under discussion and they did not want to upset Haile Selassie! If they admitted anything it was that Ethiopian subjects and troops had suffered much heavier losses in defending themselves against the British aggressors.

Sometimes it was arranged for local frontier officials to meet and confer and then, after drinking a lot of tej and arak, and hearing much false evidence, the matter was referred back to Addis and forgotten about.

In the year 1923 the present Emperor of Ethiopia as Ras Tafari became Regent. My copy of the *Encyclopedia Britannica* depicts him signing a decree awarding the death penalty for anyone taking part in the slave trade. Slavery, however, went on as usual, and approximately a decade later the emperor promised a deputation from Great Britain that he would bring it to an end in the course of another twenty years.

This was about eighty years after Theodore had abolished the slave trade and the present emperor had then been nine years 'in the saddle'; he opened many offices but we shall never know whether or not 'twenty years' meant postponement to 'the Greek Kalends'. In 1934 there occurred the Wal Wal incident which led to the invasion of Ethiopia by the Italians. Slavery by then had not abated, and I have shown in another chapter that up till then orderly administration had not yet been achieved in Menelek's conquered provinces after forty years in Habash hands. At the time of Wal Wal the Emperor's Writ, according to one of our Foreign Secretaries (Sir Samuel Hoare, afterwards Lord Templewood), 'barely ran beyond the limits of his Palace'.

The Maffey Report of 1935 appears to confirm generally the truth of this terse verdict, at least in regard to provinces bordering on British controlled territory.

It was a redeeming anomaly of our adventures in the land of Kush that the British public needed a moral basis for our aggressions abroad. Our occupation of Egypt, for instance, was intended by the moralists to put an end, in the name of the Sultan of Turkey, to the financial debauchery of the Sultan's viceroys; in the Sudan their high purpose was to end slavery and the slave trade. In Abyssinia, however, we were consistently indifferent alike to incompetent administration and to the institution of slavery; even slave raiding was a thing we tolerated so long as the slaves of the Christian Habash were not exported across the Red Sea to Arabia.

In the chapter on a dismembered nation I have traced the present emperor's imperialism in Somalia with some references to Eritrea. There seem to be no bounds to the ambitions of a negus negast who, for the past forty years, has managed to secure and hold the uncritical support of Britain and America both in his moves to dismantle the British Empire and in his extension of the Ethiopian Empire following its recovery from the Italians by British arms in 1941 and 1942.

In 1963 an American educated Somali described to me some of the methods used by the Habash in the administration of the Somali Ogaden Province.

If you don't stop at once and do exactly what you are told when someone with a rifle says 'baa Haile Selassie' you will be shot and nothing will ever be done to the man who shoots you—he is covered once he has uttered the incantation! Ha, ha, can you be surprised that only amongst Somalis are there still people in Ethiopia who run the risk of demanding freedom and proclaiming the view that they don't want to have anything to do with the man, Haile Selassie—mind you I get on well with Ethiopians individually— very good company—but this Emperor, baa! Terrible! If it wasn't for American support the Habash would have got rid of him by now!

Habash colonies seem to be in the same mess as Menelek left them after half a century of marking time.

It is doubtful whether the emperor has ever yet been in full control of his side of the frontier with Kenya. Sir Philip Mitchell, former Governor of Kenya, wrote in his book *African Afterthoughts* of 'the everlasting murderous raids from across the Abyssinian frontier'. That was in 1952, and by then the emperor had been Chief Executive for nearly thirty years. In 1962 *The Times* reported a number of Kenya tribesmen killed by Habash raiders. Some of these were in fact Samburu, and they were killed near the spot where in 1923, forty years earlier, I was instructed to establish a post for the purpose of intercepting Habash raiders.

Finally as a footnote to the article from the *New York Times* previously quoted, I quote *The Times* of London of April 1, 1964, which published two Press reports from Reuter, one from Moga-

13. *Young Turkana (Kenya) housewives (1925).*

14. *Young Turkana wife, her first baby and her first home (1925).*

15. *Young Turkana housewife cutting up fish from Lake Rudolf with her husband's wrist-knife (1965).*

dishu, the other from Addis Ababa, both of March 31. The Mogadishu report starts: 'Four Ethiopian aircraft today bombed Hargeisa for the third time and fighting was renewed all along the Somalia frontier with Ethiopia, a Government spokesman said.' The Addis Ababa report reads: 'The Ministry of Information denied Somali reports that four Ethiopian aircraft had attacked Hargeisa, but reports on air force involvement are conflicting. The general in command of the state of emergency stated in Harrar that the Ethiopian Air Force was only protecting our soldiers'.

Perhaps the emperor is not in full control of his army and air force. However that may be, it seems probable that the Somalis have escaped from their most pressing danger. In their darkest moment they appealed for justice to Britain and the United States and they appealed in vain. They tried to interest Rome and Bonn in their defence problem, but neither Bonn nor Rome were sufficiently interested. They appealed to Kenyatta who replied 'not an inch'. They received the faintest encouragement from the emperor on 'heads of State' level, but they had to meet the assault of his armed forces on the ground. They managed to interest a few members of the Organization of African Unity, but most of these have their own colonial problem which drives them to suppress self-determination in favour of territorial integrity.

In their difficulty the Somali turned from British and American and African injustice to Soviet justice. They appealed to Khrushchev and they did not appeal in vain. Dr. Shermarke was reported as dining with Khrushchev on a day when our Foreign Secretary, Lord Home, was himself in Moscow but not dining with Mr. Khrushchev. So then we must now ask: 'Is Khrushchev too among the prophets?'

I am grateful to Mr. Khrushchev for answering the cry of the oppressed to which British justice had been deaf. Yet some of those oppressed by the Habash Empire have no voice at all. In memory of Queen Warkit, therefore, I raise my own voice and cry to God, or Allah, or Jahweh, or Wak. May the Habash find an Amba for an Emperor before eighteen millions set upon those two millions of superior people and massacre the lot notwithstanding their ancient and stirring history.

M

10

THE TEN PLAGUES OF UHURU

1. *Too short a spoon*

All the new African states have flirted with the revolution—some more, others less. The revolution is of the Left, whose prophet is Karl Marx. All African nationalists like to be thought revolutionary. Revolution permeates their thought, pervades their speech and is often a preferred mode of action. All African nationalists and many Asians like to be thought Socialists and the word *socialism* crops up in their dialogue like *Alleluia* in Paschal time. 'We talk about it a great deal more than you do in England but we have a great deal less of it here,' remarked the editor of the *Financial Express* of Bombay in 1963.

Socialism's greatest practitioner is the Soviet Union, and in Moscow (or should I say Peking?) revolution still means revolution, whereas in London revolution is bloodless—the idea being that 'evolution' is a peaceful process.

Both varieties of socialism are descended from Marx, but while both still retain 'Clause 4' and the class war, London has dropped the violence, the atheism and the single party rule. But African nationalists are adaptable, willing to appear as acolytes of the revolution in Moscow, yet also visiting the shrines of Marx in London as churchgoing evolutionary agnostics. Like St. Paul they readily become all things to all men; unlike St. Paul, as I shall presently show, they have no objection to incompatible doctrines in different parts of the same charter.

In the eyes of African nationalists Belgrade is the fountain-head of non-aligned socialism, and here, too, is to be found a blueprint for getting the Western powers not only to carry out the purposes of the revolution but also to do so at their own expense. Latterly the vast unity of the Chinese People's Republic, with its non-white face and its travelling Prime Minister, has risen to co-

168

leadership of the band of blood-brothers notwithstanding Peking's brutal assault upon India.

The revolution is rather bored when independence is granted too readily. It is not amused by *uhuru* achieved with the goodwill of the colonial power, for this runs counter to its doctrine that imperialism remains entrenched to the last ditch until it is driven out forcibly by 'freedom fighters' to surrender its position.

So the revolution eggs on the nationalists towards revolutionary situations, fostering the collapse of bourgeois institutions, destruction or eviction of the intelligentsia, corruption of police forces, subversion of military forces and debauchery of agriculture. This is part of the 'price' which the revolution would like the new states to pay in order to obliterate all traces of colonialism, bourgeois society and even tribal loyalties. 'Peace founded on justice', 'settlement of disputes by negotiation'—these formulae recur unceasingly on the lips of the nationalists as they march to the tuck of a Marxist's drum sowing the seeds of war and intending to send in the account for payment by the colonial powers.

Mr. Henry Fairlie, in the *Sunday Telegraph* of October 1, 1964, gave a lucid account of part of this process, starting with the shameful blot which stained the fair fame of Jawaharlal Nehru in the last years of his life—namely his wholly unnecessary rape by violence of little Goa:

> In December, 1961, the Security Council passed a resolution which, in effect, condoned the use of force by India against Goa. Lord Home (as he then was) said: 'For the first time since its foundation a number of countries have voted publicly and without shame in favour of the use of force to achieve national ends. Such an action was a direct breach of the Charter and of international law. When the United Nations approved that, it could be, as Mr. Adlai Stevenson said, "the beginning of the end".'

But the way had been prepared with unexpected success exactly a year earlier, as Mr. Fairlie goes on to explain:

> Perhaps the moment when the Afro-Asian members were first allowed to feel their newly acquired weight was in Resolution 1514, passed by the General Assembly on December 14, 1960:
> 'Immediate steps shall be taken in Trust and non self-governing territories or territories which have not yet attained independence to transfer all powers to the people of these territories without any conditions whatever. . . . Inadequacy of political, economic, social

or educational preparedness, should never serve as a pretext for delaying independence.'

In pursuance of this resolution—or at least in the spirit thereof —the claim of Kasavubu (later to become first president of the Congo) for independence in thirty years was swept away by the 'immediate' claim of Lumumba. Mr. Fairlie continues:

We must recognise, too, that, if power is transferred to some territories without adequate 'political, economic, social or educational preparedness', a situation may occur which is such a threat to international peace that the direct intervention of the United Nations becomes necessary. This, after all, is what happened in the Congo. In that case, we must recognise that such intervention is certain to be costly, and that the member countries (especially the countries supporting the resolution) must support it financially.

This, of course, is exactly what has not happened. The essential cause of the serious budget deficit of the United Nations is the failure of a large number of members to contribute to the cost of its peace-keeping operations in the Congo and in the Middle East. These members are, for the most part, those who are largely responsible for the United Nations being there, and who most consistently use the United Nations for their own propagandist purposes. Britain remains one of the few fully-paid up members.

It is no longer independence and an orderly transfer of power that the Afro-Asian countries are seeking but 'instant Uhuru' which the revolution intends shall precipitate chaos and which the nationalists cannot delay by one hour for fear of being replaced by less scrupulous servants of the revolution.

On October 11, 1964, fifty-seven (including ten as observers) non-aligned countries meeting in Cairo broadcast the text of their resolutions. The document is *par excellence* a charter of mutually exclusive propositions proclaiming peace with passion, but incorporating also precise recommendations and a prescribed priority for campaigns of violence. It speaks of 'peace founded on justice' in terms which are unexceptionable. It prescribes methods of settling disputes by peaceful means which none could hope to better. It proclaims again and again and yet again the right of all peoples to self-determination and independence, including such small non-viable and land-locked territories as Basutoland, Swaziland and Bechuanaland—none of the three exceeding three-quarters of a million persons. It includes on the menu for 'instant Uhuru' French Somaliland, with a population of less than one-tenth of a million.

Aden, Oman, the Republic of South Africa, the Trust Territory of South-West Africa, Southern Rhodesia, Palestine, the Portuguese and Spanish Colonies—all are specifically mentioned. But the spoon has been too short, and these peace-loving peoples have been caught up in a gadarene gallop wherein the only lead that anyone dare give is: 'Faster! Faster!' 'Instant Uhuru' is the panacea, and if it does not come along instantly 'instant violence' will be used to achieve the result. Here is a relevant paragraph of the document agreed by the fifty-seven:

> Imperialism, colonialism and neo-colonialism constitute a basic source of international tension and conflict because they endanger world peace and security. The participants in the conference deplore that the declaration of the U.N. on the granting of independence to colonial countries and peoples has not been implemented everywhere and call for the unconditional, complete and final abolition of colonialism now.

This is the paragraph which invokes once again—even after the Congo debacle is before us—the U.N. General Assembly's Resolution 1514 which caused the debacle.

Another paragraph authorizes armed violence, the very violence which is outlawed in other parts of the document.

> The process of liberation is irresistible and irreversible. Colonised people may legitimately resort to arms to secure the full exercise of their right to self-determination and independence if the colonial powers persist in opposing their natural aspiration.

Not only is subversion sanctioned, it is encouraged, and the fifty-seven non-aligned countries urge one another to recognize the 'revolutionary government of Angola in exile', to supply money and arms to the 'freedom fighters' in Portuguese territories, break off all relations with Portugal and boycott all trade with Portugal. They call upon all participants to take 'all means necessary to compel Portugal' to carry out the so-called decisions of the U.N. General Assembly. All this is to be done by this self-appointed gendarme outside the machinery of the General Assembly. The 'freedom fighters' have their headquarters in a Commonwealth country—Tanganyika (now Tanzania) and the Foreign Minister of that country is chairman of the Liberation Committee of the Organization for African Unity.

Here then in black and white is an omnibus authority and a precept for fifty-seven nations to apply diplomatic, economic and military sanctions against Portugal and also to furnish, sustain and encourage armed subversion in Portugal's African colonies. Were the measures meant to be directed against South Africa there would be at least the pretext that South Africa is not moving in any way now or in the future towards the enfranchisement of an African majority; Portugal, however, *is* moving in that direction, just as Southern Rhodesia is moving in the same direction. Portugal, moreover, has to her lasting credit as a colonial power both that great country Brazil and little Goa on the flank of India. Given a few more years there will certainly be an African political majority in both Angola and Mozambique, and this majority may even possibly decide to remain Portuguese— a contingency far more objectionable to the revolution than even the wholly unnatural system of *apartheid* in South Africa.

2. *Black colonialism*

A first reading of the resolutions of the Cairo Conference of non-aligned countries is sufficient to disclose that they have no intention of applying to themselves the precepts which they urge with intemperate threats upon those who are not among the revolutionary brethren. Britain, Portugal, South Africa, Spain and France are indicted in varying degrees. Once again I quote Mr. Henry Fairlie in his commentary upon the U.N. General Assembly's resolution 1514:

> But we may take the resolution at its face value and assume that it means what it says. In that case, we must properly count among the 'territories which have not yet attained independence', Poland, Czechoslovakia, East Germany, Hungary, Rumania, Bulgaria— and, for that matter, Ghana. Even to Lenin that might have seemed a fairly general incitement to revolution.

Mr. Fairlie has overlooked three whose very identity has been extinguished—Lithuania, Latvia and Esthonia.

How is it that once again the fifty-seven varieties of non-alignment betray their true alignment by suppressing all reference to Russia's one hundred million colonial empire in Eastern Europe.

And what of China too? When I visited India in 1963 a District Magistrate referred to the lessons that India might yet learn from my viceroy grandfather. 'During Lord Lytton's term as viceroy,' he said, addressing a gathering of lawyers in Benares, 'it was said, and rightly said, that Russia in Afghanistan meant Russia on the Ganges. Today we can apply that and say that China in Tibet means China on the Ganges.'

The Chinese People's Republic had recently launched a wholly unprovoked attack upon India. Mr. Nehru's policy of neutralism lay in ruins and his armed forces suffered a severe setback. His leadership of the Asian—indeed the whole coloured—world passed to another. Mindful of little Goa I reworded to myself a scriptural proverb as follows: *He who is unfaithful in that which is least shall suffer betrayal in that which is greater.* And now I look through the record of the Cairo Conference of the non-aligned countries trying to find a hint that they are fraternally shocked at the aggressions of Peking, but there is no sign of it. The camels of the revolution are swallowed without wincing while the gnat of Djibouti produces fifty-seven gulps of protest.

The conference has upheld the right of self-determination for all peoples by every kind of emphatic and unqualified phrase. No territory is too small to be Balkanized or fragmented if the colonial power is white. But self-determination is a precept which none of the preachers intend to practise themselves. They declare that in their own case the boundaries, even those boundaries whose absurdity they have been denouncing for the past forty years, are today inviolable and the imperial principle of territorial integrity shall reign supreme over the principle of self-determination.

Mr. Shastri, possibly with Kashmir in mind, makes the vast inconsistency perfectly clear in the following paragraph:

> While we stand pledged to the right of self-determination (? for all) territories under colonial rule I would like to sound a note of caution. Self-determination is the right of any country that is dominated by another, but there can be no self-determination for different areas and regions within a sovereign and independent country, for this would lead only to fragmentation and disruption, and no country's integrity would be safe.

I wrote to him hoping to hear that he had been misreported but I have received no reply.*

The fifty-seven have deplored the fact of divided nations, but in this again they are only acting as publicists for the revolution;

* As I amend these proofs in September 1965, Pakistan is giving the answer.

they imply merely that where the China lobby has conquered half a country the rest of the country should be given to it. They demand 'instant Uhuru' for tiny French Somaliland in the name of self-determination but they refuse self-determination to Kenyan Somaliland and Ethiopian Somaliland in the name of territorial integrity. We read them as they proclaim that all imperialism must come to an end, but we note that they say nothing whatever about the ending of the least enlightened colonial empire of the lot—the Ethiopian Empire. It is evidently taboo to notice the whited sepulchre of black colonialism!

With their right hand the fifty-seven demand freedom in the following language:

> The right to complete independence, which is an inalienable right, must be recognized immediately and unconditionally as pertaining to all peoples. . . .

With their left hand they repudiate demands for freedom in the following language:

> The countries participating in the conference . . . reaffirm their determination to oppose by every means in their power any attempt to compromise their sovereignty or violate their territorial integrity. They pledge themselves to respect frontiers as they existed when the states gained independence. . . .

May there be no peace for those who base it on this injustice! Here is an example of the right hand at work in Kenya (*The Times*, June 23, 1964):

KENYA MINISTERS 'BURY' S. AFRICA

NAIROBI, June 21

About 25,000 Africans cheered and let off fire-crackers here today as Mr. Jomo Kenyatta, the Prime Minister, and Cabinet Ministers buried an effigy of the South African Government. In a massive protest demonstration Mr. Kenyatta called on his Cabinet Ministers to bring on 'the dead carcase' of Dr. Verwoerd and his friends.

Solemnly, to the chanting of 'we are burying South Africans', the Ministers of Finance, Education, Justice and Health, buried a mock coffin daubed with anti-South African slogans in a shallow grave.

Mr. Kenyatta spoke for 80 minutes on the policies of South Africa and pointed to a slogan painted on his rostrum, 'We will invade South Africa'. He *said Kenyans must be prepared to shed their blood* for their brothers in South Africa, Southern Rhodesia, and the Spanish and Portuguese colonies.

(Author's italics)

And here in quick succession both hands:

JOINT COMMUNIQUE ON HAILE SELASSIE'S VISIT TO KENYA

B.B.C. monitoring NAIROBI in English 16.00 GMT 12.6.64

Excerpts of report of communiqué:

Emperor Haile Selassie of Ethiopia left Kenya today at the end of his eight-day State visit. . . .

The communiqué said the Emperor and the Prime Minister agreed to establish a consultative body. They also reaffirmed the policies of their respective governments to continue supporting faithfully the principles enunciated in the Charter of the OAU and in the Charter of the UN. They also agreed to take joint measures, in accordance with the mutual defence treaty to defend the territorial integrity of Kenya and Ethiopia.

[This treaty is directed against the independence of Somali Provinces.]

The communiqué went on to say that the two leaders consider it necessary that appropriate measures should be undertaken immediately, in conformity with the declaration of the conference of the Heads of African States in Addis Ababa, to grant independence to all African people under colonial domination. In this connection they earnestly appealed to all independent African States and to other freedom-loving nations to assist in all possible ways the peoples of Southern Rhodesia, South Africa, Mozambique, Angola, the so-called Portuguese Guinea and all other dependent people in their struggle to liberate themselves from the yoke of colonialism.

The mailed fist of one of the brothers is disclosed in the following cutting from the *Daily Telegraph* of October 15, 1964.

KENYA TIGHTENS SECURITY LAWS

Anyone in Kenya's troubled north-eastern region can be detained without trial, it was announced today in Nairobi as Mr. Kenyatta, Prime Minister, tightened security in an attempt to end the country's war with Somalia border raiders.

Legislation published today said that anyone could be detained 'If it was necessary for the preservation of public security'. Any detained person could appeal but only through an Appeal Tribunal appointed by the Minister for Internal Security and Defence.

The African Conference on the Rule of Law held in Lagos from January 3–7, 1961, has the following on page 16 para. 7, which has a bearing on the above ruthlessness:

The Conference feel that in all cases of the exercise of emergency powers, any person who is aggrieved by the violation of his rights should have *access to the courts* for determination whether the power had been lawfully exercised.

3. 'Non-aligned' partisans

There is a valid *raison d'être* for non-alignment, but also a practical expression of it which is very satisfactory for the revolution. I have already pointed out that every defect of the non-Socialist white colonial powers is enlarged by the non-aligned and denounced out of hand, even while there is no criticism whatsoever of Russia or China whose colonialism far outstrips in scale and menace the tiny residue of their colonial empires still remaining in the hands of the decolonizers.

The fifty-seven naturally desire to contract out of the nuclear fall-out. It is a tribute, moreover, to India's deep sincerity in one of her policies that she has renounced the military exploration of nuclear power albeit knowing that China was resolved to 'have the bomb'.

The self-destroying potential of the human race concentrated in the hands of a few is so horrifying that it is a waking nightmare for all—not alone for the fifty-seven non-aligned. Some of the fifty-seven have a keen insight into the horrors, but so have we. Presumably we retain the deterrent to deter, and if by some terrible calamity it fails to deter we prefer to be dead rather than red.

The Afro-Asians are following the pattern of European nationalisms during the nineteenth century. Having renounced a weapon whose use means extinction for most people, they are following a policy of expanding the type of armaments whose use is only too likely. They castigate the deterrent whilst acknowledging that the deterrent deters, but they go ahead with the old provocative kind of armaments which everybody believes provoke. President Nasser no doubt needs armed forces to deal with Israel or Israel's Anglo-American friends. President Aboud of the Sudan, now superseded, may not wish to be swallowed by Egypt or to lose his southern provinces. The Emperor Haile Selassie is very arms-conscious; Mr. Mboya, during a visit to Addis Ababa, thought that this was a hangover from Italian invasions but others may suspect that a heterogeneous Empire with little love for Ethiopia needs quite a lot of holding down. The Somalis have already been involved in armed clashes with Ethiopia which observers have regarded as aggressions by Ethiopia. Mr. Kenyatta seems to have grandiose ideas of invading South Africa and other parts of the continent when Britain has sufficiently trained and equipped his forces. Far from universal disarmament, some African states are getting the first ship of a first navy which they do not need at all, while others are having an air arm for the first time and most of them are adding to their ground forces.

None of these nations manufacture arms, so to whom shall they go? They can only go to one of the producing nations, and they are bound to be aligned with their supplier or his patron or take the risk of having their replacements cut off at some awkward moment. Some go to an armourer in the Western bloc others to one in the Eastern bloc. One wonders if they take no account that there is an inescapable alignment between Saul and his armour-bearer, and that if their sources of arms are in the country of the Philistines they will to that extent be in the power of the Philistines?

Then there is the matter of financial affiliations; currency, banking, overseas trade and aid, some of which those who have less are beginning to demand with menaces from those who have more, using language of this sort:

'When we were your colonies you plundered us and made us poor, now that we are free you have a duty of restitution and if you do not carry out that duty there will be war.'

And if we do provide preferences in trade and actual aid, whether in friendship or in acknowledgment of the alleged duty, does it not constitute an alignment between those who bestow and those who receive? President Osman of Somalia at the Cairo Conference made some dry references to his fruitless search for a definition of non-alignment, while President Tubman, presumably aware of his extreme dependence upon the United States, declared that non-alignment did not debar anybody from associating himself with a bloc of his preference. Probably neutralism was the better term for these non-aligned countries clearly resolved to avoid being implicated in a nuclear war if they can possibly do so.

Were it not for colonialism none of the African states of today would have made such great progress in their material well-being, yet few Africans pay tribute to colonialism as the creative factor in emancipating Africans from tutelage; to most of them the jargon of the revolution implies total emancipation from those by whose hands they have in truth been lifted from darkness to the threshold of the affluent society. So, at that very door of what should be their greatest advance, they one and all seem to select as their enemy the nation which is the most willing and the most able to be their friend.

Economic neutralism is claimed by African political neophytes as a way of getting the best of both worlds, or both blocs, but there are conspicuous weaknesses in this attitude; such a policy leaves each feeble state without any substantial backer clearly dedicated to sustain its progress. Each state is urgently in need of investment capital; each asks intemperately for cash while proclaiming its total independence of the providers of cash; overseas capital investment both public and private is therefore a hesitant, patchwork and nibbling affair, featured by small-scale bids and counter-bids from East and West.

The inexperienced states themselves are apt to make a faulty assessment of their own needs, and to have less rather than more control over the pattern of their own advance.

The trouble with non-alignment is that it is often a positive alignment with the revolution; it is a renunciation, a repudiation and a cutting away of ties which already exist. It involves depicting friends and liberators as potential enemies and enslavers. Mr. Kenyatta provides an extreme example of this. On December 12, 1963, he received from Her Majesty's Government the Independence of Kenya; on January 24, 1964, the King's African Rifles mutinied and at his own request the mutiny was at once put down by British troops. On April 14, 1964, Mr. Kenyatta, speaking as Prime Minister, broadcast an address to 'the men in the Army, policemen and prison warders . . .'; he referred to the mutiny in the first sentence of this address but omitted all reference to the help given to him by friendly Britons, and his last paragraph started with the following words: 'Finally, I say this to you: We must unite and not be deceived by those imperialists who want to crush us'. It is not Mr. Kenyatta who united the sixty tribes of Kenya but Britain. In the hour of crisis he had recourse to Britain to preserve that unity, but no sooner was he delivered than he denounced as deceivers and crushers those who had just saved him from being crushed.

To bring my point to its climax is a quotation from the *Kenya Digest* of June 20, 1964, which indicates clearly how the revolution has successfully arranged that Britain shall pay for Kenya's black colonialism and her deconsolidation of land holdings.

£60,000,000 IN AID FROM BRITAIN

Kenya is to receive from Britain aid worth more than £60,000,000 in money, materials and services as an Independence settlement, it was announced in Nairobi and London this month. More than half the aid will be in the form of gifts. The discussions leading to this settlement started six months ago and were continued during the visits of the Commonwealth Secretary, Mr. Sandys, and a team of his officials to Nairobi, and more recently during a visit to London by the Minister for Finance, Mr. Gichuru. They were concluded at a meeting in Nairobi on June 3 between the Prime Minister, Mr. Kenyatta, and the British High Commissioner, Sir Geoffrey de Freitas.

The aid is in the form of military and technical assistance, money for development and settlement, assistance to the Kenya Civil Service and the cancellation of some outstanding loans. Some of it is available immediately, and the remainder will be spread over four or five years. Military assistance includes a gift of £3,500,000 worth of arms, equipment, vehicles, aircraft (including six Chipmunks, eleven Beavers and four Caribous) and such things as armoured cars and the latest infantry weapons. There will also be a gift of about £1,000,000 over the next three years towards the cost of British Army and R.A.F. training for the Kenya Armed Forces. More than £6,000,000 worth of military property and fixed assets, included Kahawa, which is the most modern British barracks in the world, is to be presented to Kenya. In addition, Britain will provide, free of charge, experts to advise on the formation of a Kenya Navy. At present, military assistance is already being provided free—for instance, the air-lift to supply the Kenya Army in the North-Eastern Region* at present costs more than £1,000 a day. During the next four years, at least £12,000,000—£4,600,000 of which is a gift—will be provided for land settlement. Later this year there will be another gift and loan for a special scheme at Ol Kalou, for which details are being discussed. Outstanding interest-free loans totalling about £6,000,000 have been cancelled. A loan of £13,600,000—£10,000,000 of it interest-free—has been provided for compensation and commuted pensions of designated officers.

The air-lift of supplies to the army of oppression costs more than the administration of the whole Northern Province in 1961, according to my record of figures obtained from Isiolo in the autumn of that year.

* Kenya's Somali Colony.

An African broadcasting in French from Leopoldville on January 7, 1965, must have the last word on this (B.B.C. monitoring January 9, 1965); here is the text of the talk, entitled 'The Rebellion in Kenya':

> Before looking at the mote that is in your neighbour's eye, look at the beam that is in thine own. This is a wise saying which Mr. Jomo Kenyatta would do well to ponder. The Kenyan Premier has given an ultimatum to the rebels [shifta] who refuse to acknowledge his authority to lay down their arms by January 12, 1965, saying: Otherwise I will liquidate you. Here, then, is the man who preached moderation, who shouted aloud from the housetops that one must never fight against a rebellion and that one must always negotiate. Here then is that great conciliator who suddenly forgets the path of negotiation and who has only one wish—to crush the rebels.
>
> In the Congo we are well placed to judge the words and actions of Mr. Kenyatta. As chairman of the OAU commission on the Congo, he could suggest only one solution: to negotiate, to negotiate with the rebels. And when our government of public salvation wanted to show him that it was not possible to talk with the murderers of Stanleyville, he could find only one answer: negotiate. And finally, when the Congolese rebels, by taking hostages and massacring defenceless civilians, sank in the eyes of the whole world to the same level as Hitler and the worst (?characters) in history, Mr. Jomo Kenyatta could again find only one word: negotiate.
>
> But this wisdom which Mr. Kenyatta displays only holds good when disorders are not taking place in his own country. It is enough that former Mau Mau fighters should refuse to obey him or for shifta to feel that they are Somalis rather than Kenyans, for the great conciliator of Africa to envisage only one solution, namely to crush the rebels in Kenya.
>
> We do not wish to give any advice to Mr. Kenyatta. We are for non-interference in the internal affairs of other states. But we simply ask Mr. Kenyatta to be logical with himself. Let him apply to himself the advice he gives or else stop giving advice. And we would ask him once again to ponder over this proverb: 'Before criticizing one's neighbour, one must sweep one's own doorstep'.

4. *Rewriting history*

The brief reign of European colonialism in north-eastern Africa is over. As we review the era of white flow and white ebb covering no more than one long lifetime it seems fitting to conclude with a summary of the experience. Looking back may help us to look forward.

The fact that powers outside the continent should for so long have raided Africa rather than occupied it is probably due to the absence of anything in the unproductive economy of Africa to attract outside interests apart from the increasingly reprobated and disreputable slave trade. There were also powerful deterrents in the shape of great distances and topographical obstacles, poor communications and the tardiness of victory over tropical diseases. Some successful missionary enterprises of the Portuguese for instance occurred centuries ago, but were brought wholly to an end by diseases to which all the missionaries succumbed. Although the west coast was more notorious as 'the White Man's grave', there were parts of the east which remained so unhealthy that up to my own time the incidence of serious and fatal illness remained high even with a turnover of personnel which aimed at relief every eighteen months.

The final impulse to occupy East Africa came, as indicated earlier in this book, when considerations of political strategy were acutely underlined by the new Suez Canal. The impulse spread up the Nile to its source, and then along the coast line of the Red Sea, the Gulf of Aden and the Indian Ocean.

During the process white rivalries more than once clashed ominously. Britain seeking a territorial corridor from Cairo to the Cape clashed with France, seeking a similar corridor from Dakar to Djibouti. First the principals clashed at Fashoda, then they clashed through their satellites in Abyssinia—Britain briefing resurgent Italy to do her work while France briefed the resurgent Habash to do hers. The success of France's satellites brought dissatisfaction to all three European invaders including France, and the rise of a Teutonic Samson brought the three of them to the conference table in 1906. Here they consolidated their spoils by acknowledging the military advantage of France's satellite together with the civilizing mission of Britain's satellite. The integrity of the heterogeneous highlands was guaranteed together with the continued dismemberment of the homogeneous desert. With these two follies in the diplomatic brief-case the three moved on to further imprudences culminating in a clash with Samson which brought about the decline of all four.

Half a century later the chastened Europeans have left the scene with the homogeneous desert still artificially forced apart, and the heterogeneous highlands still artificially forced together. It is the end of white colonialism notwithstanding the many benefits which the white invaders remained to bestow, but black colonialism receives a new lease of life notwithstanding its unenlightened oppressions.

As the Europeans depart, often with a good grace, African politicians accuse them of various 'crimes', some of which are almost the exact reverse of the truth. I have shown the extent of the truth that border tribes and even small nations were indeed truncated by absurd boundaries and that the whole Somali nation was carelessly dismembered, but, such exceptions apart, the Europeans did not divide Africans from Africans—they made political fusions out of anything from fifty to a hundred tribes, and the whole of independent Africa is today pledged to preserve those boundaries even at the points where they are most absurd.

The Europeans did not arrive in Africa to find a prosperous economy and then forthwith destroy it; they found a lowly economy and improved a great deal of it.

They did not on balance import diseases and shorten the life of Africans; on the contrary they reduced the impact of many diseases in human beings, domestic animals and plants, and they greatly extended the general expectation of life.

They did not condemn Africans to illiteracy and ignorance; Europeans found illiteracy, and what Africans are now pleased to call ignorance, and they did a great deal to educate and enlighten; they did not find African peoples thirsting for advancement in our terms, but rather a collection of nations resolved at least in part to by-pass or resist what we had to offer.

More specifically they did not deprive Ethiopia of access to the sea; they connected Ethiopia's new capital by rail to the sea for the first time.

As for the Ethiopian colonialists, Dr. Pankhurst, after enumerating ancient reports of a golden age and referring to the unchanging tradition of the Habash, declares that the primitive form of agriculture, industry and trade and social conditions, the incidence of disease and the poor schooling surviving from former times should convince even a proud patriot that the 'golden age lies not in the past but in the future . . .'.

Here we must face the crucial issue that constantly presents itself to the impartial student of the African scene—the question as to whether Africans suffer from some hereditary disability which bars their advancement beyond a comparatively low level of economic life. Some observers point to the backwardness of

Negroes in North America, others to the backwardness of Negroes in Liberia, others to the backwardness of the Habash non-negroid in the land where they have been independent for at least two thousand years. We must ask ourselves whether there is or is not an inherent propensity in Africans to retrogress, as many a white administrator, who would wish it otherwise, has repeatedly concluded. Is it a fact that, in the region under consideration in this book and in other regions of Africa, notwithstanding exceptions in antiquity such as Egypt, much evidence points to African resistance to successive waves of superior influence from outside, some of them white but others not white?

Again I consult my anthropological critic on this point and he answers:

Africa, as it happens, had a very full history, but it cannot be written in our terms. We already know a great deal about it, and as the years go by we shall know much more. It is a unique phenomenon—every part of the continent thinly inhabited by fragile, co-existing societies, handing on to one another ideas and discoveries. Great migrations, trade routes and regions of high material culture were rare. Here and there existed a flourishing culture at the end of a trade route to the coast. These were fragile and impermanent. They depended on uncertain supplies of raw materials, usually deposits of gold, and they were usually snuffed out by greedy invaders from outside. These outside invaders certainly made no attempt to civilize, rather the reverse!

This is the case of Songhai, destroyed by the Moroccans. It is the case of East African coastal culture, destroyed chiefly by Vasco da Gama and his successors, who looted them, and then failed to operate the gold trade with Monomotapa as efficiently as their Swahili predecessors. It was the case with Nubia, the land of gold, wantonly invaded and destroyed by Saladin's brother. It is again the case with the old Congo kingdom destroyed by Portugal's slaving activities.

The Portuguese and others were not interested in making colonies, they just did 'ship and castle' trading, or undertook barefaced razziahs inland.

I fail utterly to see that this can be called 'an African resistance to waves of civilization'. Rather, whenever Africa was on the verge of producing a high culture, it was destroyed (in the main) by outside interference.

I should, of course, add that Africa has not always or principally been a passive victim of invasion, which, in any case affected a small area. There have been some exceptional movements like the

N

formation of the Almoravid Empire among the Hamitic Berbers and Touaregs which ruled as far as Ghana and Spain! And there has also been the remarkable Luo migration of Nilotic peoples from the Sudan into East-Central Africa, with its creation of the Lacustrine Kingdoms. . . .

I do not think you should take as seriously as you do the modern African's appeal to his past. From my reading of modern politicians' statements, they ardently want to create an 'African image' before the eyes of the world, to give themselves dignity and self-respect. Obviously, if they succeed, it will be a new creation 'sui generis', but I do not think they are wrong to look for good inspirations from their past. There *was* much in it that was good. Also, that past is still with them in most areas of Africa. It is upon that past that they must build. The colonial epoch has been too short to make any lasting impression. It is up to the new leaders themselves, I feel, to civilize Africa in depth, and that cannot be done by ignoring the positive contribution of the past.

They obviously romanticize about their past, but that is a good thing, it shows they do not want to return to the seamy side. That is to be forgotten. The romantic vision of the past provides an ideal, and an identity which they need, if they are to build up a genuinely African civilization, as please God they may. That, at any rate, is a missionary's point of view!

It would seem that in my critic my African friends have an eloquent champion.

5. *Fraternal nepotism*

The African Negro child, *vide* Mr. Kenyatta, starts as son of so and so, with brethren who are sons and daughters of the same so and so, and cousins who are sons and daughters of another so and so, who is nonetheless one of his several 'fathers'. After a short study of kinship group relationships, the terms husband, uncle, cousin, brother and grandfather seem to the outsider to become virtually interchangeable. The kinship and age groups manage in many a solemn ceremony to bestow important rights and important obligations upon their members; should an African fall through mischance there are other Africans with a duty to raise him up; correspondingly no African's success is regarded as his alone; there is always a trail of claimants with the right to share in such success.

Accordingly African nepotism is regarded not as a personal vice but as a social virtue, and the holding of an office of reward

'under the Crown' is no solitary title to be renounced at will but
a lifeline of prosperity thrown out to the brethren of the group,
a line not to be cut by its beneficiary without the consent of them
all. It is but a short step from this to the single party state with
the exclusion of opposition parties by decree.

If a Negro parliamentarian is offered presents to do him honour,
the honour is not his alone to accept or to renounce but that also
of his extended family; a Minister who does not avail himself
of petrol or other commodities freely offered on Indian credit on
the infinitely never-never system may be thought by some of his
kinsfolk to be unfit to hold office; if a Minister takes for himself
a large slice from a government contract there is no public opinion
to say that he may not honourably accept it and there is a whole
caravan of kinsfolk to insist that it is his duty to accept.

This is New Africa still struggling in the womb of the Old;
the European who expects from Negro clerk, executive or Minister
as a matter of course the incorruptible integrity which he experienced formerly from the British Colonial Service is a fool!

With rising prosperity perhaps, and with the growth of a
substantial bourgeoisie, opportunities will arise to exorcize these
foibles; meanwhile the clan threatens to drag the successful
African down to its own level, the level to which Africa per-
petually seems to retrogress.

In 1961 I asked a senior administrator: 'We are going to hand
over to politicians who as ministers will be getting at least four
times the income they could get in any other way—won't there
be a good deal of corruption?'

The answer came immediately and was endorsed by a great
many other people with experience: 'Of course there will be
corruption—what do you think? There is no public opinion
against corruption! Corruption as we understand it does not go
by the name of corruption in Africa!'

6. *Moses without the covenant*

I take the following from the London *Times* of June 23, 1964:

AFRICAN ATTACKS 'BLACK FASCISM'
NAIROBI, June 22

A prominent Kenya African and a strong opponent of the
Government said here today that the newly independent African
states were in the grip of 'Fascist dictatorships which were worse

than that of South Africa'. The difference was that the dictatorships in the new states were run more inefficiently by black men than that run by the whites of South Africa.

Mr. Lemomo, national organizing secretary of the opposition Kenya African Democratic Union, went on: 'It is shameful that with two possible exceptions there is hardly one single so-called independent African state in 1964 under which African people are enjoying even the meagre degree of freedom that the British people got from Magna Carta 750 years ago.'

Mr. Lemomo was commenting on last week's threat by Mr. Jomo Kenyatta, the Prime Minister, to scrap the country's present constitution and put an end to the present regionalism. He said African Governments should learn to respect the constitutions of their countries before 'throwing stones' at the Governments of other states.

What follows is from the *Kenya Digest* of August 29, 1964:

The Prime Minister, Mr. Kenyatta, in his capacity as President of the Kenya African National Union, issued the following statement of August 13:

On my return from the recent London and Cairo Conferences, I stated that from now on we will work toward a one-party state. Events have shown that not only was a one-party system inevitable but it was also the most prudent method of attaining those aims and objects which our people hold so dear. The evils of colonialism and imperialism left mass poverty, illiteracy, disease and ignorance in our midst, and as we embark on the historic task of eradicating these evils today, neo-colonialism, in its many manifestations, has already reared its ugly head in our motherland.

The one-party state is a state in which the formation of other parties is punishable by law or persecution. In this it differs essentially from states where the same party is regularly returned to power by the electorate.

Ethiopia is so remote from any known version of democracy that one feels of the present emperor, '*Après lui le déluge!*' The Somalis have had two General Elections, one before independence and another after three years of independence. The Somali Youth League won the second election as it had won the first by a substantial margin. In their case not only were the elections contested by a large number of groups registered as parties— they numbered at least sixteen—but the President's invitation on the morrow of success of the party to recommend an alternative Prime Minister with a mandate to pick a completely new team was, after long debate and consultation, agreed by the ruling party. This democratic latitude is possible in the Somali Republic because of the immense strength of Somali patriotism, notwithstanding the keen and often harmful rivalry between clans with their provincial interests so often taking precedence over national interests.

In Kenya there are similar clan divisions within tribes, but the main divisions are not between clans of the same common nationality as in the case of the Somalis but between tribes which are in fact different nations. In Kenya there are also two contrasting rural economies, the cultivators and the pastoralists, who are still roughly divided racially, the pastoralists having dominated the scene up to the time we arrived and the cultivators having been enthroned in their place by means of ballot box superiority which is *our* idea of how things should be done. It seems therefore that a dictatorship relying on British bayonets is likely to be the only device occurring readily to the cultivator pen-pushers as a way of holding off the pastoral spearmen. It looks very much as though Moses is about to shed the covenant and presently, when Anno Domini has removed Moses from the scene Juda may well be seen in conflict with Israel or perhaps they will go their separate ways. Ethiopian disintegration should be a more serious matter.

7. *Back to the land*

The impression made upon a visitor to India is the pressure of people upon the land—three acres per farmer or half an acre per cultivator. Against this stark background the 'tea-cup' cow, the 'hat-rack' bullock and the use of dung as domestic fuel in a vegetarian non-slaughter continent are seen as shocking impediments to farming progress.

In Africa it is all the other way round. African husbandry is, or has been, undoubtedly bad and exceedingly resistant to change; there are many examples of over-stocking and over-cropping, and consequent erosion, but such authorities as I have been able to consult give the impression that even if the African population were to multiply threefold it could remain on the land simply by a better development of water resources, and there are hosts of other steps to be taken as well. The great necessity is not that all should be farmers but that all farmers should farm efficiently. Neither the deconsolidation of white farms into black subsistence holdings nor the Africanization of large white farms is likely to be anything but harmful to African interests. The 'stolen lands' myth is the basis of the first Kenya resettlement scheme and a notion that black farmers can easily take over the large units of Europeans is the basis of the second. Neither scheme is at all likely to succeed without much adaptation and prolonged under-pinning by expatriate skills and finance.

There are, however, primitive urges which hold men to the land and which from time to time cause them to quit urban centres in order to resume occupation of the land. These are not confined to Africa. In 1932, for example, I found them passion-ately projected by non-farming types during a tour of the Zionist settlements in Palestine; here I was conducted by the chief representative of the Jewish publicity department. I had discus-sions with Jews of various nationalities, none of them skilled on the land, who ran affairs collectively (so it seemed) through a committee, and who consigned their small children to day nurseries where, clearly, community of possession (toys) was a source of strife! My questioning brought out that in all matters of importance they did what they were told by some central agency in Jerusalem or Tel Aviv and they really controlled nothing at all. Like all non-farmers out of their environment they were having one serious trouble after another: I was in-formed that one breed of cattle, I forget which, was so subject to contagious abortion that it was being replaced by another breed at the expense of the Jewish Agency. Then it was explained that the soft fruit was being excessively damaged by a Mediterranean fruit fly which did not respond to the particular sprays which were being directed against it.

The Zionist example was followed by another in England. At the time I was associated with a small religious movement for young men, Roman Catholics, and some of them had developed Cobbett-like notions that the great industrial cities were too degrading to be acceptable for any of God's children. They quoted a Papal encyclical which proclaimed that matter emerged from the factories ennobled, and men debased. So my young friends were trying to escape from the 'Great Wen' and its products, even to the extent of refusing to use such factory products as a razor. They talked of 'mucking out' as the only Christian alternative to 'mucking in', and they fastened them-selves on to the land with intense fervour that was often not matched by competent husbandry.

Similar considerations have had their influence on the alleged 'land hunger' in Kenya. There, occupation of agricultural land by small African cultivators has been represented by the Kenyatta school as the Africans' only way of life, a *sine qua non* of welfare, a spiritual necessity, an insurance against old age and a divine right.

On the ranching side many a great pastoral nomad lightly draped in tribal dress has taken a look at other ways of life only to affirm the total superiority of his own; it is in vain that we may have remonstrated over his tribe's unnumbered and un-productive kine trampling into dust the very habitat which the tribe claims to be inviolable. In·justification of his decision, how-ever, the nomad patriarch may bring to our notice something gravely amiss with the alternative way of life displayed for his scrutiny. Behold, for instance, in Nairobi a sinister change from the time when his grandfather's herds and flocks used to water their stock and pitch their manyattas on the Engare Nairob. Today there dwells here a white tribe seeking wealth from the infertilities of concrete. Here these white people contrive riches for a few and pauperdom for many. Here again are young Africans seeking delinquency as an adventure in the stunted heritage of a jobless life! Here robbery has become the vocation of the needy and sin is hallowed by a new doctrine that the wealth of the rich, if not ill-gotten, is at least unredeemed by any precept that man is his brother's keeper; here little eleven-plus African girls without benefit of 'O' levels are propelled by hunger through an open gateway leading to life's 'oldest pro-fession'.

If Africa follows other under-occupied continents, the land hunger will pass before there is time to reconsolidate resettlement. The teenage scholar with 'O' levels will join another caste, a caste socially superior to the farming caste of his parents, and he will wish to farm no more. He will demand the town which he thought he had learned to hate or which his parents had directed him to hate. No doubt there will be some 'muckers-out', like the celebrated William Morris of Britain or like Gandhi of India, who will preach the doctrine of the village loom. I confess that I, too, am a villager rather than a city man and I like the social atmosphere of a village where everyone knows everyone else, by comparison with the atmosphere of a city where nobody knows even those who live in flats above, below or on either side of him.

But alas my examination of the problem convinces me that the village, while keeping men close together and close to the soil, also keeps them close to subsistence. If they come to crave for the toys and the glitter, the higher education for their children, the expensive treatments for illnesses, for pretty dresses and hard liquor, for the multi-machines that save labour in the home, for the joys of private motoring, for a spacious house and a lovely garden—if they *do* crave for these things, then the village loom won't do, for it is an expensive way of producing anything at all, and if you produce cheap cottons it means much work for a small income while if you produce gold-embossed silk saris as they do in Benares, then you are bound to become, like William Morris, a Socialist aiming at the needs of the poor but only succeeding in producing expensive arty-craftiness for the rich.

An inefficient factory system of this kind seems only to produce what Marx called proletarians, that is people whose only source of wealth is in their children—*proles*. It seems that restraint in procreation is a factor not of skill but of greater spending power and the growth of a spending appetite. I only wish it could be otherwise.

8. *Economic nationalism*

The fifty-seven non-aligned countries meeting in Cairo in October 1964 declared their conviction amongst other things that:

> Economic emancipation is necessary to secure elimination of political domination.
> Persistence of poverty is a threat to world peace.
> The fifty-seven have a duty to break through the barrier of under-development.
> All other nations have a similar duty.
> Existing institutions and policies have failed to reduce the disparity of income between the developed and developing nations.
> International economic co-operation is needed urgently on a basis of equality to correct this disparity by a new division of labour.

They did not formally endorse the following from President Nasser's opening speech as their Chairman:

> There are acute differences between the advanced and the under-developed states. These differences are felt the more because the under-developed people rightly believe that the prosperity of others was taken from them by the dreadful methods of imperialism.

These statements embody several flaws, the first of which has regard to the craving for absolute independence and unfettered sovereignty as a fundamental and inalienable right. But the last point is of special interest in the light of Mr. Harold Macmillan's pamphlet on the Common Market where he writes:

> The talk about loss of sovereignty becomes all the more meaningless when one remembers that practically every nation, including our own, has already been forced by pressure of the modern world to abandon large areas of sovereignty and to realise that we are now all interdependent. No country today, not even the giants of America or Russia, can pursue purely independent policies in defence, foreign affairs or the economic sphere.*

Personally I have never been convinced about the military menace to the rich of the poor and weak. It normally takes the powerful to challenge power, but I am an upholder of justice even in cases where justice does not at first sight point to peace.

The great obstacle to the co-operation which the fifty-seven demand is their insistence that it shall be on a basis of equality. President Nasser demanded co-operation without domination, (which ought to eliminate colonialism of all sorts including that of Russia and China), and without alms.

First as to equality. The fifty-seven consider 'that a new international division of labour is needed to hasten the industrialization of developing countries and the modernization of their agriculture, so as to enable them to strengthen their domestic economies and diversify their export trades'.

This is a really excellent paragraph but—exceptional cases like Palestine apart—the notion of *aid* evading the label of alms on the ground that it is merely a restitution of stolen property is arrant nonsense. If then it is a genuine trade based on some division of labour it is bound to be based on some degree of inequality. Mr. Macmillan in his Common Market pamphlet suggests a division of labour on the lines of sophisticated production, e.g. 'electronics, automatic equipment, computers, and supersonic flight' in the highly industrialized countries like our own and the simpler forms of conventional industry in the less highly industrialized states.

Whether any co-operation on these lines is ever possible seems to depend upon acceptance of differentials of many kinds and

* *Britain, the Commonwealth and Europe,* published by The Conservative and Unionist Central Office.

deciding one way or another which of the two following notions of trade is going to prevail:

Nigerian News Talk, May 26, 1964 (B.B.C. Monitoring Service):
Money given for building bridges, dams and industries, which in turn improves the living standard, should not be seen from the ideological eye. It is in this light that one can see the true significance of Mr. Khrushchev's visit. For the poor fellahin of Egypt we see in him and President Nasser the people who have freed them from the horror of starvation, hunger and want.

Cairo Home Service in Arabic, May 27, 1964:
Thirdly, economic imperialism, which has been trying, without military occupation or political domination, to achieve the aims of the imperialist states through infiltration and domination of financial institutions, means of production and natural resources in the independent countries.

9. *Hugger-muggery*

In England we speak of spacious living or gracious living as something to be envied. We pretend that the crowd-spattered beaches at Margate and Brighton are something we put up with when we cannot reach the spacious emptiness of Woolacombe bay. The precise truth of this may vary with different parts of the community, but we do seem on the whole to dislike an excess of persons to the available space; we avoid overloading our private motor cars; we do not sit one on top of the other in railway carriages or long-distance coaches or aircraft. Straphanging in tube and bus is tolerable only in the rush hour and for very short distances. But it is not like that in Negro Africa, where ten or twenty men may appear to be attempting a job more suitable for one and to be most unwilling to have their numbers reduced; where all transport seems packed out and sixteen persons will cram into a car to visit lions in the Nairobi National Park. The African Negro is 'homo gregalis'—he loves to be together—sleeping eight to a bedroom is not merely an economy for some it is even also an amenity. They want to think together and to think alike and to think aloud. Most of them would be unable to vote except as others vote. They could not vote secretly for they would suspect discovery of their secret thoughts, and they would be right because they cannot conceal from one another their secret thoughts. The opinion of the herd is the opinion of all. Just as myriads of starlings all wheel together in flight so do Africans; but the African glossy starling is not like that so I must

seek another simile, and I am reminded that at a certain season
of the year the wildebeeste (or brindled gnu) of the Serengetti
Plains assemble together so that there may be as many as a
quarter of a million altogether in a great assembly before they
swish their tails, toss their quaint heads and all go off somewhere
on safari together—perhaps to some distant saltlicks. This trait
is very African.

The French have a proverb, '*du choc des opinions sort la verité*'
or 'truth emerges from controversy'. But Negroes don't seem to
like it, and so they are very suitable raw material for 'the big
bully with the block vote' and their togetherness, while excellent
for trade union bargaining purposes, is conducive to inefficiency
in matters economic.

10. *God jolts, man jogs*

In most parts of the world the broken pieces of earthenware pots
form the time-pieces or calendars of history. Archaeologists in
our time have ceased to throw them away at least until they
have made a note of the time or the date, for the shape of earthenware pots is changed at least every fifty years. In parts of East
Africa however the rate at which African design changes its
pattern seems to the naked eye to be much slower. Like the
house-martins which build always the same kind of nest under
the eaves of our houses, so the Masai always seem to build the
same kind of Manyatta. As bees always construct the same kind
of comb so the Dorobo always seem to collect honey in the same
kind of way. Mr. Kenyatta describes the building of a Kikuyu
hut—it seems to have been always round and always the same:
'What our fathers did is good enough for us' is the authority for
meeting every challenge, and the Swahili word for it is *desturi* =
custom.

In India today demonstration is bringing about a change of
custom in a country deeply rooted in tradition. For instance, a
paddy farmer in Maharashtra had installed a plant for turning
cow dung into gas; if such gas is used for cooking it saves the
burning of dung, and the dung used for making the gas is still
available for use on the land without loss of manurial value. We
asked if they liked it for cooking. 'Let the women answer,' said
the head of the family. I asked the senior woman who replied,
'I don't like it,' and turned to attend to her pots simmering away
on the glowing dung cake. Then I turned to a young and pretty

matron and asked her. She replied, 'It has the advantage of being very clean,' and she glanced at the other woman hoping that she had given no offence.

Again in much the same area twenty paddy farmers came to meet me for a conference—half of them Hindu, half Muslims. 'The Japanese have shown you how to plant in their way, and your government has given you irrigation—do you all plant the Japanese way now?'

'We do,' they all answered.

'Does the irrigated second crop grow as well as the monsoon crop?'

'The irrigation crop is more reliable and better than the monsoon crop.'

'What is the effect upon you all of two crops and better methods in the last two years since you have had these alterations?'

'The village moneylender has left the village and gone into commerce.'

'Is there room for further progress?'

'Japanese families are coming to take over new land for five years and we shall learn more from them.'

By contrast a District Officer from Machakos in Kenya told me of the resistance to contour terracing in that area: 'We got many African cultivators to do it, but then one of their politicians visited England. On his return he said to all and sundry, "You have been misled—the Wazungu do not terrace their land in Ulaya—they are imposing on you with false husbandry theories." This indeed illustrates the dead weight of *desturi* in a country whose leaders wish it to develop fast.'

There is another millstone hanging round the neck of Africa, and it is summed up in the Swahili expression *shauri ya Mungu* = act of God. Of course there are examples with a counterpart in Europe. The home help who breaks the crockery in England will say, 'It broke in my hands,' while in Africa he will say, 'Shauri ya Mungu.' But when something goes wrong with our existence at home, be it a sick animal, or the car misfiring, or the potatoes turning black, or a smoky chimney, or the groceries beginning to run out, we 'do something about it'; few who have dealt with Africans have failed to notice how often the spirit of 'shauri ya Mungu' seems to exempt them from trying to 'do something about it'. It will be one of the obstacles in a developing country, for it is apt to become an excuse for every sort of carelessness.

MAHARAJA'S WELL

'. . . Justice is as clear as the midday sun and
truth cannot be hidden.'

(Somali poem.)

'Truth lives at the bottom of a well.'

(Popular proverb.)

Three years have passed since I promised a number of Kenya
'constituents' that I would remain a silent senator no longer, but
would comply with their request to 'say what you think but in
any case say it'. Since that time they have ceased to be my
'constituents'.

I started with a tale of two cities when Mombasa, the 'Rome'
of the Kenya coastal strip, was about to pass finally under the
dominion of Nairobi, the highland 'Carthage'. During the sittings
of a one-man commission appointed to report on the coast, the
'Carthaginians' uttered uncouth threats whereas the sultan of
'Rome' conceded with good grace his unchallenged legal title in
deference to the new and very proper priority, the wishes of
the people.

In pursuance of self-determination's priority over legal title
Kenya was accorded the very valuable harbour of Kilindini and
the ocean terminal at Mombasa of the railway built to serve
Uganda and now serving a part of Tanganyika too. Had the
people been waving flags for the sultan there might well have
been another Punic War for the 'Carthaginians' are among the
upholders of a double standard. The railway is one which would
have been scrapped long ago by some forerunner of Dr. Beeching
but for the conspicuous achievements of the white settlers.

Almost before I had been reminded of the Goans by the beauty
of one of them in Mombasa Cathedral, Goans everywhere
suffered a major disaster. The government of India under peace-
loving Jawaharlal Nehru, whose detestation of violence I have

heard him declare, marched their armed forces into the tiny four-hundred-year-old Portuguese territory of Goa. They swallowed its modest well-being down into the belly of an India whose poverty still bears the needless burden of the ox that may not be slaughtered and the man who may never rise above the contaminations of his shadow.

Perhaps it was a case of poetic justice that this wanton aggression had no sooner been consummated with the approval of the United Nations than India's great neighbour, already an imperialist trespasser in Tibet, invaded India as well. In a matter of days India's unprepared forces were overwhelmed by the adventurers from Peking, who then withdrew, taking with them the Eastern crown which had until then rested on the brows of Mr. Nehru. The victors left behind them a new burden of armaments on the poor of India and mounting friction with the brethren of Pakistan.

Under Mr. Nehru's successor India has made her *amende* by receiving the Pope as a popular and honoured guest. The time may come when Goans will discover that their sacrifice and their faith together have started a new and happier era for Christian Indians throughout all India. Certainly for most Goans that will be 'paradise enow!'

In the polemics of the Afro-Asian world, the military defeat of Mr. Nehru, even though it occurred only along a debatable line of frontier, was followed by the eclipse of India in another continent as Mr. Chou En-lai of China made a triumphal tour of African states.

In 1962 and 1963 I tried without success to stop the 'Mother of the free' from throwing some of her 'less important' African children to the wolves in her haste to dismantle her colonial empire. Excessive haste went hand in hand with incompetence of administrative planning and absence of any training worthy of the name, so that many admirable constitutions are now on the way to becoming scraps of paper in the hands of the violent.

In the course of my efforts for justice I heard with indignation the leaders of my own country proclaiming the higher priority of expediency. I watched some of my 'constituents' knocking on many doors asking only for justice, but the only door that opened to give them what they asked was the door of the Kremlin.

Shortly after Kenya's independence the revolution touched off the next phase in its routine for transferring real power from the hybrids who negotiated independence to more extreme men charged with uprooting not only the slight overlay of European culture but the foundation of *all* traditional African culture.

According to information reaching me from a very reliable source, the 'mutinies' of January 1964 in the three East African territories were intended for the following September. The prompt action of Her Majesty's Government quelled the mutinies without any difficulty and so restored the military situation. Bloodshed was prevented everywhere except in Zanzibar, where Arab/Negro tensions are much the same as in the Sudan but where numerical superiority is with the Negroes. It is not clear why this most explosive area was allowed to explode and why the lunatic fringe of the revolution was permitted to wallow in Arab blood when the massacres could have been nipped in the bud by an adequate force which was ready, waiting and wanting to go in. Perhaps in another fifty years we shall know why Britannia looked on with folded arms. Is it that only white men are worthy of rescue?

But the men of blood have achieved something more than a 'little Cuba' in Zanzibar. The vitriol of the revolution has nearly replaced the smile of President Julius Nyerere in Tanzania. In Kenya a robust and prudent common sense in the convicted manager of Mau Mau seems to stand as a barrier against the full force of the revolution, but he is certainly aware of its progress. Politically the revolution is gaining ominously in power, for the Mzee is old and the revolution occupies posts where its preparations are in hand for a take-over. The Kamba remain however at the root of law and order, always supposing that Kenya's imprudent colonialism does not saddle the forces of order with a revolt in the distant desert when they are most needed to displace some politician's private army in 'Carthage' itself.

Meanwhile the Mzee is altering the constitution so as to deprive the regions of their powers and the central government of organized opposition. A one-party state was launched on December 12, 1964, and Mr. Odinga found it prudent to remind the martial tribes of their apprehensions, which clearly remain unchanged since they gave evidence before the Regional Boundaries Commission in 1962 (Cmnd. 1899):

MINISTER GIVES LAND PLEDGE

When Kenya became a Republic no one would have his land taken away from him, the Minister for Home Affairs, Mr. Odinga, told meetings in the Western Region. Some people had been spreading rumours, he said, that the Luo and Kikuyu would take away land from other tribes. People should not listen to such rumours.

The need for British aid to extend the dispossession of white farmers is still a brake on the chariot wheel of the revolution, but when that process is further advanced the landless will still clamour for land, probably Masai land. If Mr. Odinga is not then as good as his word, it is not they who are likely to fade from the scene but Mr. Odinga.

By contrast with Kenya and Tanzania, the Baganda and the Somalis have merited the tribute paid to their intelligence by Sir Charles Eliot sixty years ago.

Quite apart from her domestic mutiny, Uganda has had to cope with the consequences of violence in her neighbouring states —in the Congo civil war, in the Sudan rebellion of the African South against the Arab North, in Rwanda tribal warfare. This I understand means no less than thirty thousand refugees from the Sudan and an unspecified number from elsewhere, with all such movements bringing in their train an atmosphere of declining respect for human life as tens of thousands of Africans are killed by other Africans.

The misfortunes of a few white men in Africa have now to be seen against the vast canvas of tragedy let loose by black men against black owing to resolution 1514 of the United Nations, owing also to the Belgians with their 'Uhuru in haste' in the Congo, and in a lesser degree to ourselves with our legacies of black colonialism. In December 1964 the African President of the Congo put the total of Africans killed in the Congo by African rebels, many of them also tortured, at eighty thousand. In these circumstances there has been a robust stability in democratic Uganda, notwithstanding the disintegration of three states with which she shares a common frontier and the advance of totalitarianism in two others. Moreover her diplomatic situation is most difficult: she cannot conceal her sympathy with the Negroes of the southern Sudan who are in rebellion against their Arab rulers in Khartoum, yet her rebellious friends have set up their headquarters in Leopoldville under the government of Mr. Tshombe, who is regarded as an outlaw by all the non-aligned countries, including Uganda.

The new state of Somalia has had trials of a different order. Across her frontiers there dwell, not aliens but brother Somalis.

In the north, France retains her colonial control over a small but important portion of the Somali nation. Ethiopia has chosen the years of freedom for Africa to enforce for the first time her jurisdiction over one-third of the Somali nation, to wit, the Ogaden province; her emperor even chose the visit of the West German president to Ethiopia in November 1964 for a speech delivered in Asmara on the inviolability of dismemberment! Happily the president of the West German Bundestag addressed the Somali National Assembly a few days later in an exactly opposite sense, declaring that Germany and Somalia must stand together for peace and the unity of their divided nations.

The Somalis have had to cope with a betrayal by Britain, a revolt in their Habash-occupied province of Ogaden, shifta operations in their Kenya-occupied province of N.F.D. and frontier aggressions by the regular Habash army. They are still democratic; they still have a number of political parties; although the same party has been returned to power at the general elections, an internal reshuffle at the instigation of the president has brought forth a new administration.

Somalis have great internal problems in many fields. Their cultural overlays during the colonial period are not one but four, with four different legal codes, four different languages, four different currency systems and all applied with differing degrees of inefficiency to a scattered population still eighty per cent nomadic. Somali nomads are still much like what the Scots were for many centuries, a community of rival clans where the clan often counts for more than the nation.

Somalis are naturally part of African Africa rather than Arab Africa. The anti-islamic and totalitarian bent of Amharic emperors are decisive barriers to the closer association of Somalis with Galla and other Ethiopian peoples who are their cousins and, in many cases, fellow-Muslims; their dispositions, therefore, after independence were to turn southwards with a view to closer relations with the Negro states of British East Africa particularly, so I understood from Dr. Shermarke, Uganda. The sorry business of the N.F.D. looks like directing their interest towards the north, where they may be dragged into three quarrels which have nothing to do with them—the Arab-Israel quarrel, the Anglo-Egyptian quarrel and the quarrel between the two halves of the Sudan.

Of greater relevance to Somalis will be the impact of a growing

o

perception inside the dark empire that there is Uhuru everywhere except in Ethiopia. When the present emperor's skill and cunning are withdrawn from the helm of his one-man administration, vast dangers seems likely to threaten even the survival of the 'superior' Amharic race and its Solomonid dynasty.

Matters such as these are of importance to Britain as a world power, and the miasma of detachment from Africa to which the ex-colonial powers have been brought by the cunningly contrived litany of the revolution will presently pass away. We are collectively concerned that people whether black, brown, yellow or white should live their own lives politically without domination by others. This is mere prudence even on the lowest basis of our own self-interest, for it seems that not only great and powerful states may acquire the weapons of mass extermination but even quite small communities may be able to acquire them too.

Here I follow the catalogue of available weapons of mass destruction as set out by my kinsman Philip Noel-Baker in his Nobel Peace Prize book *The Arms Race*. He starts with what we all know, namely that in 1945 the 'A' bomb was dropped on Hiroshima. A hundred thousand persons were killed. Another hundred thousand persons were injured and fifty thousand houses were destroyed.

Since Hiroshima there has been great 'progress' in nuclear destructive power, as *The Arms Race* indicates:

> . . . If a ten megaton bomb *clean* or *dirty* should be dropped everything would be destroyed by blast or burnt, and few human beings would survive within a circle of more than twenty miles across.

It looks then as though one of these bombs, even a 'clean' one, could be sufficient to put an end to London or New York. Perhaps the bomb will be banned after all, and we may then have to deal with the 'lesser' weapons which are available to us.

If we have no bomb we can for instance revert to fire. In 1943 the R.A.F. punished Hamburg with fire. In 1945 United States bombers did even worse to Tokyo with fire and *The Arms Race* states:

> They burned fifteen square miles of city to the ground. Eighty-three per thousand persons, most of them civilians, perished in the flames.

If we could ban fire, how safe would we be then? *The Arms Race* gives its answer in terms of biological warfare:

Any number of millions of human beings can be killed in a few hours by methods now available . . . one really competent biologist working in a small laboratory could prepare enough to be decisive in a war against any country.

So it does not seem possible any longer for a large country to buy peace with security simply by throwing the children to the wolves, for even the least of these may have 'one really competent biologist'.

President Johnson of U.S.A. declared (B.B.C. December 3, 1964) that the danger of war is present so long as Germany remains forcibly divided. That is still the big man's nightmare, for Germany is a great power, but can we be sure that even the great are safe while the small remain enslaved? The Germans, now in sackcloth and ashes as penitent ex-imperialists, have acquired a broader conception of political justice and of the dangers of suppressing it. I take the following from *The German View*, Volume 5, No. 20, October 21, 1964:

Soviet Russia's policy on German unity is a threat to free men everywhere.

Since the end of the Second World War the right of nations to self-determination has become accepted throughout the world.

Thus, for instance, 18 states formerly under British rule have claimed this right and have gained their independence, 23 have separated from France, three from Belgium, one from the United States and one from Holland.

It is therefore quite natural that the Federal Republic should also demand that this right must be granted to all Germans.

This demand is in accordance with the United Nations resolution No. 1514 (XV) of December 14, 1960, which states:

All peoples have the right to self-determination; by virtue of that right they freely determine their political status and freely pursue their economic, social and cultural development. (paragraph 2)

Any attempt aimed at the partial or total disruption of the national unity and the territorial integrity of a country is incompatible with the purposes and principles of the Charter of the United Nations. (paragraph 6)

Although the Soviet Union agreed to the above United Nations resolution, she continues to deny the right of self-determination to the German people and thus prevents Germany from reuniting in freedom.

It is not widely enough known that the Soviet Union denies this right to the German people not only in practice, but also in principle.

The now-deposed Mr. Khrushshev said on June 12, 'that the principle of self-determination cannot be applied to Germany and has nothing to do with reunification of Germany.'

Lenin had already said on January 20, 1918: 'The interests of socialism must have priority over the peoples' rights to self-determination.'

The Soviet Union has in its own sphere of interest set itself wherever possible against the principle of self-determination. Whereas many states throughout the world have gained their freedom on the basis of this right, the Soviet Union on the contrary has since the war destroyed the independence and the right to existence of whole nations.

She has annexed Esthonia, Latvia and Lithuania; in 1953 the Soviet Army crushed the people's uprising in the Soviet-occupied zone of Germany; in 1956 she crushed the revolt of Hungary. She has taken away from Czechoslovakia the Carpathian Ukraine and from Poland a third of her pre-war territory, although she was not at war with these states.

Even Mao Tse-tung said recently in a discussion with Japanese socialists: 'There are too many territories which have been occupied by the Soviet Union . . . they have taken over part of Rumania, they have separated parts of East Germany and have driven out the population there and forced them into the western part.'

They have taken away part of Poland and incorporated it into the Soviet Union. And as a compensation for this, parts of East Germany have been given to Poland.

The same thing has taken place in Finland. They have taken away everything which could be taken away . . .(*Pravda*, September 2, 1964).

The treatment which the Soviet Union has meted out to the German people and to other peoples in Eastern Europe in the question of self-determination should be a warning to the whole world. What has happened here, what is still happening, can happen to other nations. All those who value their own independent national existence and their right to self-determination must reject the Soviet Union's policy on Germany.

I call attention to the dictum of the revolution itself that the 'wishes of the people' are not to be accorded top priority save as a means of inaugurating the revolution itself when there is no other way. When the revolution already occupies the seat of power by reason of a popular vote, it must retain that power by eliminating the popular vote either directly or by proscribing any other party. In Africa they call this the method best suited to Africa. Happily not all Africa is this way inclined, and I quote in contrast from President Osman's special message to the meeting of O.A.U. in Cairo, July, 1964:

We must above all beware of accepting double standards. Those principles which we accept as necessary to eliminate colonialism are right and just, and they will continue to be right and just long after the last vestige of colonialism has been driven from our shores, so that we must never abandon them for temporary advantages of political expediency.

And the following B.B.C. monitoring of a broadcast from Lagos on February 8, 1965, has a bearing on the matter too:

In his tribute to the memory of Dr. Danquah, the well-known Ghanaian journalist and statesman who died in a detention camp last week, Dr. Azikiwe, the President of Nigeria, said: 'I am sorry that Dr. Danquah died in a detention camp. I am of the considered opinion that if independence means the substitution of indigenous tyranny for alien rule, then those who struggled for the independence of former colonial territories have not only desecrated the cause of human freedom but have betrayed their people. I wish Dr. Danquah had been tried publicly, told what offence he was alleged to have committed, given a fair opportunity to defend himself, and then either discharged or punished, depending upon the fact whether or not his innocence had been established or his guilt proved beyond any reasonable shadow of doubt.'

Dr. Azikiwe's observations do not apply to Ghana only. They may as well be applied to the situation in most independent African States today.

Today there are 35 independent African States. Of these, only in five States—Nigeria, Senegal, Morocco, Somalia and Uganda—do opposition parties enjoy full freedom of speech and assembly. In others the opposition parties have been liquidated through governmental oppression. In four States there were even undenied allegations of the mass execution of opposition leaders (?by firing squad).

Having also read what Mao Tse-tung has to say of Soviet imperialism, we await a confession of the Chinese People's Republic's sins in Tibet.

Perhaps I have devoted too much space to this question of self-determination both inside my small chosen region and in the world at large beyond it. My excuse must be that infringement of the principle has been one of the danger beacons blazing throughout the half century of my own adult life. I note that fear of being robbed of our share in this inalienable right is why we cling to the appalling deterrent. If we can take so appalling a risk to safeguard our own freedom how can we call ourselves honourable men if we tolerate in silence the continued deprivation of the same freedom for others who have an equal right to it?

Freedom frustrated is also one of the main impediments to the growth of those greater economic unities, which are pregnant in these days with a vision of pauperdom being brought to an end throughout the entire planet.

It is to this vision of world plenty that I must now turn. The African continent as a whole is so agriculturally immature that it looks at a glance to be capable of producing food, clothing and housing for a population many times greater than it at present holds. By and large it is still 'sparsely populated and miserably cultivated'. The inland highlands of my region have a superfluity of rain with many rivers which become earth-ripping torrents during the wet season while the lowlands have too little rain and their rivers rarely run at all.

Indigenous husbandry in the highlands is of a low standard, making much less than full use of the abundant rainfall and soil fertility, while desert husbandry excels in the use of terrain that many would describe as waterless, though its capacity for reaching well-water is undeveloped. So the first two ingredients of African welfare are better husbandry and more water. Since water must arrive ahead of tillage, it is of water that I want first to speak. A convenient starting point is the plea of a delegation of Turkana tribesmen making their representations to the Regional Boundaries Commission in 1962 (page 61 of that Report):

> The Turkana have no rain and would be happy to be linked with any region where there is rain.

In greater or lesser degree this shortage of water is felt in more than half of Kenya and more than three-quarters of the Somali Republic.

I know the Turkana district. Its two rivers, the Turkwell and the Kerio, typical of Africa, run above ground for no more than two weeks in fifty-two. For the rest of the time they hold water below ground. The rivers discharge into Lake Rudolf which has no outlet. There *is* rain and I have seen first-rate grazing, but forty years have gone by since then, and perhaps they too have suffered the fate of the Samburu—overstocking may well have destroyed their habitat. Turkana is now a problem land, and I do not pretend to know if it can be handled productively; remembering those lava deserts I should think as to most of it probably not.

Mr. Drysdale (*The Somali Dispute*) writes of a part of the Somali Republic one and a half times the size of England:

> The Northern Plateau, about five hundred miles wide and between a hundred and two hundred miles in depth has no river.

The plateau in question gets some rain but the rain washes the soil into muddy ridges where it cakes and is presently blown away into dust, awaiting another washing to be moved once more into further unstable shapes.

The Somali Republic has two main rivers and a coastline of exceptional length. As to the latter, the nuclear age while placing in man's hands the power to depopulate and contaminate a large part of our total habitat does equally offer the prospect of cheap fresh water and power almost without limit and merely from the oceans. From *The Arms Race* I again quote:

> The total amount of deuterium available in the oceans is so enormous that if its energy could be released under control, as that of uranium has been, it would provide many times the present rate of world energy consumption for more than a thousand million years. (Page 97.)

Again:

> Since nuclear fuel is so light and easy to transport it may bring power to remote and under-developed countries which have no oil or coal. (Page 115.)

Again:

> Another application would be for irrigation . . . in Africa . . . vast tracts of land could be made fertile if power were made available for pumping water from the wells. Also in places where no fresh water is available sea water could be distilled with the off-stream of power stations situated on the coast. (Page 115.)

The difficulties to be overcome are very great. Here is a succinct account of them:

> 'Thermo-nuclear burning,' says Professor Spitzer, 'occurs only at enormous temperatures—above one hundred million degrees Fahrenheit. To convert . . . deuterium . . . into useful power we must achieve such temperature. . . .' (Page 114.)

There follows a prediction that Australia should be able to get distilled sea water for irrigation at five shillings a million gallons and to develop her agriculture to sustain a population of two hundred million persons.

So dazzling is this prospect that I wrote to Sir John Cockcroft, asking in effect 'how near are we to all this today?' In his reply dated October 23, 1964, he wrote:

1. Whether or not the deuterium in sea-water could be used for a source of nuclear power?

The answer to this is that intensive research is proceeding in the major countries with a view to ultimately solving the problem of the application of deuterium to power development. This, however, is a very long-term project, and it is unlikely that practical results will be achieved before twenty years.

2. Whether or not nuclear power could be used to assist in the desalination of sea-water so that this water could then be used for irrigation?

The Americans are at the present time actively interested in this possibility, and we are to a somewhat lesser extent, since we regard it as a fairly long-term project. The proposal is that nuclear power stations of a very large output of the order of 500,000 kws. output, might use their surplus heat to either distil sea-water or to remove the salt by other chemical engineering methods.

I do not think that any large-scale plant of this kind is likely to come into operation before 1975. It might well first be installed in a country like Israel, which is very advanced technically and in need of water.

Short though twenty years may be in the seven thousand years of recorded human history that have gone by, and even shorter in the one thousand million years of limitless power if we do not choose rather to destroy ourselves, it is a period not to be spent in marking time, for husbandry is not a matter of water alone. Good animal management may have improved indigenous beasts five to tenfold in Kenya over fifty years, but it does not follow that the kind of beast which prospers above five thousand feet will prosper equally below three thousand feet—further pro- longed experiments will certainly be necessary. The hybriding and stabilization of a single successful hybrid plant may take many years, and meanwhile populations do not cease to increase and to demand higher and higher standards of living. Fortunately husbandry, too, is on the move, and at such a pace that the old

16. *Happy warrior (from Turkana—Kenya's own and poorest desert).*

17. Snapshot showing the Governor of Lower Juba seated between the author and his wife on the occasion when the author, without any prior 'warning', was made Freeman of the Somali port of Kismayu.

law of agricultural 'diminishing returns' must take a lower place than was formerly supposed.

So while waiting for deuterium to be brought under control I have sought information of the water resources survey in Kenya made not long ago by the World Bank. One of a number of white farmer settlers who, even after seeing for themselves the shortcomings of African settlement schemes, decided to stay on wrote in the autumn of 1963 some notes to help me in a House of Lords debate:

> Further change of land ownership in the ex-scheduled areas [this is a technical term for the former white highlands] will not contribute significantly to Kenya's economy. Therefore there must be a major effort in the high potential areas in the non-scheduled areas, which are mainly in Masai land and comprise about seventy per cent of the total high potential land in Kenya. Persuading the Masai to rent, lend, sell or develop their land makes the problem of trying to strike a safety match on a cake of soap seem simple. However, it must be done and efforts are under way.

Following this forthright report, my correspondent suggests a sensible land policy. He gives three conditions for success. One: large scale farms; two: capital from British taxpayers; three: efficient and sufficient extension service, that is vets and teams of established experts something like our present Agricultural Advisory Service, but perhaps with more of the authority of a War Agricultural Committee. He writes of existing African large farms, of which he says there are more than two hundred in the former white highlands:

> Recently I saw some African large-scale farms in the Kiambu district (presumably the Kikuyu area) which compared well with the best in Kenya, and I have just done a limited tour in the Uasin Gishu to see African farmers up there. The best are doing very well, but lean heavily on the extension service and realise it. Two were virtually illiterate (one had been a contractor and the other a farm employee) and the third was an ex-soil conservation assistant. Nevertheless, all had increased the productivity of their farms. I would like to emphasise here the difference in outlook between a successful farmer and the large and vociferous numbers of the frustrated and unsuccessful. These men had a pride in their job, themselves and their country. Given reasonable chances they will be excellent and contributive citizens. The really successful ones are estimated to be about thirty per cent only, and while this is not as high as could be wished, it demonstrates clearly that Africans can

make good large-scale farmers. (Two were Elgeyo and one a Nandi.)

Seventy per cent failure in the first year is indeed an excessive proportion of failures. Reading between the lines, it is not surprising to find matters worse at the end of another year. I quote from the *Daily Telegraph* of October 14, 1964:

NAIROBI

The majority of Africans who took over large-scale mixed farms from Europeans under settlement schemes are rapidly running out of money and experience. Many of the four hundred farms are in such a state of deterioration that they are in danger of being taken over by the government as mismanaged or semi-abandoned.

And from *The Times* of January 19, 1965:

KENYA FARMS LESS EFFICIENT
From our Correspondent
NAIROBI, January 18.

Half a million acres of Kenya's best farming land is reaping only one-third of the profit for African farmers that it reaped for European farmers who were bought out by the government in the recent land shake-up. Mr. Murgor, assistant Minister of Agriculture, revealed this to a gathering of African farmers near Eldoret 200 miles northwest of here during the weekend.

He said there were nearly 500 new large-scale African-owned farms in the Rift Valley region and the number was increasing daily. He gave a warning to farmers that all their farms were situated in the main grain and milk-producing areas of Kenya and any rundown in efficiency of those farms meant a rundown in the internal economy of Kenya. He added: 'What is extremely important at the moment is that this rundown will lead to a worsening of the already critical unemployment situation.'

Although Africanization of developed farmland is not wrong in itself, yet clearly the speed of transfer from the skilled white farmer to the African non-farmer has been unnecessary and imprudent. This is political agriculture which has never yet produced a good crop in any country.

The nomads of the low potential regions who ask merely for rain will not be edified by the squandering mismanagement of high potential land at the cost of the British taxpayer. This is *not* the way to raise the poor from their poverty, and I cannot refrain from hoping that the Portuguese, the Rhodesians and the South

Africans will take a full thirty years to establish a yeoman African farming community, skilled, responsible, content and fraternal. In farming, at any rate, we have gone too fast in our appeasement of the revolution, and we run the risk of debauching agricultural holdings just as prescribed by the revolution itself.

For Somalis there are several bright prospects. One to which I was introduced in Mogadishu is a survey of water resources 'between the rivers'—that is between the River Shebelli and the Juba. It covers an area the size of England, and is being conducted by the Food and Agriculture Organization with a Canadian firm of contractors. Until the diplomatic breach R.A.F. photography was producing contour maps of the area in question.

From information given to me by the contractors—information which the Prime Minister accepted as valid and reliable and permitted me to impart to the Somali people in a radio talk—I learned of the strong probability of finding accessible water throughout this area, which could in the fullness of time be cultivated so as to sustain three or four times the total population of all Somalia as it is today. This was not the only scheme of which I heard, but it was the largest, and on its own could in the course of time transform an economy of unstable nomadism with agricultural adjuncts into an economy of settled cultivators with nomadic adjuncts.

Agricultural advances, however, can seldom be brought about by decree. Agriculture is often the revolution's *enfant terrible*. Here large-minded officials are apt to be swept away in a cloud of dust, and smallholding enthusiasts wake up to find that the co-operative marketing machinery has nothing to market. Irrigation planners forget the last mile where the channel should be maintained by the cultivator, but which is not in fact maintained by anybody. It may be that the water when it does arrive is too saline. As to crops, carefully cultivated bananas may turn out to have skins too thin for export, while stock diseases may be found to spread because the dipping has been neglected by some or the mixture is too diluted. I have known sprays which were fully effective in one environment to be totally ineffective in a different environment. There are parts where seed is regularly consumed in large quantities by vermin. Half-trained cultivators do many foolish things, such as putting the wrong fuel into fuel tanks and being totally unable to maintain their vehicles and machines.

Every relevant experiment is worthy of careful study for a country on the threshold of great agricultural changes like Somalia. There is a notably successful scheme between the White Nile and the Blue, of which Mr. Arthur Gaitskell, my Somerset neighbour, was in his time one of the best known managers. Somalis are no doubt studying the lessons of this gezira project. There are changes in India where research and experiment are intense at the present time; some results there are of extreme interest, as they are successful in doubling and trebling and even quadrupling yields. A Somali agricultural delegation was in India during my own visit in 1963, and Indian Ministers formed much the same impression of Somali intelligence as Sir Charles Eliot did sixty years ago.

The Aray milk colony in Bombay is a splendid example of combined cultivation, animal management, factory efficiency and swift delivery. If only Indians could officially cull a cow and change over from buffalo milk to graded cows . . . but it will come; Mr. N. K. Patil, Indian Minister for Agriculture, during my visit in 1962 said to us on this subject: 'Give us time! We don't want to offend everybody all at once.' I understood him to mean amongst other things that India had been given only the years since 1947 to put her house in order—such is the more splendid spirit of *Uhuru* where the date of independence in the mid-twentieth century is looked upon as the date when sleeping giants began to wake up and shake off the shibboleths of seven thousand years.

From water for agriculture we must turn to water for power; up to the present there is no indigenous coal, gas or oil in the region of my survey. There are two major sources of water power, the White Nile and the Blue. I am assured that the Owen Falls dam in Uganda was obsolescent on the day of its opening, but that the fall of the Nile within the boundaries of Uganda alone has a sufficient potential to export the power needs of Kenya as well as meeting increasing power needs in Uganda. The building of dams is expensive anywhere, more so in primitive industrial societies where productivity per unit of power is low.

The power potential of the vast gorges of the Blue Nile is still the subject of a prolonged survey by U.S.A.; when I last enquired about it from American sources, more money had been voted but no report had yet been published.

We cannot help being reminded here of Habash emperors who

thought they had the power to turn the Blue Nile away from
Egypt, and of the current medieval belief in Egypt that this was
no vain boast. There is even the case of Lalibela, the emperor
who started earthworks with the intention of depriving Egypt of
water but who abandoned them when his monks warned him
that the diversions would only serve to enrich the even more
objectionable Muslims of Adel!

I, who do not know the Blue Nile and who am still awaiting
the American report, can only refer to the Italian version of the
still inaccessible Maffey Report, which advised His Majesty's
Government on behalf of Egypt, for whom they were then responsible, to secure the waters of Lake Tana and a corridor to control
not only the waters of the Abbai but also other Nile tributaries
such as the Sobat—that is in the event of Ethiopia ceasing to be
independent. So it would seem that the setting up of a Nile
Waters conservancy in our time might be a prudent step to make
sure that no oversight leads to the medieval anxieties of Egypt
being realized in the twentieth century and thereby *inter alia*
bringing further obloquy on the head of Mr. Khrushchev. Meantime, promising traces of oil have been found in the captive
Somali province of Ogaden, and there are hopes too of a strike
in the captive Somali N.F.D. Is this, we must ask, the reason
for some of the double standards in Addis Ababa and Nairobi?
Let us hasten the day when deuterium will enable us to pour
water on troubled oils.

If indeed workable oil is found in the Somali deserts and we
sit by nourishing the predators in Addis Ababa and Nairobi,
the Somalis will have a new reason for throwing in their lot
with the oil kings of the Arab League, and then the dis-
pensers of poetic justice, whoever they may be, may deem
it more just that Her Majesty's Government should have less
oil.

Water is the pearl of great price in the land we have offended
by our injustice. Water, including sea water, looks likely to grow
in power and importance as oil reserves decline. For the present
it looks as though we have to make use of oil while it lasts to lift
the life-giving water from the bottom of wells. At the time when
The Arms Race was written in 1958, a mere six years ago, the
unexpired portion of the oil era was thought to be no longer
than seventy years. Since then there have been many new discoveries, and a geologist—who prefers not to be quoted as the

author of what he calls a 'wild guess'—thinks the era may be extended by as much as five hundred years.

Oil or no oil, seventy years or five hundred, the key to more abundant life in the Somali lands is more water. Lack of water is the annual nightmare which comes to brood over a parched land. John Drysdale writes of this:

> Although the menfolk and their camels can usually stand up to the severest drought, the lives of the weaker ones, the old and the infirm, the women and the children, may hang by a thread. A mother can be faced with the appalling choice of having to save herself or her infant child during a severe drought.

At the end of every jilal indeed the suffering prayers of almost the whole nation rise to Allah in a single sentiment: 'We thirst.' It is not a situation that we in England's 'green and pleasant land' can *feel*, even when the picture is drawn for us.

It was with a true instinct about the value of water, I have no doubt, that a former Maharajah of Benares, grateful for the service of an English tutor, decided to make a gift to England or rather to a small village in England where the tutor happened to have his home. This is the village of Stoke Row, in Oxfordshire, whose first supply of water was from a deep well sunk by the Maharajah a hundred years ago. Until lately when 'the mains' arrived, the Maharajah's well was their only supply of drinking water.

In May 1963 my wife and I were guests at breakfast with the reigning Maharajah at Fort Ramnagar on the Ganges. We promised to attend the centenary celebrations at Stoke Row, and accordingly we were present on a glorious summer day in 1964 when a red helicopter dropped upon the tip of a red carpet laid on Stoke Row's village green and Prince Philip descended nimbly from the cockpit to preside at the ceremonies. As part of the programme Prince Philip read the lesson which describes the episode of a Samaritan woman at another important well— Jacob's well. It is one of those lessons which underline the eastern origin of the Christian faith, and the Jewish, with its emphasis on water not only as a literal fertilizer and quencher of natural thirst but as a factor of supernatural cleansing, a symbol of spiritual regeneration and even in some sense a sisterhood with the Holy Ghost in man himself—'a fountain of water springing up into life everlasting'.

It was not by any naturally therapeutic properties that the leper General Naaman was healed of his leprosy after seven dips in the unimpressive River Jordan; nor in his case was Faith a pre-requisite of healing, for he entered the water in total incredulity.

The strange pool of Bethesda remained therapeutically inert until activated by an angel to effect a single cure from time to time, and the springs at Lourdes today are hardly less frugal in the matter of visible cures; we go there mostly like snakes to shed the skin of materialism which keeps us apart from God. But aside from water in special places, we are accustomed to signing ourselves with water every time we enter a church in any part of the world, and there is no entry for us at all into the Kingdom without the sacrament of water—Baptism.

The Hindus, so sweetly Christlike in the gentleness of their faith, have the same tender sensitivity to water, the water in their case being that of the great River Ganges. At the sunset hour on the waterfront at Benares the rhythmic beating of metal and the chanting of a hymn to the holy river mark the end of each panting day, while ashes of the dead are brought in urns by the devout from all over India to be mingled with waters touched by the Godhead. The devout Hindu woman can be seen in the streets carrying on her head with inimitable grace a brass vessel with water from the holy river, and during those centenary celebrations this year water from this same Ganges was mingled with water from the Maharajah's well in Stoke Row and taken in a brass vessel from the well to the altar of the Parish Church, while we listened again to a woman's puzzled question: From whence then hast thou living water? Art thou greater than our Father Jacob, who gave us the well and drank thereof, himself and his children and his cattle?

Here I remember that in one of his speeches Mr. Kenyatta was reported to have declared that the Bible would have to be re-written in a manner less provocative to Africans. We cannot seem to get away from colour! Since then I have searched the Old Testament for evidence of this and I have touched upon this problem in the chapter entitled 'Noah's Curse'. I notice also that parts of the wonderful 'Song of Solomon' seem to be slightly colour-conscious, where for instance the spouse says, 'my beloved is white and ruddy, chosen out of thousands' (Chapter 5), or when she apologizes for being dusky and blames the sun for it

(Chapter 1). However, Solomon's father David makes at least one notable act of reparation in Psalm 67 where he writes, 'scatter thou the nations that delight in wars. Ambassadors shall come out of Egypt: Ethiopia shall soon stretch out her hands to God.' Mr. Kenyatta declares that Africans who read this passage do so with great satisfaction: their satisfaction may well be all the greater when they perceive the claims of the Habash that all Ethiopian references in Holy Writ apply to them have no real validity, and that the term invariably has a broader application.

Scrutiny of the New Testament yields nothing until we come to The Acts, where there is the remarkable episode of a trusted and distinguished public servant in the household and service of Queen Candace of Kush (Meroe). He was on his way back from Jerusalem where he had come as a worshipping pilgrim. Surely a most perplexing episode! Here was another eunuch, not this time Captain of the Egyptian Army (refer to Potiphar) but Treasurer of the Nubian Queen, or perhaps a Chamberlain. For obvious reasons he was an uncircumcized person. He was a literate man, but who knows in what language? He was observed reading the Prophet Isaiah on some scroll—what scroll? In what language—Hebrew? He was moreover reading intelligently, notwithstanding the fact that he was riding in a chariot and the chariot was on the move. Most of us would find it most difficult and sick-making to read at all in a moving chariot. Then, when accosted by a total stranger, the great official asked for an explanation of a passage which, without some explanation, must have remained totally obscure. Where had he got this text? What made him read it and get as far as he did? Why was Jerusalem a holy place to him? After a short explanation from the deacon Philip, this eunuch of the Nubian Queen made a profession of faith with all the force which St. Peter had used earlier. Not till then did the chariot come to a halt, and it only halted for as long as was necessary to baptize the eunuch, who then went on his way rejoicing, having broken through the barrier of race, colour and circumcision all in a single interview, to be joined by baptism to the brotherhood of Christ.

After referring to my Scriptural critic I abandon further attempts, for he writes:

It is a hopeless task, if I may say so, trying to search out texts favourable to the southern nations in the Bible. The vast majority of the texts are unfavourable. Even in Isaiah's universalist passages,

the Ethiopians and Egyptians will be re-united with Israel as conquered enemies and not as equals. You are right, however, to mention
the Ethiopian chamberlain of Candace. Clearly The Acts try to
show how the universalist prophecies were fulfilled. Instead of
conquest, it is by the attraction of the Spirit of love. If there was
no Ethiopian at Pentecost, there had to be one in the story somewhere.

I reflect that just as Christianity had its origins in the Middle
East, so Our Lady was a Middle Eastern woman and probably
brown in colour. There are times when a pink and white plaster
statue of a bourgeois French lady seems needlessly provocative,
for instance in a mission chapel in the Kikuyu Reserve. But there
is the further reflection that only Kamba craftsmen are available
to produce indigenous representations, and they carve in wood
which is probably as near the true colour as you can get—on the
other hand all their female heads have a Kamba caste of counten-
ance, and there is no certainty that this tribal portraiture would
excite any more devotion amongst the Kikuyu.

Colour is so interwoven with our proverbs, our maxims and
our literature that perhaps the best solution after all is that of
some of my African friends, who express their gratitude to one
another in the settlers' jargon, 'Thanks so much, old boy, you're
a white man!'

British justice is a thing I have often been assigned to represent,
and seeing the injustice we have done to the Somalis, I know
that we ought to make amends, and I am in a state of discomfort
until we have done so. I do not expect protocol to allow Her
Majesty to acknowledge any miscarriage of justice: she will continue to issue free *pardons* to innocent men and make *ex gratia*
offerings in place of paying compensation. Very well, let it then
be a gift—a Maharajah's gift of water—for peace, the fruit of
justice, and in the name of God the merciful, the compassionate.

P

MAPS

KEY TO LANGUAGE MAP

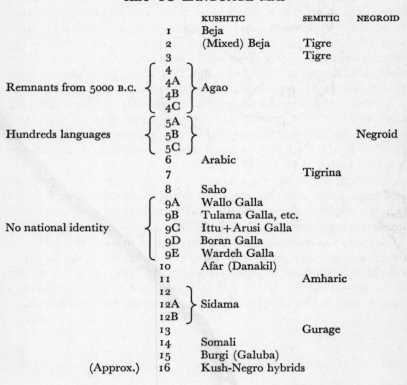

		KUSHITIC	SEMITIC	NEGROID
	1	Beja		
	2	(Mixed) Beja	Tigre	
	3		Tigre	
Remnants from 5000 B.C.	4 4A 4B 4C	} Agao		
Hundreds languages	5A 5B 5C	}		Negroid
	6	Arabic		
	7		Tigrina	
	8	Saho		
	9A	Wallo Galla		
	9B	Tulama Galla, etc.		
No national identity	9C	Ittu + Arusi Galla		
	9D	Boran Galla		
	9E	Wardeh Galla		
	10	Afar (Danakil)		
	11		Amharic	
	12 12A 12B	} Sidama		
	13		Gurage	
	14	Somali		
	15	Burgi (Galuba)		
(Approx.)	16	Kush-Negro hybrids		

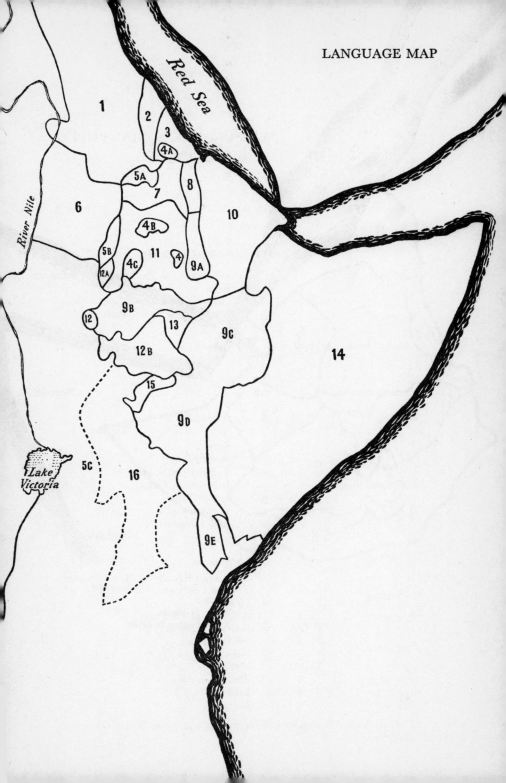

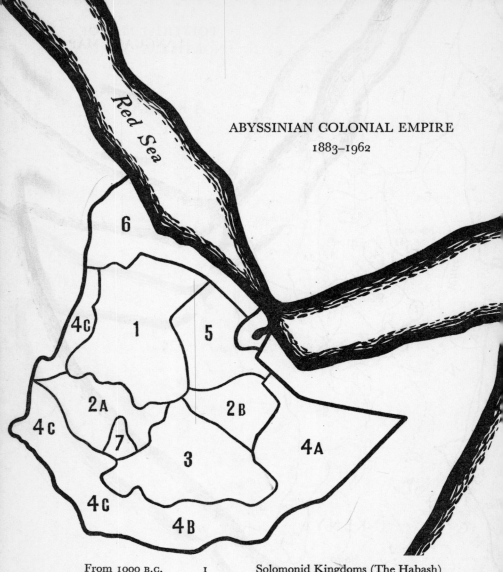

ABYSSINIAN COLONIAL EMPIRE
1883–1962

Red Sea

6

4c

1

5

2A

2B

4c

7

4c

3

4A

4c

4B

From 1000 B.C.	1	Solomonid Kingdoms (The Habash)
1883–1890 {	2A	Tuloma Galla etc.
	2B	Harar
1890–1895	3	Arusi Galla + Sidamo
1895–1900 {	*4A	Somali (Ogaden +)
	4B	Boran Galla
	4C	Negroid
	4D	Kaffa
1900–1935	5	Afar (Danakil)
1952–1962	6	Eritrea
1883–1933	7	Jimma

* Helped by five British expeditions, 1899–1920, and British control, 1941–1948.

POLITICAL MAP OF
NORTH-EAST AFRICA

ARABIA

R.Nile

Red Sea

R.Atbara

Khartoum

White

Blue

Massawa

YEMEN

Adowa

Assab   Aden

Gulf of Aden

Gondar

L.Tana

Magdala

Djibouti

Berbera

ETHIOPIA

Ankober

R.Hawash

Harar   Hargeisa

R.Sobat

Addis Ababa

SUDAN

R.Omo

R.Dawa

Ganale Doria

R.Shebeli

R.Fafan

SOMALIA

L.Rudolf

Moyale

Mandera

El Wak

Wajir

R.Juba

Mogadishu

Albert

UGANDA

KENYA

L.Victoria

Nairobi

R.Tana

Kismayu

Indian Ocean

Mombasa

N

TANZANIA

TANZANIA
(Zanzibar)

L.Tanzania

Dar-es-Salaam

0   100 200 300 Miles

APPENDIX 1

CENTENARY DIARY
THE SOMALI PROBLEM: 1864–1964

1. 1861–1865   American Civil War brings cotton prosperity to Egypt.

2. 1866   Germany overwhelms Austria and establishes herself as a first-class European power.

3. 1868   Great Britain spends the year invading Abyssinia from India: *Casus belli*—minor diplomatic muddle caused by G.B. herself. G.B. Forces destroy the Emperor Theodore in one battle. G.B. combines diplomatic mishandling with first-class military efficiency.

4. 1869   Chef d'œuvre of the Khedive Ismail—French engineer completes construction of Suez Canal, thus converting the Red Sea from a cul-de-sac into a main seaway.

5. 1870   The French are defeated by the new 'knight in shining armour' i.e., Germany, and robbed of two provinces in Europe. They seek compensation in Africa by extending French settlements in Algeria (conquered 1830), assimilating Algeria as part of metropolitan France and later extending their control into Morocco.

6. 1870   Italians achieve National Unity and find a place in the African sun at Assab (port on the Danakil coast of Eritrea).

7. 1871   Verdi's *Aïda* first performed in Cairo to celebrate the opening of the Suez Canal.

8. 1874   The sultan's Egyptian viceroy extends Turkish rule inland from Massawa (port for Tigre portion of Eritrea) also to Harar and the Somali coast along the Gulf of Aden to Guardafui.

9. 1875   G.B.'s Disraeli acquires from the Sultan's insolvent

220

Egyptian viceroy a majority shareholding in the Suez Canal Company (French), for the government of G.B.

10. 1878   Russo-Turkish War culminates in Congress of Berlin where an 'honest broker' (Bismarck) presides, and the disposal of the African Estates of the 'sick man of Europe' (Turkey) is promoted with smooth diplomacy enabling Disraeli to bring back 'peace with honour' and Cyprus as 'baksheesh' from the sick man's bed.

11. 1881–1885   The Small French Somaliland is established with the port of Djibouti, and a railway from Djibouti to Addis Ababa is planned.

12. 1882   G.B. invades Egypt—defeats patriot army under Arabi Pasha in one battle and 'restores order' in the name of the sultan who has no desire for such restoration of order, and has already decorated Arabi. G.B. remains as 'Trustee' of Egypt in the name of the sultan.

13. 1883   G.B. is defeated by the Mahdists—Hicks at El Obeyd.

14. 1884   G.B. again defeated by the Mahdists—Gordon at Khartoum.

15. 1885   Italy occupies (with approval of G.B.) part of the sultan's Egyptian Estate Massawa, of which G.B. is 'Trustee'. This has been Turkish since the sixteenth century, not Ethiopian as frequently alleged by the Emperor Haile Selassie.

16. 1885–1900   Italy occupies Benadir (otherwise known as Italian Somaliland) with the approval of Great Britain.

17. 1887   Italy is defeated by the Emperor John (successor of Theodore).

18. 1889   The Emperor John is killed by the Mahdists in the hour of Abyssinian victory, whereupon the victory passes to the Mahdists.

19. 1889   Menelek II succeeds John. (Menelek I is legendary son of Solomon King of Israel, and Belkis Queen of the Habashat or Sheba.)

20. 1889   The Italians negotiate the Treaty of Ucciali with Menelek; the Protectorate which they claim thereunder for the whole of Ethiopia is recognized by all the powers, but not by Menelek.

21. 1883–1900   Menelek, first as King of Shoa then from 1889 Negus Negasti, raises a large standing army, conquers an Empire (largely Galla), making Ethiopia four times the size of Abyssinia, 'abolishes' slavery but himself

enslaves (Leviticus as authority) more free men than any previous emperor.

22. 1890–1900   G.B. occupies Northern Somaliland (to keep others out), Uganda (to protect the source of the White Nile from less scrupulous exploiters) and Kenya (communicating corridor between the Indian Ocean and the source of the White Nile).

23. 1896   Menelek, prompted by the French and well supplied with arms by both the French and Italians, denounces the so-called Protectorate and Treaty of Ucciali.

24. 1896   At Adowa Menelek defeats the Italians with heavy losses on both sides. The Treaty of Ucciali is thereafter scrapped.

25. 1896–1898   G.B. conquers the Sudan in order to secure the whole length of the White Nile. The Northern Sudan is Hamitic, or possibly even Arabian, and certainly Mohammedan, and is known in history as Nubia, or Ethiopia (the Abyssinians have misappropriated the name of Ethiopia for themselves). Today the Southern Sudan (four million) is pagan Nilotic Negro (half a million recent Christian converts). The Sudan was conquered by Egypt in 1820–22, and from 1883 to 1906 Mahdi after Mahdi rose up to struggle for independence once more.

26. 1898   Desecration of the Mahdi's tomb. His remains are scattered on the Nile like those of Joan of Arc on the Seine some centuries earlier.

27. 1898   Fashoda Incident. France is squeezed out of the Nile Valley.

28. 1891   G.B. in effect conducts the major dismemberment of the Somali Nation—the only large homogeneous region of Africa. They consist of one race (Hamitic in blood, Semitic in culture)—one name, Somali (compare Galla which is a name for a group of separate peoples); one spoken language, Somali; one written language, Arabic; one religion, Islam; one variety of Islam, Sufi; one method of applying Islamic law; one economy, pastoral and nomadic. The worst feature of this partition is the allocation of one-third of the population to a debased Abyssinian colonial power of which the best one can say is 'Nemo dat quod non habet.'

29. 1899–1920   Desperate Somali National resistance under Mohammed Abdille Hasan (the 'Mad Mullah') without help from any power. Five British campaigns and four

Ethiopian fail to quell the Mullah until he is bombed from the air by the R.A.F.

30. 1905 High Commissioner for Kenya (East Africa Protectorate then) writes in a book that it would be right (if only it were not impracticable) to place all the Somali lands in a single province so that this people, talented above the average of East Africa, might follow their different way of life together.

31. 1906 Three rival White European Empires decide, in order to avoid disputes between themselves and to exclude Germany, to preserve the undesirable integrity of a Black African Empire, that is the historic collection of petty Abyssinian Kingdoms which have tottered through thirty centuries of history, plus the ill-gotten and ill-managed gains of Menelek II. They decide to respect mutually their own separate interests in Ethiopia. These are:
(a) *G.B.* The Blue Nile and certain Somali grazings.
(b) *France.* Any railway from the coast through Abyssinia, possibly on to French Equatorial possessions.
(c) *Italy.* All Ethiopia a sphere of Italian influence. (A kind of Monroe Doctrine for the region in place of the defunct Treaty of Ucciali.)

32. 1907–1913 Decline and death of Menelek II: At his death the only flicker of light in the darkness of Abyssinian history for centuries past goes out. Chaos as usual reigns in Abyssinia, while chaos worse than usual reigns in the new Empire which it is unable to administer.

33. 1914–1918 Honest Brokers and Honourable Peacemakers come to blows—the First World War ending in U.S.A. presidential homilies worthy of St. Paul, but a peace scarcely worthy of Carthage. During this war two men of military renown (Von Lettow Vorbeck and Jan Smuts) display to their African Askaris and colonial subjects the secrets and limitations of 'White Magic'.

34. 1918 The Addis Ababa railway chugs into life—three days to arrive, no night travel owing to bandits by night.

35. 1920 The gallant 'Mad Mullah' is bombed into defeat after fighting a galaxy of empires for an unprecedented period (21 years). (The writer of these notes had the pleasure of congratulating the Mullah's son in Mogadishu during May 1963.) Syed Mohammed

retires to the Ogaden after being bombed by the
R.A.F., and in the Ethiopian sphere of his country
he is safe, for there is no effective control on the part
of Ethiopia.

36. 1921   Syed Mohammed dies of old age. During his campaigns his followers, even when his fortunes were at
their lowest ebb, invoked his name in the heat of
battle and at 'the cold hour of execution'.

37. 1923   Ras Tafari becomes Regent after sixteen years of
worse Ethiopian chaos than ever before. Ethiopia is
then admitted to the League of Nations with Franco-
Italian support but with Anglo-American misgivings
(U.S.A. not a member of the League). . . . Massacre,
mutilation, torture, enslavement and looting are
indeed not very good credentials for admission.

38. 1923   Ras Tafari abolishes the slave trade, imposing the
death penalty for infringements, but slavery goes on
as before. The Ogaden Somali province is still a lawless area with Ethiopian Tigre (bandits), and Somali
Shifta (bandits) looting across the frontier.

39. 1924–1925   G.B. gives Somali Jubaland to Italy without in any
way consulting the wishes of the Somali inhabitants
—more baksheesh, this time for Italy's assistance
during the First World War. (One of President
Wilson's homilies comes to mind 'Peoples and provinces shall not be bartered about from sovereignty
to sovereignty like chattels or pawns in a game.')

40. 1932   Emperor Haile Selassie (Ras Tafari with a crown on),
pressed by G.B. anti-slavery interests, promises to
bring slavery to an end in Ethiopia by the end of the
next twenty years. Offices open all over the place,
but *plus ça change, plus c'est la même chose*'.

41. 1934   Mussolini settles his African issues with France and
from France receives a 'nihil obstat' for Italian action
in Ethiopia, notwithstanding the covenant of the
League of Nations, the Kellog-Briand Pact, etc.
(these I term the obligates).

42. 1935   Mussolini, having squared France, approaches G.B.
under Clause 4 of the Tripartite Treaty of 1906,
saying in effect: 'I am in mind to occupy a part, or
perhaps even the whole of Ethiopia. I desire, before
I begin, to respect your interests, pray tell me what
those interests are?'

43. 1935   G.B. reacts to Mussolini's enquiry without shock,
surprise, censure or any reference whatsoever to the

obligates. She sets about finding out what interests she has, so that she can inform Mussolini in reply to his enquiry. A high-powered inter-departmental Commission under Sir John Maffey is asked in its terms of reference how British interests would be affected if Italy occupied (a) the Somali portion of Ethiopia, or (b) the whole of Ethiopia. At Stresa the three conspirators confer on other matters without a single reference to Mussolini's enquiry about Ethiopia.

44. 1935   The Maffey Commission reports in May. It declares that G.B. has no interest in preserving the integrity of Ethiopia. It acknowledges the Tripartite division of interests. It describes the misrule and non rule of Ethiopia over its conquered provinces, mentioning specifically the Somali Ogaden as an illustration of maladministration. It finds that an Italian occupation of either a part or the whole of Ethiopia would be advantageous from every point of view.

45. 1935   Mussolini's agents photograph the Maffey Report (which in 1965 is still restricted in England) in our Embassy in Rome. Mussolini derives from this report a clear 'nihil obstat' from G.B. having regard to what has passed hitherto and the terms of reference addressed to the commission.

46. 1935   October. Mussolini invades Ethiopia.

47. 1936   February 12. Oil experts report the impossibility of stopping Mussolini by means of oil sanctions without the co-operation of U.S.A. Everyone except Anthony Eden knows quite well that U.S.A. is totally Isolationist.

48. 1936   February 20. The *Giornale D'Italia* prints the Maffey Report in Italian (the only version from which today the author of these notes is permitted to quote).

49. 1936   The policy of sanctions against Italy is pursued. ('Bad cases break good law.') Italy concludes victorious campaign and annexes Ethiopia. Somali liberation movement starts in Ogaden.

50. 1936   March 7. Germany reoccupies the Rhineland in defiance of her obligation under the Carthaginian Treaty (Versailles). Peace breaks out between Hitler and Mussolini. Strained relations break out between the Allies and the League; Anglo-French disunity and unpreparedness thereby disclosed to both the dictators. (All set for World War Two.)

51. 1938   At Munich a belated decision is made in favour of

self-determination for Sudeten Germans in Czechoslovakia where they should never have been placed.

52. 1939   World war breaks out again.

53. 1941   G.B. invades Ethiopia to liberate it from the Italians.

54. 1941   The Emperor Haile Selassie persuades the R.A.F. to
drop leaflets on occupied Eritrea and Benadir proclaiming Ethiopia's claim on historic grounds to these
two territories. He announces that his arrival to
incorporate them in the Ethiopian Empire is being
supported by British arms.

55. 1941–1948   The whole of the Somali nation except the small
French part is under one British administration.
Everyone who has anything to do with the Somalis
at this time knows that they wish to remain united
and not to be dismembered again.

56. 1945   The atomic bomb transforms international relationships.

57. 1946   G.B.'s Foreign Secretary suggests to the powers that
British Somaliland, Italian Somaliland and Ethiopian
Somaliland shall be 'lumped together' as a Trust
Territory.

58. 1946   The Emperor of Ethiopia objects to the foregoing
proposals. He claims Ethiopian Somaliland on historical and strategical grounds, and says it is Ethiopia's internal affair and no business of anyone else.
The Soviet Union, suspecting British colonial
aggrandisement, vetoes the proposal.

59. 1946   The Emperor of Ethiopia addresses a memorandum
to the United Nations claiming Eritrea and Benadir
on his usual incorrect historical basis.

60. 1948   The Somalis claim their unity in accordance with
principles of self-determination, but the emperor
objects to their claim and U.N.O. rejects it.

61. 1948   G.B. returns the Somali Ogaden to Ethiopia. G.B.
officials at this time declare 'we don't believe the
Somalis will ever forgive us'. Somali resistance goes
underground.

62. 1950   The United Nations sets up a Trust Territory of
Italian Somaliland to be known as Somalia, to
become independent in 1960, and meanwhile Italy
to be the Trustee.

63. 1950   The Emperor of Ethiopia protests to the United
Nations, alleging that it has infringed the principle
of self-determination [sic] by not appointing Ethiopia
in place of Italy as Trustee for Somalia.

64. 1952   The emperor is virtually presented with Eritrea under a feeble federal constitution.

65. 1956   A major Franco-British mistake is made over the Suez affair. Britain invades Egypt on the back of Israel. The whole position of G.B. east of Suez deteriorates.

66. 1956   With Somalia independence only four years ahead, the emperor makes a speech in the Ogaden announcing his support for Greater Somalia 'for then our country will be larger and stronger'. The emperor by 'our country' means Ethiopia and he has in mind the 'Eritrean solution'.

67. 1956–1960 The Emperor of Ethiopia objects to the inclusion of British Somaliland in Somalia.

68. 1959   G.B., under pressure from her Somali subjects in Somaliland, agrees to permit their union with Somalia, but the emperor secures a pledge from the British Prime Minister, Mr. Macmillan.

69. 1960   April 11. In the House of Commons Mr. Macmillan renounces the right of H.M.G. to permit secession of the Somali N.F.D. in Kenya to Somalia. He supports the integrity of the Somali colonies of Ethiopia and France. He thus pledges H.M.G. to support continued dismemberment of the Somali nation.

70. 1960   July 1. Somalia is born with a Constitution giving her the duty to consolidate and preserve the freedom of the Somali nation.

71. 1961   In November Mr. Kenyatta of Kenya, lately released from some years of detention for managing Mau Mau, visits Addis Ababa as guest of the emperor. He arranges a secret defence pact with the emperor not to let Somali N.F.D. join Somalia.

72. 1962   At the Kenya Constitutional Conference in London Mr. Maudling, British Colonial Secretary, allows the delegates of the Somali N.F.D. to attend the conference.

73. 1962   Mr. Maudling issues a White Paper undertaking to send a commission to the Somali N.F.D. to ascertain the people's wishes regarding their future. A White Paper promises a *decision on* the findings, *before* Kenya internal self-government, *before* changing the status of the N.F.D.

74. 1962   Mr. Kenyatta and Mr. Ngala both object to this commission.

75. 1962　　　Anyone who reads the White Paper (Command 1700) understands it as being tantamount to a pledge in advance of self-determination for the N.F.D.—Mr. Kenyatta, understanding it in that way, threatens to go to war to recover the N.F.D. if it is allowed to secede. The Emperor of Ethiopia objects to it and reminds Macmillan of his pledge.

76. 1962　　　In pursuance of the emperor's intervention (presumably) H.M.G. address a private letter to the members of their own N.F.D. Commission modifying the published terms of their own White Paper.

77. 1962　　　A second commission is set up to advise on regional boundaries in Kenya.

78. 1962　　　Mr. Kenyatta and Mr. Ngala of Kenya, the only two possible leaders of the future independent Kenya, are both successively invited to visit Somalia as guests of the government. On arrival they are treated as heroes, but both refuse to consider agreeing to N.F.D. secession, even if the commission reports that in the light of self-determination this is a proper solution.

79. 1962　　　Both commissions report a homogeneous Somali region in the major part of the N.F.D. of Kenya, with some 250,000 Somalis, in a semi-desert area one-quarter the size of Kenya, almost unanimous in wishing to join with Somalia.

80. 1962　　　Mr. Kenyatta threatens war if Somali N.F.D. is allowed to join Somalia.

81. 1963　　　March 8. Mr. Sandys, British Colonial Secretary, announces in Nairobi that the Somali N.F.D. will not be allowed to join Somalia in accordance with the wishes of the people as ascertained by the N.F.D. Commission, but will be put in a separate region as suggested by the Regional Boundaries Commission. This is a device for keeping the region inside Kenya.

82. 1963　　　On March 12, in the House of Commons, Mr. Sandys makes it clear that the prospect of violent reactions and political non-co-operation in Kenya made any other course in regard to the N.F.D. impossible. So justice for Somalis is sacrificed to appease Mr. Kenyatta as well as the Emperor of Ethiopia.

83. 1963　　　Dismay in Somalia. Somalia breaks off diplomatic relations after continuous session of the National Assembly for more than a week.

84. 1963   Dismay in the Somali N.F.D. Boycott of the Elections is 100 per cent successful, except in the mixed township of Isiolo where G.B. security forces quell riots by shooting Somalis armed only with stones.

85. 1963   In May Lord and Lady Lytton are guests of the Somali Government in Somali Republic. Lord Lytton ascertains from the Prime Minister that in given circumstances the Somali Government would consider joining the British Commonwealth.

86. 1963   The African Summit Conference is held at Addis Ababa. Somalia is rebuffed by the emperor and by some other delegates of the Pan-African Organization, but president and emperor agree to negotiate at some later date.

87. 1963   July. N.F.D. delegates are in London. Rebuffed by the Colonial Secretary, invite *inter alia*, Lord Lytton to meet them to discuss their problems. Later, a delegate writes to Lord Lytton asking if he can persuade the Somali Prime Minister to attend a conference in Rome. (Request not passed on.)

88. 1963   August. The Rome Conference is held. G.B. informs Somalia that she is not prepared to permit the N.F.D. to join Somalia unless Kenya (already pledged in an opposite sense to the Emperor of Ethiopia) can be persuaded to agree.

89. 1963   September 25. N.F.D. delegate writes to Lord Lytton saying the only language H.M.G. understand is terrorism.

90. 1963   The Prime Minister of Somalia visits Moscow and Peking with satisfactory results.

91. 1963   December 12. Kenya Independence includes Somali N.F.D. inside the boundaries of Independent Kenya.

92. 1963   Mr. Kenyatta announces the Defence Pact with Ethiopia. Repeats 'not an inch' to the Somalia Foreign Minister.

93. 1963–1964   Somalia relations with Kenya and Ethiopia deteriorate. There is a major Somali rebellion in the Ogaden, and Ethiopian military aggression in Somali territory. The Somalis defend themselves robustly.

94. 1964   In January there is subversion of the Army in three East African territories, and a revolution in Zanzibar which overthrows the sultan.

95. 1964   Chou En-lai visits Somalia and declares that the revolutionary conditions in Africa are excellent.

96. 1964   The Somalis appeal to the Security Council and the emperor appeals to the Organization of African Unity. Discussions of O.A.U. at Dar es Salaam and Lagos followed by discussions between Ethiopia and Somalia under an 'honest broker' at Khartoum.

97. 1964   Somali resistance in the N.F.D. begins to develop, with African Kenya's new colonialism actively supported by H.M.G.

98. 1964   Position of H.M.G. in Aden and Cyprus deteriorates.

99. 1964   Position of H.M.G. in Zanzibar and Tanganyika deteriorates.

100. 1964   Republic of Somalia faced with dilemma of suporting Somali insurgents in Ogaden and N.F.D., of which hitherto she has been incorrectly accused, or standing by while 'The Revolution' (probably Peking) takes over.

APPENDIX 2

IDENTIKIT MEMORANDUM
'THE REVOLUTION'

'Know your enemy' is a military maxim upon which I have been trained and accordingly I now draw up a mirror, as I see it, of the enemy mind.

PLANS FOR EAST AFRICA.

'An Excellent Revolutionary Situation Exists in Africa' (Chou En-lai in Mogadishu, February 3, 1964, reported by B.B.C.)

Here now I have composed a 'brief' for the revolution to its agents:

By every possible means the achievement of Independence in Africa must everywhere be depicted in Algerian terms as a desperate revolutionary act by subject peoples directing their campaign against a single enemy—the hostile white colonial power. (*Vide* Tom Mboya page 61.) The Somali dictum that colonialism has no colour is a heresy. To this end the colonial power must be represented as having divided African peoples who were formerly united. (*Vide* Mr. Kenyatta and Dr. Nkrumah in their books.) The revolution must take every opportunity to show the imperialists as generating hostility between peoples who were formerly friendly, of bringing poverty to peoples who were formerly well off, of depriving Africans of education, of stealing their land and of robbing them of their wealth; once independence has been achieved the imperialists must be accused of seeking to substitute dollar colonialism for Colonial Office colonialism and of fomenting inter-state friction in such a manner as to provide them with an excuse to return to Africa and inaugurate a second phase of colonial exploitation.

During the independence campaign each colony must be united within its own colonial boundaries by a single watch-word connoting freedom without any attempt to define the concept—let everyone put into the word whatever his desires may be (*vide* Tom Mboya)—the campaign must be given a supra-tribal national spirit focused upon a single father-figure. Any local loyalties of tribe or race must be ruthlessly suppressed as impediments to the revolution. Self-determination is to be the charter for obtaining independence, but territorial integrity must be the charter for preserving it. So, when independence is a fact, self-determination must become taboo. Potential gainers equally with potential losers must resist all secessionist movements as they divert energy from the next phase of the revolution. Moreover any diminution of territory must detract from the prestige of one of our important leaders, therefore each father-figure must rule precisely wherever the white colonialist ruled before him—not an inch less and no poaching. All tribalism is an enemy of the revolution, which seeks to make new men initiated on to a plateau of living where the standards of the revolution entirely replace all traditional standards, such as circumcision, baptism, kinship allegiances and all age-group alliances except that of the one revolutionary youth group. Leadership of the youth group must on no account be left to youth, but must be in the hands of mature men worthy of our confidence. Tribal names will become taboo in conversation. A Danakil African may differ from a Luo as drastically as a Scotsman differs from a Chinese, but for the purposes of the revolution both are one, to wit African. There is but one acceptable division, that between Africans and Europeans, freedom fighters and imperialists.

'*Break the shackles of Colonialism in the political, military, economic and cultural fields.*' (Chou En-lai in Mogadishu, February 3, 1964.)

In order to inflate the importance of weak African revolutionary states on the international plane, they are to be given the semblance of unity on every possible occasion. During the struggle for independence they are to proclaim as their target in the immediate future a Pan-Africa, or United States of Africa. The revolution intends, however, that these multiple sovereignties shall remain independent of one another as well as independent of the white imperialists. Accordingly those leaders who have talked of federations during the struggle for independence must be encouraged to find excuses for postponing the federations after they have acquired independence. Exceptions may perhaps be tolerated in regions where the revolution seems unlikely to make sufficiently rapid progress—in such cases one flag at U.N.O. serves the revolution rather better than five.

In order to achieve the total insulation of Africa from white imperialists, in order further to sustain the revolutionary impetus after independence has been achieved, and finally in order to liquidate the remaining pockets of white settlement in Africa, the Organization of African Unity is a most suitable agency to control. The revolution sees O.A.U. as an excellent organ for by-passing U.N.O. where such obsolete principles as self-determination are still embalmed. In Africa's revolution O.A.U. enables liberating states to give a 'hands off' signal to white imperialists, thus safeguarding their revolutionary independence. The Organization will enable a measure of fusion in the field for action to take place in Africa, while fostering fission in the rest of the world. African states must preserve their sovereignty if only to retain their numerical strength in U.N.O. with the object of paralysing or even subverting the imperialist influence in that organ.

There is no need for the revolution in Africa to be conducted by Communist parties and there are disadvantages in such parties. Socialism, for example, is a word well loved in half the white imperialists' world, and tolerated by the other half, while Communism is as yet under suspicion even in revolutionary Africa. Therefore the word Communism and the Communist Party alike should be dropped for the time being.

The leaders of the independence phase of African liberation are to be regarded as expendable. They are the revolutionary hybrids with a foot in both camps, who are due eventually for replacement. The purpose of the revolution will be carried out by our chosen representatives who will exercise power as it passes from the hybrids, even while these hybrids continue to hold office.

Newly independent African states have an aptitude for single-party rule. Everyone in office, for example, will be earning ten times as much as he could possibly earn out of office, therefore he cannot afford to leave. Moreover, there is little more than half a front bench available for managing affairs in any case; there are, for instance, no Africans of education, no African colleges of professors, no centres of African learning worthy of the name. There is no African bourgeois class with the know-how of managing affairs; there is no substantial African yeoman farmer class; there are virtually no African business executives of any standing, no African bureaucracy, no true African press, no African economists of repute, no African officers in the army or police with more than two years commissioned experience. The conclusion, as we see it, is that there is no substantial opposition of which we have to rid society. The Europeans have left a power vacuum into which lightheaded masses have advanced to freedom on a single watch-word which promises them everything in a society where there is hardly anything to give. Those who purport to regulate this empty society are petty men whom we can intimidate or subvert or even by-pass with the greatest of ease, so long as opposition parties are made illegal, and effective opposition outside of the one party is treated as treason, while the police, the military and the Civil Service are selected from properly conditioned party members.

The retention of a few whites in positions they would never reach in their own country will help to give us an entrée on the word of a white man.

The solidarity of the one-party police state is the better able to purge itself of colonialism and neo-colonialism if it has a dissatisfied minority: An insoluble unemployment problem is an excellent condition while it lasts. A Kashmir in every new state is a long-term boon

to the revolution, for it helps to preserve the tempo of internal unification at the decisive point. The fashioning of a security service,
nominally for defence or for the preservation of some secessionist
province, is a useful means of raising a force whose main purpose will
be the suppression of the revolution's enemies inside the camp.

In the region of the Nile Valley there is a whole portfolio of grievances, all of which are serving the purpose of the revolution in this
way. In the extreme north, for example, almost all peoples of Arab
stock, and indeed even the whole Moslem world, have been estranged
from the European imperialists by the establishment of Zion in Arab
Palestine, and have been even more exasperated than we could have
hoped by the Anglo-French-Israeli invasion of Egypt in 1956. Officially
we are pro-Arab, but it would not suit the revolution if Israel were to
disappear. In the extreme south we can rely on white South Africa, and
her kindred satellites, to fight for survival for a generation and this
will preserve the anti-white mania in a continent which is already
ninety-nine per cent black. In the middle there is Ethiopia, which is
the worst of the white imperialisms, and survives under a black agent
of the imperialists. The unenlightened oppression of the rule of a small
superior race of Amharas is throwing the Horn of Africa, Moslem and
Galla alike, into the hands of the revolution.

So it is that our main allies are Israel in the north, Capetown in
the south and the emperor in the middle, all doing very good work
for us. There are subsidiary areas where the situation is especially
satisfactory to us, in Kenya, for example, the fate of the more able
Hamitic minorities has been placed in the hands of the incompetent
Negro majority. Here the slaves are now lording it over the free. In
the Sudan, by contrast, it is the other way round—there the Moslem
Hamites of the north are riding rough-shod over the pagan Negroes
of the south. In Kenya, Uganda, Tanganyika and Zanzibar Negro
incompetence touched off, at the beginning of 1964, a new phase
which was not due to open until September 1964, when British
military thinning out would have been far advanced in East Africa
and the base at Aden might well have been further undermined:
however, in Zanzibar we have acquired a little Cuba on the flank
of Africa, and its very insularity is going to be quite useful to us.
Conditions on the mainland, particularly in Kenya, are promising.
A swarming population has established a locust army squatting on
the verges of the white farms, rustling the white man's stock and
pilfering the white man's equipment and waiting to move in to the
vacated white men's lands without having any competence to manage
them. This will ruin white farming. Agricultural output from this
mixed farm sector is bound to fall without appreciably absorbing the
large force of unemployed. The temperament of the Kikuyu, always
prone to grievance, has been fanned by its principal leader for more

than a generation. The land freedom army, the freedom fighters, the lawless, the landless, the jobless and common bandits are all making common cause demanding fulfilment of the promises of Uhuru which nobody can possibly fulfil.

The Somalis in the Horn are unique in several ways, for example, where other states are unities contrived out of a hundred separate tribes by the colonial powers, the Somalis are a nation dismembered by the colonial powers. In the case of the Somalis a black imperialist has injured them more than three white imperialists. In 1963 a departing white imperialist gave away a part of their nation to a second black imperialist. Now the Somalis occupy one-quarter of Kenya, and perhaps one-sixth of Ethiopia. As Hamites, moreover, in a racial sense they are akin to four-fifths of Kenya and three-quarters of Ethiopia. They have a large settlement in Aden which it will be useful to have disaffected towards the British authority. They have a colony in French Jibouti. They are close to the Danakil of Eritrea, and they have small colonies in many of the ports of the Western imperialists. They are intelligent, hardy and brave. They are passionately attached to freedom and stand in no need of Tom Mboya's mass rallies to wake them up. They have an excellent military record. They resisted the imperialist longer than anyone else. They have lately been rebuffed in Washington, London and Bonn. Even as late as May 1963 they were still prepared to join the British Commonwealth, but in August they were rebuffed again in Rome and they appealed to us for help. The revolution has responded immediately and generously to that appeal. We will make special use of the Somalis.

APPENDIX 3

Author's translation of the French version of the Emperor Menelek's letter of April 1891 (photocopy reproduced facing page 23).

TRANSLATION

Conquering Lion of the tribe of Juda, Menelek II, elect of the Lord King of Kings of Ethiopia.

To Our Friend Her Majesty Queen Victoria, Queen of Great Britain and Ireland, Defender of the Faith, Empress of India.

Greetings!

We ask most especially for news of Your precious health.

I wrote a letter to Your Majesty dated *25 Maskaram 1883*; but I do not know if it reached You.

The great English Power being up to this day the friend of the Ethiopian Empire, and in recognition of Your goodwill to her, We express to You Our gratitude.

Seeing that We wish to acquaint the friendly Powers of Europe in writing with the boundaries of Ethiopia, We hereby write to Your Majesty in the same sense, and We are hopeful that You may bestow Your benevolent consideration upon what follows:

Boundaries of Ethiopia:

(*Here follows a page of descriptive details of the boundary claimed by Menelek.*)
In pointing out the exact boundaries of My Empire as they exist today I signify My Intention, if God (*le bon Dieu*) graciously grants Me life and strength, to re-establish the ancient frontiers of Ethiopia as far as Kartoum and Lake Nyanza [*sic: presumably Victoria*], with all the Galla territories.

I have not the least intention of remaining a disinterested onlooker if Powers from a distance come with the notion of dividing Africa between themselves, Ethiopia having been, during the course of quite fourteen centuries, an island inhabited by Christians in a sea of Pagans.

Just as Almighty God (*le Tout-Puissant*) has protected Ethiopia up to

236

the present time, so also I am confident that He will be her Guardian today and will also add to her territory in the future, and I have no reason to contemplate that He will divide up Ethiopia amongst other Powers.

Formerly the boundary of Ethiopia was the sea. Because of lack of strength on Our own part and because of the failure of other Christians to come to Our aid, Our frontier on the seaward side fell into the hands of the Muslims (*Musulmans*). Today We make no pretence of seeking to recover Our seaward frontier by force; but We hope that the Christian Powers, guided by Our Lord Jesus Christ, may yield Us Our frontiers on the sea, or that at least they may give Us some points on the coast.

Done at '*Adis-Abéba, le 14 Miazzia
l'an 1883 de la miséricorde*' (April 1891).
        In
India office of July 9/91

APPENDIX 4

SELECT BIBLIOGRAPHY AND SOURCES OF REFERENCE

AVON, EARL OF, *The Eden Memoirs*, Vols. 1 and 2 (Cassell, 1960, 1962).

BAKER, R. ST. BARBE, *Sahara Challenge* (Lutterworth, 1954).

BALFOUR, E. B., *The Living Soil* (Faber, 1943).

BLUNT, W. S., *My Diaries* (Martin Secker, 1919).

BLUNT, W. S., *Secret History of the English Occupation of Egypt* (T. Fisher Unwin, 1907).

BUDGE, SIR E. A. WALLIS, *A History of Ethiopia* (Methuen, 1928).

CHURCHILL, WINSTON S., *The River War* (Longmans, 1899).

COLE, D. H., *Imperial Military Geography* (Sifton Praed, various editions).

COUPLAND, R., *East Africa and its Invaders* (O.U.P., 1956).

DRYSDALE, JOHN, *The Somali Dispute* (Pall Mall, 1964).

ELIOT, SIR CHARLES, *The East Africa Protectorate* (E. Arnold, 1905).

FARSON, NEGLEY, *The Last Chance in Africa* (Gollancz, 1949).

GORDON, *The Journals of Maj. Gen. G. C. Gordon* (Kegan Paul, 1885).

HILL, DR. G. BIRKBECK, *Colonel Gordon in Central Africa, 1874–1879* (De La Rue, 1881).

HODSON, SIR ARNOLD, *Seven Years in Southern Abyssinia* (T. Fisher Unwin, 1927).

HOLT, P. M., *The Mahdist State in the Sudan, 1881–1898* (O.U.P., 1958).

HUDDLESTON, TREVOR, *Naught For Your Comfort* (Collins, 1956).

HUXLEY, ELSPETH, *White Man's Country* (Chatto, 1953, new edition).

JARDINE, D. J., *The Mad Mullah of Somaliland* (Herbert Jenkins, 1923).

JONES, A. H. M., and MONROE, ELIZABETH, *History of Ethiopia* (O.U.P. reprint, 1960).

KARIUKI, J. M., *Mau Mau Detainee* (O.U.P., 1963).

KENYATTA, JOMO, *Facing Mount Kenya* (Secker, 1938).

KEYNES, J. M., *The Economic Consequences of the Peace* (Macmillan, 1919).

LAURENCE, MARGARET, *The Prophet's Camel Bell* (Macmillan, 1963).

LEAKEY, DR. L. S. B., *Mau Mau and the Kikuyu* (Methuen, 1952).

LEWIS, DR. I. M., *A Pastoral Democracy* (International African Institute: O.U.P., 1961).

LUGARD, SIR FREDERICK, *The Dual Mandate in British Tropical Africa* (William Blackwood, 1922).

MAGNUS, SIR PHILIP, *Kitchener* (Murray, 1958).
MASON, P., *The Birth of a Dilemma* (O.U.P., 1958).
MATHESON, ALASTAIR, *Land of Wide Horizons* (Macdonald, 1962).
MATHEW, DAVID, *Ethiopia* (Eyre & Spottiswoode, 1947).
MBOYA, TOM, *Freedom and After* (André Deutsch, 1963).
MEINERTZHAGEN, R., *Kenya Diary, 1902–06* (Oliver & Boyd, 1957).
MILNER, ALFRED, *England in Egypt* (Edward Arnold, 1892).
MITCHELL, SIR PHILIP, *African Afterthoughts* (Hutchinson, 1954).
MOOREHEAD, ALAN, *The Blue Nile* (Hamish Hamilton, 1962).
MOOREHEAD, ALAN, *The White Nile* (Hamish Hamilton, 1960).
MOSLEY, LEONARD, *Duel for Kilimanjaro* (Weidenfeld and Nicolson, 1963).
MOYSE-BARLETT, LT. COL. H., *History of the King's African Rifles* (Gale & Polden, 1956).
NKRUMAH, DR. KWAME, *Autobiography* (Nelson, 1957).
NOEL-BAKER, PHILIP, *The Arms Race* (Atlantic Book Publishing Co., 1958).
OTTER, ERIK VON, *Som officer och Stotviltsägare i Turkana* (Albert Bonnier, 1930).
PANKHURST, R., *An Introduction to the Economic History of Ethiopia* (Lalibela, 1961).
PERHAM, M., *The Government of Ethiopia* (Faber, 1948).
REECE, ALYS, *To My Wife 50 Camels* (Harvill Press, 1963).
ROBINSON, R., and GALLAGHER J., *Africa and the Victorians* (Macmillan, 1961).
SIMON, NOEL, *Between the Sunlight and the Thunder* (Collins, 1962).
STAMP, JOSIAH, *The Financial Aftermath of War* (Ernest Benn, 1932).
SUN YAT-SEN, DR., *San Min Chui, The Three Principles of the People* (The Commercial Press Ltd., Shanghai, China, 1930).
SWAYNE, CAPT. H. G. C., *Seventeen Trips Through Somaliland* (R. Ward, 1895).
TEMPLEWOOD, LORD, *Nine Troubled Years* (Collins, 1954).
TRIMINGHAM, J. SPENCER, *Islam in Ethiopia* (O.U.P., 1952).
TURNBULL, SIR RICHARD, *The Darod Invasion* (printed privately).

Pamphlets, Periodicals and Reports

Annual:
Kenya Labour Department, 1959.
Kenya Department of Agriculture.
Triennial:
Kenya Education Department, 1959–1960.
Others:
F.O. Report on Abyssinia, 1920.
African Conference on the Rule of Law—Lagos, Jan. 3–7, 1961 (International Commission of Jurists, Geneva).

Britain, the Commonwealth and Europe, Harold Macmillan, published by the Conservative and Unionist Central Office, 1961.
Carter Commission (East Africa Royal), 1953–1955 (H.M.S.O. Cmnd 9475).
Corfield Report, 1960 (H.M.S.O. Cmnd 1030).
Denning, 1963 (H.M.S.O. Cmnd 2152).
Kenya Coastal Strip, 1961 (Cmnd 1585).
Kenya Coastal Strip, 1962 (Cmnd 1701).
Kenya Coastal Strip, 1963 (Cmnd 2161).
Kenya Regional Boundaries Commission, 1962 (H.M.S.O. Cmnd 1899).
Kenya Statistical Abstract, 1960.
Maffey, 1935 (*Giornale d'Italia*).
N.F.D. Commission, 1962 (H.M.S.O. Cmnd 1900).
The Issue of the N.F.D., Somali Government, 1963.
The Problem of the N.F.D. of Kenya, Dr. I. M. Lewis (*Race*, Vol. 5, No. 1, July 1963).
The Somali Conquest of the Horn of Africa, Dr. I. M. Lewis (*Journal of African History*, Vol. 1, No. 2, 1960).
A General Survey of the Somaliland Protectorate, 1944–1950, J. A. Hunt.
The Somali Peninsula, Information Service, Somali Government, 1962.

APPENDIX 5

ACKNOWLEDGEMENTS

Amongst the hundreds to whom I am grateful for hospitality, support, information, help, criticism, patience or advice in the task described in this book are the following: H.E. Aden Abdulla Osman, President of the Somali Republic; H.E. Dr. Abdirashid Ali Shermarke, former Premier of the Somali Republic; H.E. The American Ambassador at Mogadishu; H.E. Mr. Arraleh, former Somali Ambassador in London; H.E. Dr. Ahmed Gelle, Somali Minister of Justice; H.E. Abdulcadir Mohamed Aden, Somali Minister of Finance; Mr. Jama Abdullahi Galib, President of the Somali National Assembly; Dr. Abdi Aden, President of the Somali National Bank; Mr. Ahmed Dahir; Mr. Dennis Akumu of the Mombasa Dockworkers' Union; Professor B. J. Andrzejewski; H.E. the British Ambassador at Addis Ababa; Dr. Ahmed Shire Lawaha; Mr. Bille Issa; Commander David Blunt; Miss Enid Blackmore; Lady Eleanor Cole; Sir F. Cavendish-Bentinck; Mr. P. Carrel; the Duke of Devonshire; Mr. Christopher Dobson; Mr. John Drysdale; the Earl of Enniskillen; Mr. Malcolm Elwin; the Lord Faringdon; Mr. Musa Galal; Mrs. Hugh Grant; the late General Daud Abdulla Hersi; Mrs. E. D. Hughes; Mr. Peter Henderson; the Lord Huntingdon; Mr. J. A. Hunt; Mr. Douglas Hinde; Brigadier the Hon. Miles Fitzalan Howard; Mr. Tony Irwin; Mr. John Knight; Mr. Nikita Krushchev; Dr. I. M. Lewis; the Liwali of the Coast; the Marquess of Lansdowne; Mr. Abd-er-Rahman Lutz; Dr. Kannedid Ahmed; Mr. Mohamed Musse; H.E. Mohamed Abdi Nur, Somali Minister of Interior; Mr. Mohamed Ali Dar; Major-General Mohamed Abscir, Somali Chief of Police; Mr. Mohamed Abdalla; Mr. A. Mussa; Dr. Syed Mahmud; Colonel Mans; Mr. and Mrs. Michael Mariano; the Most Rev. J. J. McCarthy, Archbishop of Nairobi; the Rt. Hon. Reginald Maudling; Mr. C. J. Martin of the B.B.C.; Mr. D. Mohamed; Miss Kadisha Mohamed; H.E. Hillo Maalim, Somali Minister of Defence; N.F.D. delegates in London; Mrs. D. Partridge; Mr. and Mrs. W. E. Powys; Mrs. Paxton, H.E. the Portuguese Ambassador in London; Mr. J. N. Perks; Dr. Rana; Sir

241

Patrick Renison; Sir Gerald Reece; Sir Richard Turnbull; Mr. and Mrs. Noel Solly; Mr. J. C. Sainty; the Lord Somers; the Rev. A. Shorter; Mr. A. Scawin; Sir Arthur Kirby; Miss Rosamond Wardrop; Mr. Walters; Mr. J. F. C. Williams; Mr. J. G. Williams; Mr. John Williams; the Italian Consul-General at Kismayu; the Somali Community in Aden; Hunter Surveys at Mogadishu; the Student Entertainment Group (Afgoi); Somalia Radio; the Ministry of Information of the Somali Republic; journalists at Nairobi and Mogadishu.

Others not named have sent me information for use on a non-attributable basis.

I acknowledge the considerable quotations I have made from the Summary of World Broadcasts, Part 4, 'The Middle East and Africa,' which the B.B.C. print under the following safeguarding clause: 'The B.B.C. can accept by responsibility for any claim for defamation or for infringement of copyright arising out of their publication'.

Finally I gratefully acknowledge permission to quote or reproduce copyright material from the following sources: *The Times* and the *Daily Telegraph* for news items; the *New York Times* for a special article on the Somali rebellion (1963) against Ethiopian rule in the Ogaden and the undeclared border war between Ethiopia and the Somali Republic in the same year; the *Sunday Telegraph* for Henry Fairlie's article of 1st October 1964; Mr. C. J. Martin for photographs of Somali notables; Mr. John Knight for photographs illustrating soil erosion due to overstocking during the Colonial period; Sir John Cockcroft for his opinion on the development of nuclear power in relation to water resources; the Public Record Office for copies in Amharic and French of the letter of 1891 written by the Emperor Menelek II; the *Daily Mirror* for the only good up-to-date picture I have been able to find of the Emperor Haile Selassie and for a photograph of President Kenyatta; Dr. Lawaha for a photograph of President Osman; the editor of the *Giornale d'Italia* for an Italian version of the Maffey Report and the Government Whips' Office of the House of Lords for ascertaining that there would be no objection to printing my translation into English; the author and publishers of *The Arms Race*, by Philip Noel-Baker (Sweet & Maxwell); the author and publishers of *Ethiopia*, by David Mathew (Eyre & Spottiswoode); the authors and publishers of *History of Ethiopia* by A. H. M. Jones and E. Monroe (Clarendon Press, Oxford); the author and publishers of *History of Ethiopia*, by Sir E. Wallis Budge (Methuen & Co.); Curzon Publicity Ltd. and the Federal German Embassy for *The German View*, vol. 5, no. 20, 21st October 1964; the Kenya High Commissioner for *Kenya Digest*; the author and publishers of *Islam in Ethiopia*, by J. Spencer Trimingham (Oxford University Press) for maps; Mr. R. I. M. Campbell and Mr. D. Bartlett of Armand Denis Productions for photographs.

INDEX

Abbai, river, 211
Abba Kierlos Cyrille, 22
Aboud, ex-president, 158, 176
Abraha, viceroy, 34
Abuna, 22, 146, 149, 150, 153, 154, 158, 159
Abyssinia, 20–26, 30–38, 118–126, 134–149, 158–166, 181, 220–223. *See also* Habash, Ethiopia
Addis Ababa, 26, 102, 104, 105, 110, 134, 140, 164, 165, 167, 175, 176, 182, 211, 221, 223, 227, 229
Adel, 30, 35, 211
Aden, 30, 68, 93, 95, 110, 159, 171, 181, 220, 230
Adjuran, 164
Adoulis, 29, 30
Adowa, 135, 222
Afar, 24
African Afterthoughts, 166
Africa, Africans: agricultural improvement in Africa, 207; democracy and self-determination thwarted, 201–203; desert toil, 96, 97; dialogue on inherited disabilities, 118 et seq; dismemberings, 99 et seq; disordered borders, 140 et seq; foibles of new Africa, 168 et seq; four Emperors, 152–160; highlands and lowlands, 17, 18; poor husbandry, 3, 204, 208; in 'White' schools, 13; Kikuyu customs, Ch. 3; mass rallies, 2, 64; Maffey Report suppressed, 139; 'mixed' races, 23, 94; 'Negro' and other terms, 128; politicians, 5; racial movements, 26, 27; relations with Indians, 8, 9, with 'White' settlers, Ch. 4; unpromising human material, 94, 119, contra, 131, 183; water and power, 204–215; 'White' failure to modernize nomadic economy, 88–91
Agau, 118
Agumba, 130
Ahamed Gran, Emir of Harar, 31
Ahmed Arabi, 57, 58, 221
Aithiopis, 20
Akaba, 56
Aksum, 20, 22, 23, 26, 29, 30, 35, 158
Aksumawi, 20
Akumu, Dennis, 4
Alexandria, 22, 58
Algeria, 87, 107, 220

Ali bin Salim, Sheykh, 1, 2
Almoravid, 184
Alwah, 149
Amalek, 155
Amba, 27, 144, 150, 167
America, 93, 117, 119, 124, 137, 155, 156, 166, 167, 183, 191, 205, 220, 224
Amhara, 21, 23, 26, 87, 92, 110, 139, 151, 152, 158, 164, 200
Amphilla, 158
Angola, 171, 172, 175
D'Annunzio, Gabriel, 135
Arab League, 211
Arabia, 20, 22, 23, 27, 126, 166, 222
Arak, 155, 165
Arms Race, The, 200, 205, 211
Arraleh, H. E. Mr., 109
Assab, 220
Asmara, 199
Askari, 68
Atatie, 37
Atbara, 25
Athanasius, 148
Atlantic Charter, 101
Austria, 132, 133, 143, 220
Azande, 54
Azikiwe, Dr., 203

Bab el Mandeb, 16
Baccu, 162
Baganda, 96, 93, 120, 198
Bako, 165
Balkans, 56, 57
Banks Mission, 165
Bantu, 24, 52, 93, 119–121, 128–130
Baobab, 68
Baragoi, 81, 90
Basutoland, 105, 170
Bathsheba, 146
B.B.C., x, 63, 64, 65, 110, 175, 180, 192, 201, 203
Bechuanaland, 105, 170
Bedja, 26, 121
Beeching, Dr. (Lord), 59, 195
Beghemder, 26
Belgrade, 168
Belkis (Queen of Sheba), 22, 221
Benadir, 104, 221, 226
Benares, 93, 173, 190, 212, 213
Benjamin, 22, 146, 152
Berbera, 159
Berbers, 19, 126, 127, 184

Berlin Congress, 57, 221
Bethesda, 213
Bevin, Ernest, 103, 104, 106
Bismarck, 57, 221
Blue Nile, 25, 26, 33, 133, 134, 161
Blunt, (W.S. and Lady Anne), 58
Bogos, 158, 159
Bombay, 70, 168, 210
Boran, 37, 38, 82, 83, 87, 161, 163–165
Boyd of Merton, Lord, 66
Brahmin, 69
Brazil, 15, 172
Britain: accused of cruelty, 93; aid to Kenya, 179; Bevin champions Somali unity, 103; brilliant invasion of Ethiopia for absurd reasons, 157; campaigns against 'Mad Mullah', 99; conquest of Sudan, 58; criticism of policy in Africa, 143; Duncan Sandys 'bomb', 114; Eden Policy, 143; effect of British occupation of Egypt, 158; F.O. 'always appease the Habash', 135; halting the Habash, 161; halting the Somalis, 34; Imperial motives, 58, 59; Macmillan underwrites Somali dismemberment, 112; Maffey Report ignored, 137, terms of, 138 et seq; Maudling supports Somali self-determination, 111; offer of land to Zionists, 61; policy of white settlement, 60, 61; renunciation of power, 1, 4; sustains black colonialism, 117; takes lead in Somali dismemberment, 99; transfers Somali Jubaland to Italians, 102; victims of Habash raiders, 163, 164, 166
British Colonial service, 66, 67, 101
Brown, L. H., 62, 72
Bruce, 33, 36
Budge, Sir E. Wallis, 20, 21, 23, 24, 35, 36 98, 118
Bundestag, 199
Byron, 48

Cairo, 107, 170, 172, 173, 177, 181, 186, 190, 192, 203, 220
Calvin, 154
Cameron, Consul, 156
Canada, 209
Candace, 20, 125, 214, 215
Canterbury, Archbishop of, 146
Cape of Good Hope, 32, 84, 181
Cape Town, 105
Cardiff, 95
Carpathian Ukraine, 202

Carthage, 195, 197, 215, 223
Central African Federation, 106
Central Powers, 132
Chad, 126
Cham = Ham, 124
Chanaan, 123–126, 151
Changalla, 119
Changallos, 158
Charters:
 Addis Ababa, 102
 Atlantic, 101
 United Nations, 101, 168, 201
China, 29, 107, 109, 172–174, 176, 191
Chinese People's Republic, 168, 173, 203
Chou En-lai, 96, 196, 229
Cockcroft, Sir John, 205
Cole, Lady Eleanor, 241
Collins, Michael, 117
Colonial Office, 100, 104, 113, 135, 142 185, 229
Colorado, Grand Cañon, 25
C. in C., K.R.A., 75
Commissions and Reports:
 Banks, 165
 Corfield, 240
 Kenya Coastal Strip, 240
 Kenya N.F.D., 113, 228
 Kenya Regional Boundaries, 113, 197, 204, 228
 Maffey, 165, Ch. 8
Common Market, 191
Commons, House of, 76
Communism, 6, 108, 109
Communist Manifesto, 39
Commonwealth, 137, 143, 171, 179, 191, 229
Congo, 130, 170, 171, 180, 183, 198
Congola, 159
Constantinople, 31
Coptic Church, 22, 148, 149
Coryndon, Sir Robert, 75
Coulbeaux, Father, 22, 149
Cuba, 197
Cyprus, 57, 221, 230
Czechoslovakia, 172, 202, 213, 214, 226

Dahir, Muktal, 107
Daily Telegraph, 175, 208
Dakar, 181
Danakil, 17, 24, 26, 29, 110, 123, 220
D'Annunzio, Gabriel, 135
Danquah, Dr., 203
Dar-es-Salaam, 4, 109, 230
Darley, Major, 162
Darod Invasion, The, 34

David, King of Israel, 145, 147, 214
Debra Tabor, 158
De Freitas, Sir Geoffrey, 179
Delamere, Lord, 69, 72, 73
Delhi, 93, 106, 111
Desert and The Green, The, 85, 90, 95
Desthuri, 72, 194
Devonshire, Duke of, 75, 76
Dinka, 41
Disraeli, 35, 57, 100, 220, 221
Djibouti, 104, 105, 107, 173, 174, 181, 221
Dongola, 149
Dorobo, 193
Drysdale, John, 116, 205, 212
Dual Mandate, The, 162
Duka, 8, 89
Duka-wallah, 68
Dundee, Earl of, 111

East Africa, 20, 24, 37, 60, 67, 95, 121, 130, 161, 162, 181, 183, 192, 199, 223, 229
East African Federation, 112
Eastern Hamites, 19, 24, 121
Eden Memoirs, The, 143
Eden, Sir Anthony (Lord Avon), 76, 77, 104, 138, 143, 225
Edward VII, 133
Egypt, 22, 29–31, 57, 58, 108, 123, 125, 126, 142, 146, 148–150, 152, 154, 158–160, 165, 183, 192, 211, 214, 215, 220, 221, 227
Eire, 77
El Barta, 90
Eldoret, 209
Elgeyo, 208
Eliot, Sir Charles, 24, 60, 61, 94, 95, 100, 102, 119, 120, 131, 161, 198, 210
Elizabeth II, 146
El Molo, 81, 82, 83
El Obeyd, 221
El Wak, 161
Emir of Harar, 31
Enarya, 26
Enniskillen, Earl of, 115, 116
Eritrea, 104, 106, 152, 166, 220, 226, 227
Erythriotes, 127
Esthonia, 172, 202
Ethiopia: Size, topography, climate, 17; meanings of word 'Ethiopia' ancient and modern, 19, 20, 125; black Colonialism, 117; Britain's brilliant but absurd invasion, 157; 'Chosen

race' rule, 151; 'Divine right', 151; Emperor-Status, 143–162; 'Eritrean solution' as a substitute for Somali independence, 106; erroneous version of history, 194; four emperors, 152–160; F.O. report 1920, 121; from legend to history, 22; Galla movements, 35–38, 101; Habash movements, 24–27; imperialism, 131; German influence, 134; Italy invades, 143; Italy's assignment to civilize, 102; Lalibela and the Nile, 211; lawlessness, 99; Lebna Dengel and the Portuguese, 31, 32, 156; Maffey Report, 139–142; maladministration, 135; Mboya's Myopia or black colonialism, 107; Muslim movements, 28–35; Negroes at the bottom of society, 118, 119; predators, 99; rebellion in Ogaden 107; 'Shame of Adowa', 135; slavery and slave raiding, 160–166; tribes, 98; Tripartite Agreement of 1906, 134
Europeans: Africanization, effects, 2; allegedly bellicose, 42; Brown craftsmen of white settlers, 68; 'Crash' into pagan society, 54, 55; crossbreeding European bulls, 37; decision to fill empty highlands with white settlers, 61; departing Europeans dishonoured mainly for their virtues, their cash demanded by those who dishonour them, 63, 64, 180–184; Devonshire declaration 1923 renews white privilege to black advantage against brown, 76; European Africans, 7; European features of some black African races, 19; falsely accused by Kenyatta, 56; halt Habash and Somali, 101; halt Hamitization, 121; increase African longevity, 45; 'land-hunger' a 'groundless' passion of ill-will, 66, 187 et seq; leprosy of white society—unemployment, 70; the Revolution whips in anti-European hounds, 168–172; ruthless invaders, brilliant cultivators, 7; settlers hostile to Jews, 73; to Administration, 73; to Indians, 74; to Parliament, 75; tyranny strides forward preaching democracy, 172–176
Eutyches, 147, 148
Evans-Pritchard, Professor, 50, 54
Exmoor, 17, 40, 85

Facing Mount Kenya, 39, 56
Fairlie, Henry, 169, 170, 172

Falasha, 131
Faringdon, Lord, 115
Far East, 32
Fashoda, 181, 222
Financial Express (Bombay), 168
Financial Times (London), 105
Finland, 202
First World War, 133, 162, 223, 224
Fitzalan-Howard, Brigadier The Hon. Miles, 11
Foreign Office, 24, 104, 135, 136, 138, 140, 142, 156, 165, 167
'Fort Jesus' (Mombasa), 1
'Fort Ramnagar' (Benares), 212
France, French, 31, 38, 57, 87, 99, 100, 102–104, 107, 108, 132, 133, 136, 143, 152, 160, 171, 172, 174, 180, 181, 192, 199, 201, 215, 220–222, 224–227
Frumentius, St., 22
Fundi, 68, 78

Gabbra, 164
Gabredare, 106
Gaitskell, Arthur, 210
Gala, 163
Galla (peoples), 17, 23, 24, 26, 27, 32–38, 100, 101, 104, 110, 121, 127, 139, 151, 152, 155, 158–161, 199, 221, 222
Gandhi, Mahatma, 189
Ganges, 173, 212, 213
Geez, 20
Gelubba, 164, 165
General Assembly (U.N.), 169
Genesis, 43, 122–126
George III, 93
Gerenuk, 19
German View, The, 201
Germany, Germans, 19, 57, 87, 88, 102, 107, 132–134, 137, 199, 201, 202, 220, 223, 225, 226
Ghana, 98, 172, 184, 203
Gichuru, Mr., 65, 179
Gikuyu = Kikuyu, 43
Giornale d'Italia, 138, 225
Giriama, 4
Goans, 4, 68, 77, 79, 169, 172, 173, 195, 196
Gojjam, 26
Gordon of Khartoum, 158, 221
Gran = Ahamed Gran
Grand Cañon of the Colorado, 25
Great Britain = Britain
Greece, Greek, 20, 29, 56, 57, 87, 94, 143, 156

Guardafui, Cape, 16, 56, 220
Gulf of Aden, 30
Gurreh, 164

Habash: 'Abyssinia' not 'Ethiopia' of antiquity nor the modern empire, 20, 21; habitat and consolidation up to rise of Islam, 25–29; American support, 166; Imperialism in blood, 29; Ethiopianism, 150; expansion halted north of Blue Nile 16th century, 26; fine physique of men and beautiful women, 23; Habash Kings and Emperors, 144; weakness, 26, 33, 37; Menelek's letter 104; mixed cultural customs, 145; myth-history, 104; nearly overwhelmed by Islam (1643), 31; no 'golden age' in past, 182; religion, 22, 149; rise of modern Empire, 152–161; slavery, 161; 300 years pressed by Galla tribes, 27; unreliable historians, 21
Haile Selassie, Emperor, 100, 107, 108, 135, 158, 165, 175, 176, 186, 221, 224, 226, 227
Ham (son of Noah), 20–22, 35, 118, 120, 123–127
Hamburg, 200
Hamites, 19, 23, 27, 35, 94, 121, 122, 126–130, 184, 222
Harar, 139, 140, 158, 159, 167, 220
Hargeisa, 167
Haud, 93, 100
Hebrews, 20, 23, 122, 124, 125, 144, 150, 151, 214
Hedjaz, 31
Hehe, 38, 121
Hindus, 86, 145, 194, 213
Hiroshima, 200
Hitler, Adolf, 132, 137, 143, 180, 225
H.M.G., 92, 101, 105, 111—114, 116, 142, 178, 197, 211, 228, 230
Hoare, Sir Samuel (Lord Templewood), 136, 165
Hoare-Laval plan, 143
Hodson, Sir Arnold, 118, 162–164
Holland, 201
Holy Ghost, the, 212
Holy War = Jihad, 28, 108
Home, Earl of, 111, 167, 168
Homer, 20, 36
Horn of Africa, 16, 28, 29, 32, 57, 92, 100, 102, 103, 109, 121, 135, 158
House of Commons, 114, 115, 227, 228
House of Lords, 110, 111, 114, 207, 208

Hungary, 172, 202
Huntingdon (Earl of), 114
Huxley, Elspeth, 94

India, Indians, 2–5, 8, 9, 17, 20, 24, 29, 57, 58, 69, 74–77, 93, 106, 151, 169, 172, 173, 176, 185, 187, 189, 193, 195, 196, 210, 213, 220
Indian Ocean, 58, 72, 104, 181, 222
Indus, river, 20
Ireland, 4
Isaiah, 214
Islam, 28–33, 35, 56, 99, 145, 150, 151, 153, 156, 158, 160, 222
Isiolo, 109, 179, 229
Ismail, Khedive, 158, 220
Israel, 21, 22, 125, 145–147, 155, 176, 187, 206, 215, 221, 227
Italy, 19, 99, 102, 103, 104, 107, 132–141, 159, 160, 164–166, 181, 211, 220–226

Jahweh, 23, 52, 145, 146, 147, 155, 167
Jacob, 149, 213
Jacob's Well, 212
Japan, 120, 137, 194
Jedda, 30
Jembe (hoe), 71
Jeroboam, 147
Jerusalem, 150, 153, 188, 214
Jews, 4, 61, 73, 76, 122, 124, 125, 145, 146, 150, 151, 188, 212
Jibouti = Djibouti, 173
Jihad = Holy War, 28, 108
Jilal, 212
Jimma, 26, 162
Joab, 147
Joan of Arc, St., 222
John, St., 149
John IV, Emperor, 158, 159, 160, 221
Johnson, Martin, 81
Johnson, Lyndon B., 201
Jones and Monroe, 30
Jordan, river, 33, 209
Jubaland, 99, 103, 135, 224
Juba, river, 33, 209
Judah, 149, 187

K.A.D.U., 186
Kaffa, 87, 162
Kalávryta, 88
Kalenjin, 12
Kamba, 11, 68, 197, 215
K.A.N.U., 6, 7, 186
K.A.R., 10, 11, 60, 68, 83, 127, 178
Karani, 68

Karl Marx, 168
Karnak, 28
Kasavubu, ex-President, 170
Kashmir, 173
Kassa, 152–154, 156, 158
Kavirondo, 68
Kebra Negast, 21
Kellogg-Briand pact, 136, 137, 224
Kenya: achievement of white settlers, 18; African delusion, 63; blood and husbandry, 187; blood and language, 118 et seq; Britain's vast support, 179; corridor from ocean to Nile, 58; crafts: black at bottom, 69, brown in middle, 68, white at top with perpetual privilege pledge, 67; culling vows, forty years of failure, 88–91; 'dead carcase' of Dr. Verwoerd, 174; defence of negro religion, 131; desert disciplines, 95–97; 'everlasting murderous raids from over Habash frontier', 164–166; flaws in 'land-hunger' 66; Galla in north, 35; 'Happy Valley', 78; Highlands, 25; Ian Smith's forerunner, 75; Kenya's black imperialism 94, 100; justice expounded by Mboya, 106, 107; least founded charge against white settlers, 56; loyal rebels, 76; 'mutinies', 178; Nile power, 210; nomadic ranching, 80 et seq; Odinga's land pledge, 197; 'one party' State, 197; over-stocking and erosion, 90, 91; pact with Ethiopia, 112; pledges (white) renewed (1923, 1932), 76; prototype rebels, 74; review of Kenyatta book on Kikuyu, 39–55; retrogression in agriculture, 208; savage lip-licking, 65; segregation all sorts, 73; settlers' farming victories, 62, 63; Somalis on Tana river, 33; Somali patriotism becomes treason, ix; 'stolen lands' myth, 188; Uganda railway, 56; wasteful indigenous husbandry, 6; white man's country, 60
Kenya Digest, 178, 186
Kenya Independence Bill, 115
Kenya Mountain, 40, 43, 52, 161
Kenya Rebel Army, 74
Kenya Statistical Abstract, 91
Kenyatta, Jomo = Mzee, first President of Kenya Republic, ix, Ch. 1, 13, 18, 25, 33–45, 58–69, 73–81, 88, 90, 92, 94, 98, 100, 103, 107, 111–115, 120, 144, 150, 167, 174–180, 184, 186, 189, 193, 213, 214, 227–229

Kenyattaland, 39
Kerenyaga, 52
Kerio, 204
Khartoum, 129, 160, 198, 221, 230
Khedive, 159
Kiama, 144
Kiambu, 68, 208
Kikuyu, 6–8, 34, 39–46, 50–52, 67–70, 82, 83, 86, 87, 92, 94, 98, 99, 120, 130, 144, 193, 208, 215
Kilindini, 1, 195, 198
Kirby, Sir Arthur, 109
Kisumu, 59
Kitchener, Lord, 160
Kremlin, 196
Kruschev, Nikita, 167, 192, 202, 211
Kush, 18, 23–25, 28, 32, 35, 37, 38, 101, 118, 120, 121, 123, 125–127, 139, 165, 214

Labour Party, 74, 75
Lacustrine Kingdoms, 130, 184
Lagos, 175, 203
Laikipia, 82
Lakes:
    Rudolf, 26, 81–83, 86, 121, 165, 204
    Stefanie, 26
    Tana, 211
    Victoria, 94
Lalibela, Emperor, 211
Lansdowne, Marquess of, 114
Lasta, 26
Latvia, 172, 202
Laval, 143
League of Nations, 136, 137, 143, 224, 225
Leakey, Dr. E. S. B., 39, 41–45
Lebna Dengel, Emperor, 31, 156
'Leg. Co.', = Kenya Legislative Council, 13, 62
Lemomo, Mr., 186
Lenin, 202
Lennox Boyd = Boyd
Leopoldville, 180, 198
Lepanto, 32
Letter of Theodore III, 156
Lettow, Von, 223
Levantines, 152
Leviticus, 32, 145, 220
Lewis, Dr. I., 33, 34, 144
Lex talionis, 51, 145
Liberia, 183
Lion of the Tribe of Judah, 148, 149
Listowel, Earl of, 114, 115
Lithuania, 172, 202

Liwali, 13
Lloyd George, 74, 137
Lodwar, 60, 93, 161
London, 95, 131, 168, 179, 186, 200, 229
Lorian Swamp, 93
Los Angeles, 73
Lourdes, 213
Loyangalani, 82
Lucerne, 71
Lugard, Sir F. (Lord), 60
Lumumba, Patrice, 170
Luo Tribe, 4, 6, 68, 98, 99, 130, 184, 198
Lytton, 1st Earl of, 172

Machakos, 68, 194,
Macmillan, Harold, 77, 104, 112, 113, 116, 117, 191, 227, 228
'Mad Mullah', 99, 109, 157, 220, 223
Maffey, Sir John, 138, 142, 225
Maffey Report, 138, 142, 143, 165, 211, 225
Mafia, 132
Magdala, 157
Magnus, Sir Philip, 160
Maharajah, Benares, 212
Maharajah's Well, 195, 212, 213, 215
Maharashtra, 186
Mahdi, 157–159, 221, 222
Mahmud, Dr. Syed, 111
Maji, 158, 165
Makeda, or Belkis, Queen of Sheba, 22
Makurrah, 149
Malawi, 98
Mangasha, Ras, 159
Mann, Tom, 75
Manyatta, 84, 97, 193
Mao Tse-tung, 202, 203
Mariano, Michael, 82
Marsabit, 81, 164
Marx, Karl, 169–190
Masai, 6, 38, 40, 44, 52, 68, 69, 72, 78, 81–83, 86, 94, 95, 98, 101, 120, 121, 128, 131, 193, 198, 208
Massawa, 26, 29–31, 104, 158–160, 220, 221
Mathew, Archbishop David, 26, 27
Mathews Range, 81
Maudling, Reginald, 110, 111, 113, 116, 227
Mau Mau, 2, 12, 70, 87, 88, 180, 197, 227
Mau Plateau, 60
Mboya, Tom, 6, 7, 13, 61, 64, 66, 87, 93, 94, 106, 107, 176
McKenzie, 65
Mecca, 30, 34

Medina, 28
Meinertzhagen, Colonel, 59, 71
Menelek I, 22, 221
Menelek II, 100, 104, 106, 133, 134, 153, 158–161, 164, 165, 221–223
Merile, 164
Meroe, 20, 125, 214
Meru, 80
Mesopotamia, 20
Metemna, 158
Michol, 145
Mitchell, Sir Philip, 166
Mizraim, 123, 125
Mogadishu, 82, 96, 107, 108, 112, 115, 117, 158, 167, 209, 223
Mohammed, the prophet, 23, 28
Mohammed Abdille Hassan, 99, 222, 234
Mohammed Ali, 160
Mohammedan, 26
Mombasa, 1–5, 59, 70, 195
Monneret de Villard, 149
Monomotapa, 183
'Monroe doctrine', 223
Moombi, 43
Moorehead, Alan, 157
Moors, 94
Morocco, 133, 183, 203, 220
Moscow, 167, 168, 229
Moses, 185, 187
Moyale, 163
Mozambique, 172, 175
Mswake, 95
Mtwapa Creek, 2
Mungu, Murungu, 52, 72
Munich, 225
Murgor, Mr., 208
Muslim, 19, 23, 24, 26, 28–32, 35, 37, 84, 111, 126, 152, 153, 160, 194, 199, 211
Mussolini, Benito, 100, 132, 143, 224, 225
Mutesa, King, 58
Muthaiga Country Club, 12, 73

Naaman the Leper, 213
Nairobi, 1, 5–7, 12, 13, 59, 65, 70, 73–75, 83, 114, 115, 174, 175, 179, 185, 189, 192, 195, 208, 211, 228; Archbishop of, 14
Nandi, 68, 208
Nanyuki, 11, 78
Napoleon I, 152
Narok, 40
Nasser, Gamal abd er, 190–192
Nathan the Prophet, 147

Negro, negroid, 18, 23, 24, 27, 33, 35, 65, 69, 94, 119–122, 125–131, 183–185, 192, 197–199, 220; foundation stock, 118; bottom of social scale, 118; limitations of, 119; slaves of Habash, 119
Negus, 144
Negus Negast, 147, 152, 153, 158, 166, 221
Nehru, Jawaharlal, 79, 169, 173, 195, 196
New York, 93, 95, 200
New York Times, 107, 166
N.F.D., ix, 12, 34, 80, 81, 92, 94, 100, 109–116, 199, 211, 227–230
Ngai, 41, 43, 47, 52
Ngala, Ronald, 111, 112, 227, 228
'Ngweko', 48–50
Nigeria, 192–203
Nile, 20, 25, 59, 121, 133, 142, 181, 220; Blue, 25, 33, 133, 134, 161, 210, 211, 223; Delta, 58; Upper, 58; White, 58, 67, 210, 220
Nkrumah, Dr. Kwame, 150
Noah, 21, 35, 118, 122–125, 213
Nobel Peace Prize, 200
Noel-Baker, Rt. Hon., Philip, M.P., 200
North Africa, 28, 56
North-East Africa, 121, 123, 125–127
North-Eastern Hamites, 127–129
North-East Region, 92, 113, 115, 179
Northern Province, 80–82, 88, 91, 92, 109, 179
Northern Rhodesia, 106
Northey, Sir Edward, 73
Nubia, 20, 121, 123, 125, 149, 159, 183, 220
Nuer, 41

Organization for African Unity (O.A.U.), 102, 108, 167, 171, 175, 180, 203, 330
Odinga, Mr., 65, 197, 198
Ogaden (Ethiopian Somaliland), 35, 100, 103, 106–108, 139, 140, 161, 166, 199, 211, 224, 225, 227, 229, 230
Oglie, 37
Ogmore, Lord, 115
Oman, 171
Orma, Oroma, 35
Osa, 81
Osman, President of Somalia, 108, 177, 203
Ottoman Turks, 29, 31, 32, 56
Owen Falls, 210

Pakistan, 4, 173, 196
Palestine, 22, 30, 56, 61, 123, 171, 188
PAMFECA, 105
Pankhurst, Dr. R., 182
Patel, 8
Patil N.K., 210
Paul, St., 168, 223
Peking, 96, 168, 169, 173, 196, 229, 230
Perham, Dame Margery, 150
Periplus, 130
Persia, 149
Persian Gulf, 57
Peter, St. 145, 214
Philip, the deacon, 214
Philip, H.R.H. Prince, 212
Phut, 123
Pilate, 114, 124
Poland, 172, 202
Pontine marshes, 132
Pope, H. H. the, 146, 151, 188, 196
Pope Pius V, 32
Port Sudan, 2
Portugal, 1, 12, 29, 31, 32, 68, 151, 156,
    171, 172, 174, 175, 181, 183, 196, 208
Posho, 69
Potiphar, 214
Pravda, 202
Prester John, 148, 149
Prussia, 132

Queens: Belkis or Makeda of Sheba, 110,
    147, 154, 221; Candace, 214; Eliza-
    beth II, 5, 11; Victoria, 151, 156, 157;
    Warkit, 155
'Queen of the South', 22

R.A.F., 200, 208, 223, 224
Railways: Addis Ababa–Jibouti, 104,
    105, 223; Mombasa–Kisumu, 59, 67,
    195
Rameses II, 28
Ramnagar Fort, 212
Rases, 27, 139, 140, 144, 152, 155, 160,
    161, 165
Ras Tafari, 135, 224
Redmond, John, 117
Red Sea, 17, 18, 20, 29, 31, 32, 104, 159,
    166, 181, 220
Reece, Sir Gerald, 34, 35, 109
Rendille Tribe, 82, 113, 164
Rennell of Rodd, Lord, 104
Rhineland, 225
Rhodes, Cecil, 59
Rhodesia, 171–175, 208
Richard I, 153

Robeson, Paul, 18, 19
Roman Empire, 29
Rome, 94, 138, 195, 225, 229
Royal Charters, 5
Royal Chronicles, 21
Royal Navy, 2, 57, 58
Rubbia, Alderman Joseph, 92
Rudolf, Lake, 81, 121, 165
Rufiji, 130
Rumania, 172, 202
Russia, 57, 132, 172, 173, 176, 191
Russo-Turkish War (1877–78), 56, 221
Rwanda, 198

Saba = Sheba, Habsha, Habash, etc.
Sabbath, 145, 154
Sahara, 129
Saints:
    Athanasius, 148
    Augustine of Hippo, 55
    Frumentius, 22
    Joan of Arc, 222
    John, Evangelist, 149
    Matthew, Evangelist, 45
    Paul, Apostle to the Gentiles, 168, 223
    Peter, Chief of the Apostles, 145, 214
    Thomas, Apostle, 22
    Thomas, Aquinas, 55
Saladin, 183
Salisbury, Marquess of, 110
Samburu Tribe, 81–90, 166, 204
Samson, 181
Samuel, 146, 155
Sana, 30
Sandhurst, 11, 98
Sandys, Rt. Hon. Duncan, M.P., 114,
    115, 179, 228
Saudi Arabia, 81
Saul, 146, 147, 152, 154, 165, 177
Security Council, 169, 230
Seligman, 126
Selim I, 31
Sem, 22
Semites, Semitic, 21, 121, 124–129, 139
Senaar, 159
Senegal, 203
Septuagint, 125
Serengetti, 193
Servia, 56
Severus of Antioch, 149
Shangalla, 119
Shastri, Lal Bahadur, 173
Shauri ya Mungu, 2, 194
Sheba = Saba, etc.
Sheba, Queen of, 110, 147, 154

Shebeli (leopard), river, 209
Shermarke, Dr. Abdi Rashid Ali, 110–114, 119
Sheridan, Sir Joseph, 73
Shifta, 164
Shoa, 23, 26, 30, 158, 160, 162, 221
Sidama, 101, 129, 165
Sikhs, 68
Single Somali Government (1905), 102
Smuts, Jan, 223
Snowdon, Mount, 59
S.O.A.S., 131
Sobat, river, 142, 211
Solomon, King of Israel, 21, 22, 30, 45, 49, 147, 149, 150, 200, 214
Somali: Africans, not Arabs, 199; Ahamed Gran, 31; aptitude for trading 3, 68; assimilating power (blood), 28, transmitting powers (culture), 28; beautiful features, 24; Bevin's plea (1946) for united Somali nation, 103; Eliot's similar ideas (1905), 102; clothing, women not veiled, 84; cult of superiority injures, 151; development to present day, 32; dismembered, Ch. VI; Eliot castigates method of handling, 100; 'Eden tradition', 143; globe trotters, 95; grazing rights, 134; Haile Selassie supports 'Greater Somalia' as part of 'Greater Ethiopia', 107; halted by British, 34; homogeneous, 99; Kenya's Somali region ix, resolved to join Mother Country, 12; Kushitic in speech, 19; 'knowledge of law', 24; low rainfall, 81; Mohammed Abdille Hassan ('Mad Mullah') 99; Macmillan's unhappy pledge, 29; N.F.D. fiasco, 111 et seq; security laws, 175; origins in Africa, 28; Ogaden and N.F.D., 100, 139, 161; oil 'strikes'?, 211; pastoral nomads, 82; Osman on non-alignment, 177; Republic breaks with U.K., 114; Somali interests regularly sacrificed by F.O., 135; triangular balance of power, 152; 'talented race', 24; unsupported by Kenya settlers, 78; water resources, 205; 'whited sepulchres', 174
Somalia, 30, 78, 94, 107, 108, 114, 142, 175
'Somali Peninsula', 109
Somali Republic, 80, 92, 100, 101, 113, 116, 198, 205
'Somali Republic and African Unity', 112

Somers, Lord, 115
Songhai, 183
'Song of Solomon', 213
South Africa, 75, 171, 172, 174, 175, 177
South-West Africa, 171
Southern Province, 92
Soviet Union, 107, 167, 168, 201, 202, 226
Spain, 31, 94, 171, 172, 174, 184
Spitzer, Professor, 205
Stanley, 59
Stanleyville, 180
Stefanie, Lake, 26
Stoke Row, 212
Strabo, 20
Stresa, 127
Sudan, 41, 58, 142, 152, 156, 159, 165, 184, 197, 198, 199, 222
'Sudeten', 94, 226
Suez, 56–58, 110, 138, 157, 221, 226
Sufi, 222
Sultan of Turkey, 56
  Muhammad II, 31
  Selim I, 31
  Suleiman the Magnificent, 31
Sultan of Zanzibar, 1, 4, 229
Sunday Telegraph, 169
Sura, 163
Suzannah, 52
Swahili, 2–6, 14, 21, 52, 183, 193
Swaziland, 105, 170
Syed Mahmud, Dr. 111
Syria, 20, 22, 30, 56

Tafari, Ras, 135, 224
Takaze, river, 25, 26
Tana, Lake, 211
Tana, river, 33, 82
Tanganyika, 14, 17, 78, 88, 171, 195, 230
Tanzania, 171, 197, 198
Teita Tribe, 64
Tej, 155, 165
Tel Aviv, 188
Templewood, Lord, 136, 163, 165
Theodore III, 153–159, 161, 165, 220, 221
Thomas, St., Apostle, 22
Tiber, 196, 203
Tigre, 22, 23, 26, 110, 152, 158, 163, 164, 220, 224
Times, The, London, 105, 110, 114, 166, 174, 185, 208
Tokyo, 200
Touaregs, 127, 184

Trans-Nzoia, 61, 73
Trevor, 127
Tripartite treaty (1906), 132, 134, 136, 138, 139, 143, 224
Triple Alliance, 133
Trust Territory, 171
Tshombe, Moyse, 198
Tubman, President, 173
Tunis, 133
Turkana Tribe, 2, 60, 81, 82–84, 86, 88, 95, 96, 204
Turkey, Turks, 27, 31–33, 56, 104, 152, 156, 158, 161, 165, 221
Turkwell, river, 204
Turnbull, Sir Richard, 38, 88, 109

Uasin Gishu, 161, 208
Ucciali, Treaty of, 159, 221, 222, 223
Uganda, 58, 60, 67, 195, 203, 210, 222
'Uhuru', 2, 6, 8, 11, 15, 168–170, 198, 220, 210
Uhuru, instant, 1960, 174
Ukraine, 202
Ulaya = England, 194
Union of South Africa, see S.A.
United Kenya Club, 7
United Nations, 77, 79, 101, 170, 171, 175, 196, 198, 201, 226

Verwoerd, Dr., 174
Victoria, Lake, 4, 59, 60
Victoria, Queen, 105, 151, 156, 157, 160
Vitetti, Signor, 138
Voice of Free Africa, 63
Volstead Act, 155
Von Lettow Vorbeck, 223

Wahehe Tribe, 38, 121
Wak, 37, 167
Walters, Mr., 109
Wal Wal, 135, 136, 138, 165
Wandorobo Tribe, 43, 81, 82, 84
Wardeh Tribe, 34, 82
Warkit, Queen, 155
Waruhiu, Chief, 5
Weekend Telegraph, 93
White Berbers, 19
World Bank, 7, 208
World War II, 201, 226

Yaman, 20
Yemen, 22, 23, 25, 28, 29

Zambesi, 130
Zanj, 130
Zanzibar, 1, 4, 16, 197, 229, 230
Zeila, 158
Zion, 150